God's Renaissance Man

Abraham Kuyper at the age of forty-five

God's
Renaissance Man

The life and work of
Abraham Kuyper

by
James Edward McGoldrick

 EVANGELICAL PRESS

EVANGELICAL PRESS
Faverdale North Industrial Estate, Darlington, DL3 0PH, England

Evangelical Press USA
P. O. Box 84, Auburn, MA 01501, USA

e-mail: sales@evangelical-press.org

web: www.evangelical-press.org

First published 2000

British Library Cataloguing in Publication Data available

ISBN 0 85234 446 5

Printed and bound in Great Britain by Creative Print and Design Wales, Ebbw Vale

Contents

Preface

When the apostle Paul wrote to Christians in Corinth, in about A.D. 55, he explained that God's method for building his church was, for the most part, to employ common people who had little acquaintance with worldly wisdom. He declared, 'Brothers, think of what you were when you were called. Not many of you were wise by human standards; not many were influential; not many were of noble birth' (1 Corinthians 1:26). The most distinguished Jews and Gentiles of the first century regarded the message of Christ as foolishness, and scorned it accordingly, but the fact that Paul wrote this description of the situation is evidence that *some* people of learning, influence and nobility believed the gospel and became its zealous exponents. Paul had been a very prominent Pharisee and erudite rabbi and a citizen of the Roman Empire by birth, one whose significance for the development of the Christian faith is almost incalculable.

Although Paul ministered to, and with, throngs of ordinary people, he was a leader of extraordinary knowledge, faith and energy, the first in a succession of such figures whose careers would grace the pages of church history. While common people have always been the backbone and mainstay of the church, exceptional leaders such as Augustine of Hippo, Bernard of Clairvaux, John Wycliffe, Martin Luther and John Calvin have appeared at crucial times to serve their undistinguished brothers and sisters in the faith. Such a champion of Christianity appeared in the second half of the nineteenth century when Abraham Kuyper became the dynamic leader of Protestants in the Netherlands.

Like his predecessors in church history, Kuyper was a person of massive intelligence, immense learning, terrific energy and zealous faith. He nevertheless received great adulation from his beloved *kleine luyden* (little people) of the working and lower middle classes, many of whom struggled to survive economically and few of whom could afford a higher education. Throughout his long career as a pastor, journalist, educator and political leader, Kuyper maintained close contact with the common people and communicated with them effectively, even though he was far above them in intellect and formal learning.

There have been only two substantial efforts to narrate the life of Abraham Kuyper in English. Frank Vanden Berg, a high school teacher and novelist, produced *Abraham Kuyper* in 1960, and Louis Praamsma wrote *Let Christ be King, Reflections on the Life and Times of Abraham Kuyper*, published in 1985.[1] The first of these works adopts the format of conventional biography and it covers the subject's entire life. It is, however, entirely without documentation, and the author's admiration for Kuyper prevented him from being duly critical.

Praamsma was a respected church historian who employed a scholarly method in research, and he did not neglect to indicate Kuyper's weaknesses and failures. His account is briefer than that of Vanden Berg, but it is much more insightful and balanced in appraising the great leader's significance. Both books are out of print, so the time seems auspicious for another examination of Kuyper's life and legacy.

The present study builds upon the work of its predecessors, in some ways to expand their coverage and, at some points, to differ with their interpretations. Since this is a book for English-language readers, the documentation is in English except in cases where the material remains untranslated. Citations from French and German sources reflect my own unaided reading of those items, but I have received assistance in rendering material from Dutch into English. Responsibility for everything in the book, including translations, is, of course mine alone.

Many people deserve thanks for their contributions to this project, and foremost among them is McKendree R. Langley of Westminster Theological Seminary, the leading American authority on Kuyper. The many entries in the bibliography relating to Langley's writings bear witness to this. He has been a great encouragement from the beginning of this endeavour. His aid in translation has been particularly helpful, and I still enjoy a delightful correspondence that has developed with him in connection with this book. Harry Van Dyke of Redeemer College provided helpful material and suggestions, as did Irving Hexham of the University of Calgary, J. de Bruijn of the Free University of Amsterdam, James W. Skillen of the Centre for Public Justice, Michael Morbey of Ottawa, Del Ratzsch of Calvin College, Wayne Kobes of Dordt College and Pastors Cornelis Pronk and Carl Schouls of the Free Reformed Church. Robert Decker and Herman Hanko of the Protestant Reformed Seminary provided copies of documents difficult to find.

No scholar could accomplish much without the assistance of librarians, and in this case their contributions have been invaluable. At Cedarville College Ruth Martin, Melinda Howard and Hope Morris deserve special recognition. Conrad Bult at Calvin College went well beyond my expectations to render help in locating documents, as did William Harris of Princeton Theological Seminary.

James E. McGoldrick

Introduction

The principles of great thinkers have often induced their disciples to make interpretations and applications of those concepts which the thinkers themselves did not foresee. This appears to have been the case with some of the ideas of Abraham Kuyper. His doctrines of common grace and presumed regeneration, in particular, have given rise to views and practices which have carried the movement he founded to lengths he might not have approved. Although a substantial study of his teachings on these subjects appears in chapters 11 and 12, it is fitting at the outset to indicate in some measure how Kuyper's ideas have influenced certain unwholesome developments within Christian bodies which claim him as their mentor.

Common grace[1]

Kuyper's understanding of common grace went far beyond that of earlier theologians in that he gave greater emphasis than they had done to the redemption of culture and the universe. It had long been conventional belief among Christians that God blesses the whole creation with unmerited material and temporal benefits, such as the fertility of the soil, sunshine and rain, and the enjoyment of productive intellectual and manual talents. These gifts are common to humanity, since God has conferred them without regard to the recipients' faith, or lack of it. Kuyper, of course, gratefully acknowledged these provisions of common grace, but he maintained that this principle has broad and deep implications for the practices of Christians as they relate to creation and society. Kuyper's understanding of this matter has caused considerable debate, even among his fellow adherents to the Reformed expression of the Christian faith. Some of his critics regard Kuyper's doctrine of common grace as an unwarranted elevation of social responsibilities over the biblical mandate to evangelize the world, and there is evidence that some Kuyperians have erred in that direction. The tendency to do so seems especially appealing to intellectuals who find Kuyper's world-view satisfying because of its comprehensive vista of human relations and social obligations.

Kuyper had a deep concern for the material well-being of all humans, and he urged Christian social action as a means to help people in need. He did not thereby intend to diminish the urgency of confronting sinners with the demands of God's law and calling them to believe the gospel and to embrace salvation in Christ. To whatever extent later disciples of Kuyper's teaching about common grace have failed in the work of evangelism, to that degree they have deviated from the legacy he has left them.

Another unfortunate consequence of misunderstanding and misapplying the concept of common grace has appeared in the way some professing Christians have tried to justify their conformity to worldly ideas and practices that Kuyper would not have endorsed. Dr Kuyper was a brilliant intellectual, but he never portrayed the Christian faith in cold, formal, academic ways. Most of his writings are devotional in character, designed for ordinary readers as helps to arouse their love for Christ and to impel them to put it into action by ministering to both the spiritual and material needs of their neighbours. Although there have been misuses, and even abuses, of Kuyper's teaching, the excesses which pertain to his view of common grace appear, for the most part, to be due to faulty understanding of his intent.

Perhaps he was not sufficiently explicit in explaining himself, but still it seems inappropriate to hold him responsible for developments he could not have foreseen.

Baptism and regeneration

The second area of concern about harmful effects of some of Kuyper's beliefs relates to the doctrine of presumed regeneration, which occupies a substantial portion of chapter 11, and which appears again in chapter 18 as a critique of Kuyper's position.

Abraham Kuyper contended vigorously for the validity of infant baptism as the sign of a child's induction into the community of God's people, and he maintained that the Holy Spirit's work of regenerating the infant precedes the sacrament. He made the necessary distinction between regeneration as a silent work of the Holy Spirit and conversion as an overt experience when a person actually receives Christ. Kuyper's teaching, however, led some people to conclude that baptism assures salvation. As a result, numbers of children reared in Christian homes and under the care of Christian churches have failed to realize the need for personal faith and repentance. While this is very distressing, it is, once more, an example of misapplying Kuyper's doctrine. His view of regeneration is at odds with Reformed theology, and his peculiar position on this subject has produced detrimental effects. This is clear, but a more careful reading of Kuyper might have prevented some of the harmful consequences of his strange teaching about baptism.

With the above cautions in mind, it is fitting to turn to the life and career of 'God's Renaissance Man'.

I.
Home and heritage

Abraham Kuyper entered this world on 29 October 1837 at the manse of the Dutch Reformed Church in Maasluis, Holland. He was the first son but third child of Jan Frederik and Henriette Kuyper (née Huber). His father had become pastor of the Great Church in Maasluis in 1834.

Early days

Because of his unusually large head, Abraham's parents feared he was a victim of hydrocephalus (water on the brain), but a physician assured them that nothing was wrong. His mother made hats for 'Bram', as his parents called him, and other children sometimes ridiculed him because of his appearance.

In 1841 Jan Frederik Kuyper accepted the position of pastor at a congregation of the National Church in Middelburg, Zeeland, where Bram was to spend most of his childhood. His parents did a fine job of educating him at home, so he did not attend elementary school in Maasluis. Under their instruction he learned French and English and became an avid reader.

While living in Middelburg, young Kuyper became fascinated with ships and enjoyed talking with seamen. Sometimes he distributed religious tracts and tried to preach to the sailors. He dreamed of becoming a sea captain.

In 1849, when Pastor Kuyper moved his family to Leiden, his son Abraham attended school there. He was then twelve years old. His performance in school was outstanding and he demonstrated such facility in the German language that he delivered the valedictory address in that tongue. In 1855 he entered the University of Leiden to study philosophy and theology. His father had obtained his own theological education at Leiden, the most distinguished of the Dutch universities, but a stronghold of the anti-supernatural religious movement which came to be known as modernism. The precise theological beliefs of the elder Kuyper are not clear, but it appears that he did not subscribe wholeheartedly to the historic doctrines of the Reformed faith as expressed in the official standards of the Dutch Reformed Church. When orthodox believers within that body protested against deviations from its doctrines, Jan Kuyper did not support them.[1]

A diligent student

While an undergraduate at Leiden, Abraham Kuyper studied ancient languages, the mastery of which he added to his previous fluency in English, French, German and Dutch. Unlike many frivolous students at the university, Kuyper avoided distractions and pursued his studies with diligence. He was awarded the Bachelor of Arts degree, with highest honours, in 1858. His major subjects were classics, philosophy and literature. About the time of his graduation Kuyper became engaged to Johanna Hendrika Schaay (1842-99), whom he would marry in 1863.

Whatever may have been the religious legacy he received from his father, Kuyper became enamoured of modernist scepticism with regard to the miraculous features of Christian belief. He related in later years that, as a student at Leiden, he joined with others in applauding Professor L. W. Rauwenhoff when he denied the bodily resurrection of Christ.[2] Writing in 1873, Kuyper lamented his spiritual condition while a student of theology: 'In the academic world I had no defence against the powers of theological negation. I was robbed of my childhood faith. I was unconverted, proud, and open to doubting.'[3]

The influence of John à Lasco and Charlotte Yonge

During his time at Leiden Kuyper developed a great appreciation for Professor M. de Vries (1820-92), a specialist in Dutch literature. De Vries urged him to enter a contest under the auspices of the University of Groningen by writing an essay in which he compared the views of John Calvin and the Polish Reformer John à Lasco (1499-1560) on the doctrine of the church. This led Kuyper to search for the printed works of à Lasco, which were extremely rare. After an arduous, unrewarding quest, his mentor directed Kuyper to look at de Vries' father's extensive collection of books on church history, and there he found what was perhaps the only extant set of à Lasco's works. Kuyper's essay won first prize — a gold medal — and it is significant to note that, in writing to gain that honour, he expressed strong disdain for Calvin's theology.[4] The essay became his doctoral dissertation, and in 1866 Kuyper published the works of à Lasco with his own introduction and critical preparation. Church historians hailed his achievement.

After his conversion, Abraham Kuyper often reflected on the manner in which he discovered à Lasco's writings, and he attributed it to the working of God in his life to draw him towards salvation. The experience implanted within him a strong conviction about divine providence. He explained: 'I know very well that such a conviction is not conversion, but it is, nevertheless, an encountering of the living, working, directing God in the pathway of our lives, and the impression made on my heart by this almost incredible experience was so deep and abiding that whenever I recall the seeking love of my God, I go back continually … to the remembrance of that marvellous providence of the *Lasciana*.'[5]

About the same time that he found the works of à Lasco, Kuyper read *The Heir of Redcliffe,* a novel by English author Charlotte Yonge (1823-1901), a participant in the Oxford Movement.[6] This was a revival of religious fervour within the Church of England led by scholars such as E. B. Pusey, John Henry Newman and John Keble. Describing themselves as Anglo-Catholics, the Oxford leaders opposed modernist theology and stressed the validity of the Bible and Christian traditions. Miss Yonge was an avid student of the Christian faith and a Bible teacher in her congregation.

While reading *The Heir of Redcliffe*, Kuyper found in the figure of Philip de Morville a picture of his own character. He saw Philip collapse under the weight of self-accusation, and that humbled Kuyper and made him think about his own sinfulness, although he did not, at that point, understand the gospel. In his own words he related what had happened: 'What my soul lived through at that time I have only later fully understood; but yet in that hour, from that very moment, I despised what I formerly admired, sought what I formerly held in no esteem.'[7]

The spiritual turmoil that accompanied the reading of *The Heir of Redcliffe* occurred at a time when overwork had led Kuyper into nervous exhaustion. He temporarily lost his memory of many academic matters, and as therapy he built model ships, one of which, the *Johanna*, he kept on display in his office.

In 1863 Abraham Kuyper received the Doctor of Theology degree at the University of Leiden, even though, under the influence of Professor de Vries, he had sometimes shown more interest in literature than in dogmatics. For most of his time at the university he had refrained from praying and giving thanks to God because he had dismissed belief in divine providence as a superstition. His reading of Charlotte Yonge's book had, however, effected a profound change in his thinking. By 1860 he had recovered mental and emotional stability and was, therefore, able to complete his doctoral studies with his usual distinction.

Marriage and first pastorate

In the summer following graduation he married Johanna Schaay, with whom he moved to the Gelderland village of Beesd to begin his career as a pastor in the Dutch Reformed Church. There he was to encounter criticism from a faction within the congregation that found his doctrine and preaching unaccept-able because his beliefs and sermons were not biblical. In order to understand Kuyper's views at that time and to realize the condition of the National Church of which he was a minister, some examination of the church scene in the Netherlands of the nineteenth century is necessary, and that is the subject of the next chapter.

2.

The fall of a great church

During the sixteenth century, when the Low Countries were part of the Spanish Empire, Lutheran influences from Germany initiated the Protestant Reformation which the Spanish monarchs Charles I (1516-56) and Philip II (1556-98) determined to destroy. The oppressive political and economic policies of Philip aroused resolute opposition from Roman Catholic as well as Protestant noblemen, and by 1568 resistance was underway. At that time the Protestant population of the Netherlands was small and situated mostly in the south, where Calvinism had begun to supplant Lutheranism as the dominant expression of the Protestant faith.

The Eighty Years' War (1568-1648) began as a struggle to preserve traditional aristocratic autonomy and to combat excessive taxation at the hands of Spanish revenue agents, but it eventually became a war for independence in which Dutch Calvinists exerted decisive leadership. The seven provinces north of the River Rhine eventually became the Dutch Republic, where the Reformed faith was dominant.

The establishment of a national Reformed church

During the struggle against Spain, Reformed Christians (Calvinists) conducted vigorous evangelism among the Catholics, even as they fled north to escape Spanish attacks. The brutality of the Spanish Inquisition, which Philip II had introduced into the Low Countries, created much sympathy for its victims and actually swelled the ranks of the supporters of Protestantism. A synod of Reformed leaders in 1571 adopted the Presbyterian form of government for their church and subscribed to the *Belgic Confession of Faith* (1561) and the *Heidelberg Catechism* (1562) as its doctrinal standards. These documents affirm and expound the teachings of Reformed theology known commonly as Calvinism.

Because the Reformed faith provided the ideology for independence, the Reformed Church enjoyed the support of political and military leaders who helped to establish it as the official religion of the Netherlands. This has had a pronounced effect upon church-state relations ever since. In 1575, while the war against Spain was in progress, William of Orange (1533-84), known as 'the Silent', the leader of the struggle, rewarded the city of Leiden for its defence against the Spaniards by authorizing the creation of a university for the education of Reformed pastors and learned laymen to serve the Dutch state. City magistrates were to control the university and to appoint professors of theology. When the pastors complained that some of the magistrates were not truly Reformed in belief and, therefore, not qualified to select theologians to teach, the city government established a *collegium theologicum* for ministerial students which, the magistrates agreed, should promote Reformed orthodoxy and defend it against contrary teachings.

Despite these provisions, in 1602 the city rulers appointed Jacob Arminius (1560-1609) as professor of theology, overruling the opposition of pastors who questioned his doctrine. When a bitter dispute erupted between Arminius and fellow professor Franz Gomarus (1563-1641), Reformed pastors appealed to the government to convene a national synod of their church to resolve the controversy. This meant that church and state together would decide the issue. The Synod of Dort (also known

as Dordt or Dordrecht, 1618-19), which included representatives from Reformed bodies across Europe, affirmed strict Calvinist orthodoxy, as taught in the *Belgic Confession* and the
Heidelberg Catechism, and it issued its own rebuttal of the
Arminian faction in the *Canons of Dort*, which became the last
of the Three Forms of Unity, the official theological statements
of the Dutch Reformed Church. The state paid all expenses for
the synod and agreed to underwrite production of a Dutch-
language edition of the Scriptures thereafter known as the
Statenbijbel.

Moves away from the Reformed position

State support for the Dutch Reformed Church seemed desirable to ecclesiastical leaders, so long as civil authorities used
their influence on behalf of the church to preserve its teaching.
Soon after Dort, however, the magistrates refused to require
university professors to subscribe to the *Canons of Dort*, and
the States-General (the national parliament) prohibited the calling of national synods, and thereby inhibited the clergymen
from asserting authority over church affairs. When the magistrates allowed non-Reformed teaching to occur in the university, the church had no effective means of combating it. In the
eighteenth century a militantly anti-Christian rationalism became apparent in the country's schools, and pastors of the
National Church often imbibed it and then expounded its ten-
ets to their congregations. Modernist theology had made its
début in the Netherlands.[1] The province of Holland became
the centre of resistance to orthodoxy, perhaps because the
merchants there had regular contacts with other countries and
foreign religious ideas. As they enjoyed their material comforts,
members of the middle class developed a tolerance towards
religious diversity based upon a growing indifference towards
spiritual matters.

In the face of a growing liberalism within the National Church, some orthodox Christians found an anti-cultural pietism attractive. This was especially so among common people, who sometimes formed societies meeting in homes, where lay preachers taught them Reformed doctrines to thwart the influence of liberal pastors. Although this reactionary movement was loyal to its Calvinistic heritage, it encouraged withdrawal from society rather than a vigorous defence of the faith. Its very character rendered it ineffective to stem the tide of scepticism.

By the late eighteenth century, rationalism as a world-view had become popular among Dutch intellectuals, as among their counterparts across Europe. France was the dynamic centre of this ideology, and when that country exploded in revolution in 1789, most Dutch liberals hailed the event as a great step forwards in the enlightenment of humanity, as they toasted the coming of democracy and religious diversity. It was not long, however, before the French translated their ideology into imperialism and sent their armies to impose French rule upon other nations. In 1794 they occupied the Netherlands, ending her independence and forcing the House of Orange, the most prestigious political family in the realm, to flee to Britain. The next year the French declared the creation there of the Batavian Republic, a regime subservient to its conquerors. In 1806 Louis Bonaparte, brother of Napoleon, became King of the Netherlands, and in 1810 France absorbed the Dutch kingdom as an integral part of its empire.

In 1796 the Batavian Republic had disestablished the Dutch Reformed Church, thereby depriving it of state support. The National Church then languished, as a law of that year promulgated the equality of all religions, including Roman Catholicism and Judaism. King Louis Bonaparte favoured Catholics, so they were generally supportive of his regime, as were Dutch Jews.[2] Napoleon, however, aroused resentment in the Netherlands by imposing a state police, forced military service, the French law code and the French language. When an alliance of France's enemies defeated him at Leipzig, in Germany (1813), large numbers of Dutchmen rejoiced. The Netherlands regained independence after the defeat of Napoleon, and the Congress of Vienna, an international body that constructed the post-war settlement, recognized the Prince of Orange as King William I and awarded the Netherlands control over Roman Catholic Belgium.

As monarch, William I (1825-40) displayed a poor understanding of church affairs, but he assumed much authority nevertheless. He abolished the provincial synods of the Reformed Church and established an annual national synod with extensive jurisdiction over provincial churches. William imposed these changes without the agreement of the church, but there was little resistance, perhaps because people were weary from long years of war. Rationalist theologians in the universities did not regard church polity as a crucial matter. On the contrary, they sought a broadly inclusive church with Arminian doctrine which would function as a department of the state. In 1816 the first national synod discarded the *Canons of Dort*, which was a harbinger of the abandonment of the historic Reformed faith that was to come.

Revival leads to secession

In the period after the defeat of Napoleon, religious revivals occurred in several parts of Europe, beginning in French Switzerland, where the movement was known as the *réveil*. It was in part a reaction against the rationalism of the German *Aufklärung* (Enlightenment), which had infected the Swiss churches. In Geneva the *Vénérable Compagnie des Pasteurs* (the principal ecclesiastical body) prohibited preaching of traditional doctrines, such as original sin, predestination and the deity of Christ. The *Compagnie* removed Calvin's catechism and replaced it with one of a rationalist slant. Leaders of the *réveil* protested and formed the Evangelical Society to spread Reformed teaching throughout French-speaking lands. This group founded the Evangelical Theological Seminary in Geneva, where J. H. Merle d'Aubigné (1794-1872) became a professor. He had been chaplain to the Dutch royal family until 1830, when the royal court had to leave Brussels after the Belgians had revolted successfully against Dutch rule. Merle d'Aubigné helped to establish the Free Church of Geneva, and he became famous as the author of a comprehensive *History of the Reformation of the Sixteenth Century.*

When the influence of the *réveil* arrived in the Netherlands, it stimulated great interest in promoting conformity to orthodoxy. Willem Bilderdijk (1756-1831), a poet, was a firm Calvinist who led a study group that aspired to restore the influence of the Reformed faith in the kingdom. Isaak da Costa (1798-1860) was one of Bilderdijk's converts who abandoned deism and then began denouncing secular humanism. He assailed rationalists within the Dutch Reformed Church as Sadducees. Dutch evangelicals knew about the Swiss *réveil,* and some of them went there to confer with Reformed leaders. A few Swiss believers travelled to the Netherlands to encourage the *réveil* there.[3]

The Dutch *réveil* produced many criticisms of the *Hervormde Kerk* (Dutch Reformed, or National Church) because of its departure from biblical teachings. Hendrik de Cock (1801-42) had been educated in modernism, but he became a strong exponent of the Reformed faith while a pastor at Ulrum, Groningen. The devout faith of his parishioners led to his conversion. They urged him to read an annotated edition of the *Statenbijbel,* Calvin's *Institutes of the Christian Religion* and the *Canons of Dort.* He did so and then became a champion of orthodoxy, but his efforts to promote his newly found faith incurred criticism from liberal pastors and led to his suspension from the ministry for complaining about the errors of other clergymen. Similar consequences ensued for others who followed de Cock's example, but some young university students took up the cause of reformation and provided leadership for it.[4]

Hendrik de Cock and most of his congregation withdrew from the National Church, and soon four more pastors joined them in the *Afscheiding*, or Secession (1834). All declared their loyalty to the historic Three Forms of Unity, and they called all truly Reformed believers to unite in forming a Free Reformed Church separated from state control. The first synod of the seceded congregations convened in Amsterdam in March 1836, a meeting which marks the birth of the Christian Reformed Church.[5] By then de Cock had exhausted all means of redress from the Dutch Reformed Church, and his congregation was more eager than he to withdraw. By 1835 seventy local churches had joined the *Afscheiding*, and pastors of the movement were almost overwhelmed with requests to preach in various parts of the country.[6]

Official reactions to the *Afscheiding* were swift and severe. The synodal committee of the National Church asked civil authorities to suppress unauthorized religious meetings by application of an article in the *Code Napoléon* that prohibited gatherings of more than twenty people without permission of the government. When offenders stood trial, they had to pay court costs for proceedings against them, and fines and imprisonments were common. Seceders' services were sometimes disrupted by mob violence, and when the state sent troops to restore order, it sometimes quartered them in homes of families who supported the *Afscheiding*. It appears that the king took personal affront at the secession because it contradicted his idea of a broad ecumenical church. As he had done in the case of the separatists of 1822 (see note 5), William I denied that the constitutional guarantee of freedom of religion applied to the seceders, because their church did not exist at the time the constitution took effect. Courts almost always decided against dissenters, and those who could not pay the fines suffered confiscation of their property. Hendrik de Cock spent three months in jail. Reformed believers in other nations supported their persecuted brethren in the Netherlands and appealed to the Dutch government to cease molesting them.

In severing their connection with the *Hervormde Kerk*, adherents to the *Afscheiding* argued that they were continuing the historic Reformed faith in the Netherlands and so were not establishing a new church. They disavowed rebellion and offered to return to the National Church if it would reaffirm the Reformed doctrinal standards and restore its historic character.[7]

Groen van Prinsterer

Most supporters of the secession were rural people of little political influence whose rights the state ignored. One figure of national prominence, however, came to their defence. He was Guillaume Groen van Prinsterer (1801-76), a skilful lawyer and historian, secretary of the king's cabinet, a man who held doctorates in law and literature. Groen had defended his two dissertations for those degrees on the same day.[8] Groen did not approve of the separation from the National Church, but he affirmed the rights of the *Afscheiding* and decried the persecution of its adherents. In 1828 Groen had heard J. H. Merle d'Aubigné preach in Brussels, and the Swiss scholar's influence had led him to question his own liberal political and religious beliefs. He later hailed Merle d'Aubigné as God's agent to change his life and lead him to embrace the Reformed faith, although as a student at the University of Leiden he had earlier come under the influence of Bilderdijk.[9]

In 1837 Groen wrote a defence of the seceders in terms of constitutional law, together with a critique of the National Church as reconstituted by royal policy in 1816. He decried the king's programme for religious unity without regard for doctrine, and he called for allegiance to the historic Reformed creeds. Groen cited the national synod's indifference towards truth as the cause of the separation, but he remained within the Dutch Reformed Church until he died. His eloquent appeals for equality under the law at first fell on deaf ears, and the oppression of orthodox Calvinists continued until 1840, when the government of William II (1840-49) began removing prohibitions against nonconformity within Reformed ranks. William II was a pragmatic, flexible king whose policies led to revisions of the constitution that made the Netherlands a more truly parliamentary state. The spiritual condition of the Dutch Reformed Church continued to decline, as modernism prevailed in the universities and its exponents presided in ecclesiastical bodies. The historic Reformed faith was under relentless attack. While Groen and others worked for a revival of orthodoxy within the National Church, the Christian Reformed Church opened a seminary at Kampen to educate its pastors in the theology of the Protestant Reformation.

3.
The decline of a great theology

In order to appreciate the generally decadent condition of the Dutch Reformed Church by the nineteenth century, it is necessary to consider in some detail the exact character of Dutch theology in its several varieties of liberalism or modernism. Theological liberalism began as an effort to revise traditional beliefs, so as to make Christianity acceptable to the world-view of a scientific age. All versions of this movement proceeded from basic assumptions — in this case, from a relativistic concept of truth. Liberals often denied the possibility of miracles and regarded the Christian faith as only the current stage of development in the evolution of religion.

Liberalism (modernism) appeared in the Netherlands about 1840, when Dutch scholars began to study German philosophy and German Higher Criticism of the Bible. Dutch disciples of German mentors were numerous within the National Church, but they appeared among Lutherans, Mennonites and Remonstrants (Arminians) as well. The three major schools of liberalism were the Groningers, the Ethicals and the Moderns.[1]

The Groningers

Theologians at the University of Groningen exerted powerful influence upon the Dutch Reformed Church to lead it away from Reformed doctrinal standards, as their numerous disciples filled pulpits across the land. Until about 1860 the Groningen view of Christianity dominated the National Church. These scholars held that Christ had come to lead humanity to God's will, but Christ is not God, and God is not a Trinity. Christ's death did not satisfy divine justice on behalf of sinners and Christianity is the best religion, but not the only true one.[2] This was the first academic effort in the Netherlands to harmonize Christianity with the theories of the rationalism popular among Europe's intellectuals. Despite their obvious departure from biblical teachings, Groningen theologians claimed their deviations were both necessary and beneficial for the church.[3]

P. Hofstede de Groot (1802-1886) was the foremost Groningen theologian. As author of *Natural Theology*, he appealed for a religion of feelings and veneration of Christ as the supreme religious teacher and moral example. He and other scholars at his university published the journal *Truth in Love*, which they directed at 'cultured Christians', to whom they presented what they regarded as a reasonable faith.

Groningen professors were slow to accept German Higher Criticism, with its attacks upon the authenticity of some books of the Bible, and they affirmed the historicity of the Jesus of the New Testament, which German critics denied.[4] For some time the Groningers resisted the philosophic influence of Willem Opzoomer (1821-92) of Utrecht also.

Opzoomer, a professor of philosophy at the University of Utrecht, was vigorously anti-supernatural in his teaching, and he delighted to criticize theologians. Although he rejected all historic Christian dogmas, Opzoomer claimed to be a Christian because he preserved 'the essence' of Christianity. Actually he was a naturalist who explained all phenomena in terms of cause and effect. Since the Groningen theologians adjusted Christian beliefs to accommodate the arguments of anti-Christian scholars, they could not effectively blunt the philosophy of naturalism or the assaults of Higher Criticism. Their approach to the faith enjoyed considerable popularity among intellectuals and the upper classes for a while, but it provoked the protests that led to the *Afscheiding.* In the last third of the nineteenth century the Groningen school abandoned its reservations about radical criticism of the Bible and joined the Moderns (modernists) in opposition to a resurgent orthodoxy within the Dutch Reformed Church.

The Ethicals

Within the framework of religious liberalism, Ethical Theology was the second major threat to orthodoxy in the nineteenth-century Netherlands. This movement aspired to achieve a *Vermittelungs-theologie,* a mediating theology. The progenitor of this movement was Daniel Chantepie de la Saussaye (1818-74), pastor of a Walloon congregation in Leiden and author of *La Crise Religieuse en Holland.*[5] Chantepie and his followers published a magazine entitled *Ernst en Vrede (Sincerity and Peace)* through which they contended that orthodox Calvinism lacked inner personal faith, which the term 'ethical' signified for them.

Ethicals accepted all critical theories about the origins, composition and reliability of the Bible, and they argued that Scripture *becomes* the Word of God for an individual when it speaks to his or her conscience. Chantepie and his disciples assumed the autonomy of the human moral consciousness and denied the corruption of human nature that is a fundamental tenet of historic Christianity.[6]

Chantepie came from a French Huguenot family that had migrated to the Netherlands in the eighteenth century. He studied at the University of Leiden with professors who espoused the Groningen theology and some other unorthodox views.

After serving pastorates in three cities, he became a professor at Groningen.

Although he maintained a liberal perspective on Christianity, Chantepie regarded the *réveil* as a sign of vitality in the church, a work of the Holy Spirit. He believed, however, that the *réveil* lacked an adequate doctrinal formulation and, over against the orthodox party within the Dutch Reformed Church, he argued that the traditional Forms of Unity should be replaced with a new statement of faith.[7] Chantepie professed to be a Calvinist, but he proposed to strip Calvin's teachings of 'Scholastic' interpretations that he thought had encrusted them.[8] He tried to mediate between the contending interpretations of Christianity coming from the Universities of Leiden and Utrecht, neither of which espoused the historic Christian faith. Chantepie de la Saussaye fought both orthodox Calvinists and modernists, but his awkward manner of writing impaired the communication of his ideas. The Ethical school of thought that he led failed to achieve any significant mediation.[9]

The Moderns

The Moderns comprised the third and most radical opposition to the Reformed faith in the Netherlands. The University of Leiden was the centre of this teaching, where Professor J. N. Scholten (1811-85) was its most vigorous spokesman. Moderns regarded themselves as agents of enlightenment, as they espoused Darwin's hypothesis of evolution and critical theories about the Bible. They believed they were progressives leading church and society forward so as to make the Christian faith compatible with a naturalistic world-view.

Building on the work of Opzoomer, the Moderns imbibed much influence from the University of Tübingen, where radical German scholars were assailing the foundations of Christian belief. Scholten's inaugural address at the University of Franeker in 1840 attacked the Groningen theology, as well as that of historic orthodoxy, and called for further revisions of Christian belief prompted by the influence of German idealist philosophy. He portrayed Jesus as the ideal human being whose example leads people to love one another.

In 1848, when he was a professor at Leiden, Scholten published *The Doctrine of the Reformed Church*, in which he affirmed belief in a personal God and asserted a concept of predestination. He rejected the Calvinist view of election and argued for universal salvation which God has predestined for all humanity. He maintained that God's Word is *within* the Bible, and the Holy Spirit enables people to find it. The biblical word always agrees with the revelation that comes through reason and conscience. He explained the witness of the Holy Spirit to believers as pertaining not to the Bible as history, but to its religious message. This message is that people should follow their moral and rational faculties, which lead them to true freedom.[10]

Concerning the matter of redemption, Scholten taught that sin is real, but guilt is not. The *feeling* of guilt will disappear when people realize that God has predestined everybody for salvation. This is the conclusion of reason, which he regarded as the all-sufficient authority.[11]

In addition to his *Doctrine of the Reformed Church*, Scholten produced a critical introduction to the New Testament and he supported the work of Old Testament scholar Abraham Kuenen (1828-91), his colleague at Leiden, who joined the faculty in 1854.

Kuenen rejected supernaturalism and explained the Christian faith in terms of the evolutionary development of religion. He held that it is necessary to redefine Christianity from time to time in the light of scientific advances. He denied the Mosaic authorship of the Pentateuch and explained the books of the

Old Testament as products of Israel's evolution in religious thinking. His teaching enjoyed much acceptance at Leiden, and his
students spread it through the National Church.[12]

The scene set for battle

Religious liberalism in its varied expressions held sway in all
Dutch universities by the time Abraham Kuyper was ready to
begin his higher education in 1855. Some liberals claimed that
they were faithful to the Reformation heritage by subjecting all
traditional beliefs to critical re-examination, even though that
led them to reject all historic confessions of faith. They denied
everything they found contrary to reason, or offensive to their
consciences and, therefore, scorned miracles, because they
would not believe in divine interventions into history. They had
no place for a doctrine of original sin or the need for atonement. Their God was not triune, and their Christ was humanity's
ideal of a good person and wise teacher. As one influential
liberal put it, the Genesis accounts of creation are 'nothing more
than legends of a very high religious inspiration but absolutely
devoid of historical or scientific authority'.[13] He summarized
the whole basis of liberalism when he wrote, 'The very idea of
a religious authority *external* to man is based on a childish
psychology.'[14]

Many people in the Netherlands received liberalism gladly
because they had adopted the assumptions of its world-view
with which orthodoxy is irreconcilable. Although some liberals
claimed they wanted to tell the truth about religion and thereby
to stimulate piety, their teaching led to scepticism and indifference towards the church. By the mid-nineteenth century the
schools of religious thought described above were ascendant in
the theological faculties of the Dutch universities, where they
educated almost all pastors of the Dutch Reformed Church.

Opposition to this trend came from within the National Church from Guillaume Groen van Prinsterer, of whom Abraham Kuyper, after his conversion, became an ally. By about 1870 a strong resurgence of orthodoxy was underway in Reformed circles. There was much less resistance to liberalism in Lutheran, Mennonite and Remonstrant (Arminian) churches. Some liberal pastors encountered such opposition from orthodox congregations that they left the Dutch Reformed Church to become Remonstrant ministers. A battle for the minds and souls of the Dutch people was inevitable, a battle in which Abraham Kuyper became the leader of the orthodox forces.

4.
The rise of a great defence

When Abraham Kuyper arrived in Beesd to commence his first pastorate, he brought with him a sceptical attitude towards the truths it was his duty to expound. The congregation there was diverse in its beliefs. Some people seemed to be indifferent towards doctrine, while others ascribed value only to the moral principles of the Christian faith, but some members were vigorously orthodox and therefore critical of pastors who did not preach the gospel. Kuyper at first thought of the fervently Reformed parishioners as malcontents. Later, however, he confessed that God had used those 'malcontents' as instruments in his conversion.[1]

Conversion

Kuyper soon discovered that the people he disdained because of the rigour of their beliefs were theologically literate and prepared to confront him in matters of doctrine. The one who exerted the greatest influence upon his career was Pietje Baltus (1830-1914), who said to him bluntly, 'You do not give us the true bread of life.'[2] She witnessed to the grace of God in her own life and explained to her pastor how her beliefs differed from his, as she presented him with the historic Reformed confessions and related their teachings to him. Kuyper spent many hours listening to a peasant woman instruct him in the faith. Later he related that he had tried to argue with her and with other orthodox believers, but, as he put it, 'I began to listen more than talk.'[3] Although a distinguished Doctor of Theology, Kuyper attended eagerly to the teaching of common people who demonstrated great learning accompanied by fervent love for Christ.

At the suggestion of Pietje Baltus, Abraham Kuyper read John Calvin's *Institutes of the Christian Religion* regularly, and that reading reinforced her testimony to him. His conversion followed, as believers in his congregation prayed for him and sought his salvation. In Calvin's *Institutes* he found the concept of God as Father and the church as mother of believers, which he thought was similar to what he had read in *The Heir of Redcliffe*. After his conversion he said, 'My life goal was now the restoration of a church that could be our mother.'[4]

For the rest of his life Kuyper kept a photo of Pietje Baltus on his desk. He remained in Beesd until 1867, and while there he published a critical edition of John à Lasco's works, a project that assured him recognition as a scholar.[5] When he was leaving Beesd he confessed to his congregation that he had begun there uncertain about God's truth and with an empty heart. One of his last appeals as pastor there occurred when he besought a child to see the Saviour.[6]

The move to Utrecht

Although Dr Kuyper had always cherished the *kleine luyden* (common people) at Beesd, the culture of a small village was not one in which he and Johanna could live comfortably, and in November 1867 they moved to Utrecht, where Kuyper was installed as a pastor at the *Domkerk*, a large cathedral-type church, the central structure of the Dutch Reformed Church in that city. With ten other ministers he had responsibility for the entire membership of the National Church in that urban community. He delivered his first sermon there on 10 November, as he expounded the text: 'The Word of God became flesh and dwelt among us' (John 1:14). It was clear that he no longer entertained doubts about the miracle of the incarnation.[7] His eloquent scriptural preaching harmonized well with the orthodox views of the elders who formed the consistory, the ecclesiastical ruling body in Utrecht.

The Dutch Reformed Church in Utrecht had a reputation for being solidly orthodox, so Kuyper went there expecting to find its leaders engaged in a vigorous defence of the faith. To his dismay, however, they appeared feeble in the face of the challenge from liberalism, and some of them tried to avoid controversy about disputed issues. It was a great disappointment when he learned that some of his colleagues in the ministry were modernists, who refused to baptize 'in the name of the Father and of the Son and of the Holy Spirit'. Instead they administered the sacrament in the name of 'faith, hope and love'.[8]

When confronted with false teaching in his church, Abraham Kuyper called for a vigorous response, and he decried the attitude that sought peace in the church at the expense of truth. He said, 'We cannot be passive and silent towards those who reject God's Word and our holy faith.'[9] He then wrote a pamphlet in which he argued that local congregations should have the right to call pastors without permission from the National Church officials, and he urged congregations to employ only men of orthodox persuasion. He assailed the decadent moral condition of many professing Christians and criticized the church for its failure to discipline them. In this way Kuyper made his début into national life and thereby initiated a struggle to reform the National Church that lasted until 1886, when he and a large number of orthodox believers withdrew from it to preserve the Reformed faith in a separate church body.

The struggle to reform the National Church

The effort to combat liberalism and to restore the historic character of the Dutch Reformed Church began with a frontal challenge to the authority of national ecclesiastical officials. Kuyper
and the consistory of elders refused to co-operate with a 'visitation' by National Church authorities and at the same time protested against the liberal theology of church leaders. This situation became tense and almost led to a formal trial of the
dissidents in the *Domkerk*, but the authorities chose not to press
the matter. With much boldness Kuyper asserted that every congregation should be free to determine its own ecclesiastical
affiliations. [10]

By this time Kuyper had become leader of the orthodox
party within the Dutch Reformed Church and a national figure
with numerous supporters and detractors. Few people could be
neutral where Kuyper was concerned, and he regarded neutrality as an abomination. He wrote, 'When principles that run
against your deepest convictions begin to win the day, then
battle is your calling, and peace has become sin; you must, at
the price of dearest peace, lay your convictions bare before
friend and enemy with all the fire of your faith.'[11]

Kuyper's call for reforms in church government was not an
innovation. He sought to return to the system in effect before
1816, when King William I had imposed synodical control.
Kuyper wanted ecclesiastical authority entirely in the hands of
elders and deacons chosen by the congregations, and he held
that every local congregation should have the right to withdraw
from the National Church body without penalties. He believed
that a revival of the Dutch Reformed Church could not occur
without such changes. He said the church should support itself
and not depend upon state subsidies.[12]

It is evident that Kuyper hoped a revived Reformed Church
would become a counterweight against the growing authority
of central government in the Netherlands. He feared the statist

world-view that had been growing since the French Revolution, and he thought that a stable church united in faith could thwart the movement towards authoritarian civil government. To accomplish that he promoted a new reformation that featured a return to historic theology and the adoption of a free, independent church polity. He cited the Free Church in Scotland as a model.[13]

Kuyper joins with Groen van Prinsterer

While in the course of organizing a defence of Reformed doctrine and local church autonomy, Abraham Kuyper met Guillaume Groen van Prinsterer (1810-76) in May 1869 at the *Domkerk*, and the two became friends and co-workers in the cause of reformation.

Groen had already come to believe that secular humanism in the wake of the French Revolution had created an antithesis to Christianity, so that opposing world-views were contending for the souls of the Dutch people. In 1860 he had published a plea for a consistently Christian world-view that applied divine laws to all of life, personal and national. He found both Conservatism and Liberalism unacceptable as political philosophies because they were not Christian. Since about 1840 Groen had been urging revisions of the constitution so as to make the government responsible to parliament rather than to the king, and he sought a reorganization of education that would have created a Protestant school system with state support. In 1857, however, the Primary Education Act encouraged secularism in the schools by diluting the teaching so as to promote a lowest-common-denominator understanding of religion. Groen, then a member of parliament, voted against the measure, but it passed by forty-seven votes to thirteen. Groen resigned from parliament in disgust and realized, perhaps for the first time, that the Dutch kingdom was not a Christian nation. Later he returned to parliament and resumed the struggle for Christian education.

Groen van Prinsterer was the first Reformed scholar to compose a thorough analysis of the problems that secular humanism had created. He described his own *Weltanschauung* (worldview) as anti-revolutionary and Christian historical and, like Augustine of Hippo (354-430) and John Calvin (1509-64), Groen maintained that there is an antithesis between the City of God and the City of Man that began at Adam's fall and will continue until the return of Christ. In Groen's day that meant a contest between the Reformation principle of obedience to the authority of Scripture and the humanist rejection of all authority external to man.

In Groen's judgement the decadent condition of the Dutch Reformed Church and the increasing authoritarianism of the national government were consequences of humanism and anti-Christian religion generated by French intellectuals known as *philosophes* and spread by the conquests of French revolutionary armies. He wanted the gradual implementation of Christian principles in society and the state without repressive policies towards non-believers. He held that political conflicts are due to underlying spiritual conflicts — clashes of principles. Groen wanted Christians to compose political programmes on the basis of faith, as opposed to all forms of humanism — liberal, conservative, Marxist, socialist, etc. He warned that secular humanism leads to tyranny.[14]

Despite his intelligence, great learning, social standing and tireless resolution, Groen was not an effective leader. He appeared at times to be a general without an army, but that situation changed when Abraham Kuyper, a leader of exceptional abilities, joined his course and 'transformed the small intellectual group organized by Groen into a mass movement with slogans, popular campaigns, and party publications. His ideal was total rebirth. Not only the political predominance of the liberals, but also their intellectual monopoly was to be broken.'[15]

Groen and Kuyper shared a keen sense of social responsibility towards the poor, the sick and the oppressed. They believed that society's problems required Christian solutions. With Kuyper in the lead as spokesman for the Association for Christian National Schools, they struggled on behalf of Christian education, which is one of the subjects in the next chapter.

Pastor in Amsterdam

Kuyper ended his pastorate in Utrecht in March 1870, when he accepted a call to Amsterdam, the chief city of the Netherlands, the place where he was likely to have maximum opportunities to promote his cause. Over half the population of Amsterdam belonged to the Dutch Reformed Church, and one city-wide consistory of elders governed its ecclesiastical affairs. The National Church there had been deeply infected with theological liberalism, which orthodox believers had been unable to combat until 1867. In that year a governmental change in the church made it possible to place convinced Reformed pastors, elders and deacons on the consistory as vacancies occurred. An electoral commission was to nominate officials, and its first choice was Abraham Kuyper. His inaugural sermon, *Rooted and Grounded*, was an application of Ephesians 3:17-18, 'that Christ may dwell in your hearts through faith ... that you, being rooted and established in love, may have power ... to grasp how wide and long and high and deep is the love of Christ'. He made this an appeal for the reform of the National Church, a call for the restoration of historic Christianity, as expressed in the confessions of the Protestant Reformation. He made it clear that he sought, not a broadly evangelical church, but one that was specifically Reformed in belief and practice.[16]

The vigour with which Kuyper declared his purpose in Amsterdam delighted the orthodox members of the churches, but it provoked a backlash from those who had adopted a liberal interpretation of the faith. Kuyper's second sermon in his new church was 'The Comfort of Eternal Election', in which he proclaimed the doctrine of predestination to salvation, a subject previous pastors had ignored for a long time. Another Amsterdam minister attacked him from the pulpit, even though Kuyper's position on the doctrine in question was the teaching of the Dutch Reformed Church's official statements of faith. Kuyper went to Amsterdam to wage war against unbelief, and the battles began almost as soon as he arrived. Due to the changes of 1867, he did not stand alone. The consistory of Amsterdam was in the control of his supporters, so prospects for a successful reform of the church seemed promising. The opponents of orthodoxy had, however, just begun to fight.

As a preacher at Amsterdam's New Church, Kuyper attracted large audiences with his eloquent but simple proclamation of biblical truth. He had a remarkable ability to minister effectively to people from all classes of society and levels of education. Even those who disagreed with him knew that Kuyper loved Christ and his people and therefore spoke with evident conviction.

The struggle for reformation of the National Church

Kuyper understood church history well, and he diagnosed the condition of the Dutch Reformed Church accurately, so he fully expected that his efforts to restore the Reformed faith would lead to confrontation with officials of the National Church. An early sign of trouble appeared when he turned to dealing with the religious instruction of children in a municipal orphanage. A very liberal clergyman had been conducting catechism classes there for some time, and Kuyper decided to challenge him by inviting the orphans to study with him in his home. When the liberal minister retired, Kuyper led the orphanage committee to adopt a policy that assigned all religious instruction thereafter to orthodox teachers, although the committee allowed students to attend classes elsewhere if they chose.[17] The fact that a learned theologian cared about orphans and could teach them on their own level of understanding is evidence that Abraham Kuyper had a pastor's heart.

Kuyper's actions with regard to the orphans took place at the same time as he was contending with liberal opponents in the Amsterdam consistory. In 1872 he wrote in defence of seventeen elders who had declared their refusal to participate in church services and ecclesiastical affairs with liberal pastors. The elders had become incensed that some liberals from their pulpits had denied Christ's bodily resurrection, and church officials had refused to discipline the offenders. The protesting elders urged believers to follow their example, and so the church in Amsterdam became embroiled in controversy.

Kuyper's defence of the dissident elders presented a compilation of documents to verify the charges the elders had levied against the liberals, and it hailed the courage of the elders, whom he portrayed as guardians of the Reformed faith. He then began to enlist orthodox members of the consistory to organize for a systematic approach to reform of the National Church. Kuyper complained that only one-sixth of the Dutch Reformed Church members in Amsterdam attended services regularly, and he estimated that not more than one-tenth of them had received adequate catechetical instruction.[18] He called for vigorous evangelism through 'Sunday Schools, Bible and tract distribution, special meetings, and personal visitation'.[19] Some strictly Reformed believers at that point urged Kuyper to leave the National Church, but he argued that the liberals were still in a minority, as were those who thought the church had room for conflicting understandings of the faith. He hoped to rally the orthodox members and thereby to gain the support that could produce a reformation.[20]

In Kuyper's opinion the success of his efforts required a drastic change in the government of the church, so he called for a return to the presbyterian structure that had been in effect until King William I had imposed the rule of the National Synod in 1816. In a terse, pointed manner Kuyper asserted, 'The Synodical system of spiritual oppression is as illegitimate as Rome's coercion of souls. The church must be governed democratically. I want the oppressive Synodical system of 1816 abolished.'[21]

By 1873 it was evident that Abraham Kuyper and the orthodox party within the Dutch Reformed Church were prepared for the struggle to restore the historic character of that body. Bold declarations supported by resolute actions comprised their plan of action, and journalism, education and frequent protests were their methods.

· 5.

Reformation through journalism, education and political action

Soon after arriving in Amsterdam, Abraham Kuyper began writing articles for *De Heraut (The Herald)*, a weekly newspaper that provided an organ for the dissemination of his beliefs about theological, ecclesiastical, social and political matters. He formed the *Heraut* Society as an organization of committed Reformed believers who purchased the paper and chose him as editor-in-chief.

Although this publication gave Kuyper the means to spread his ideas widely, he believed that a daily Christian newspaper was essential to accomplish his objectives. In 1872 his organization began producing *De Standaard (The Standard)* every day, and *De Heraut* became the Saturday edition which featured coverage of religious matters in some detail. For the rest of his career Kuyper used his newspapers as the major instruments by which to promote his Christian world-view as it applied to all areas of life. *De Standaard* became a very effective organ for the Anti-Revolutionary Party, a Christian political movement of which Dr Kuyper became the leader.

At first Kuyper's articles in *De Standaard* appeared without his signature, and some of them provoked criticisms because he was still a pastor at the time. He justified his journalism as necessary to expound and defend the cause of orthodox Christianity and to consolidate and preserve the Reformed community in the Dutch kingdom.[1] He wrote thousands of articles on issues pertaining to the proper role of Christians in responding to national issues, and along with them he published devotional items that reflect his deep Christian piety and his longing for a great revival of biblical religion across the land. Journalism was Kuyper's broadest effort to educate Christians about conditions in church and society and to summon them to organized action in defence of their heritage.

The 'mirage' of modernism

At the same time that he was writing newspaper articles, Abraham Kuyper was boldly attacking modern contradictions of the historic Christian faith by means of lectures he presented as forums became available. In March 1871 he delivered an oration entitled 'Modernism, a Fata Morgana in the Christian World', which he later printed for wide circulation.[2] In this essay the author depicted theological modernism as an alluring belief like a fairy mirage that appears as Morgana in an Arthurian romance. It seems to be beautiful to behold, but 'it lacks the reality of the truth'.[3]

According to Kuyper, modernism exerts a great appeal to people who regard themselves as learned and worldly-wise, people to whom orthodox Christianity seems absurd. They dismiss miracles as impossible and turn to modernist religion as an alternative belief that satisfies their desire for ethical values without straining their credulity. They think they have embraced truth, but actually they have attributed reality to a mirage, a fairy tale. 'As the Morgana is nothing else than the refraction of the light in nature, so heresy is but the necessary refraction of the light of Christianity in the spiritual atmosphere of an age.'[4]

Dr Kuyper contended that the root of heresy is in the moral condition of human hearts estranged from God by sin, and heretics seek to dominate Christ's church by altering its confession so as to make it compatible with their modern anti-supernatural views. As he explained, 'In each age of renewed spiritual enquiry some heresy or other finds its congenial soil in the ideas prevalent in such an age and is fed by them. Hence, such error acquires a dominating position; such error is to be explained from the refraction of Christianity in the spirit of that age.'[5]

In the context of the nineteenth century Kuyper cited modernism as the current mirage. It claimed to be Protestant, but it was actually a religious form of rationalism which denied the basis of authority for Protestant Christianity. 'Modernism has no right to deck itself with the honours of the Reformation,' he argued.[6] Modernists worship an abstraction of their own creation; they do not deal with reality where God is concerned, for they do not accept God's revelation of himself in Scripture.

Kuyper challenged the modernists to consider the implications of their own beliefs, for their view of God leads to a false understanding of mankind. If, as modernists contend, humanity is the product of evolution, there can be no firm basis for morality: 'For, if man's moral nature is derived from his animal nature, which stands, of course, on the lower plane, the separation between the natures of both [animals and men] is removed, and thus the absolute or specific character of *ethical* life falls away.'[7] Modernists claimed to be free thinkers, champions of tolerance, but Kuyper said they were 'the most stiff-necked dogmatists', for they aspired to make their beliefs universal, and they ridiculed those who disagreed with them. They professed to accept a Jesus who was a rabbi (teacher) but not the divine Christ. They believed, not in the sinfulness of human nature, but in its inherent goodness. 'Their dogmas ... are merely an abstract of ideas current in the market place of life... For in modernism public opinion has taken the place of the testimony of the Holy Spirit.'[8]

Into the political arena

Having once been a modernist himself, Abraham Kuyper was well equipped to understand and to evaluate its theology and its entire world-view. He did so often, with authority and un-usual effectiveness. Liberal theologians across the country and officials of the National Synod realized that they faced a potent and determined adversary, and their battles with Kuyper had just begun when he left the pastorate in the spring of 1874 to enter politics.

Kuyper's decision came as a result of his conviction that the reform of church and society required a systematic, compre-hensive effort to assert the claims of Christ over all areas of life, public as well as private. He regarded Christian education as indispensable to the success of his endeavours, and as a mem-ber of parliament he could strive to free Christians from de-pendence upon public schools, where humanism prevailed, and could work to relieve them from the financial burden of paying taxes for schools that taught things contrary to their faith. In May 1869 Dr Kuyper addressed the Congress of the Associa-tion for National Christian Education, where he delivered 'An Appeal to the Conscience of the People'. He explained the an-tithesis between Christian and secular concepts of education and asserted that Reformed believers had a responsibility to provide education in truth. If the state would not do this, Chris-tians would have to establish their own schools. He wanted Christian political action to seek government approval for pri-vate schools supported from tax revenues. He demanded the right for citizens to operate various types of private schools, Roman Catholic and Protestant, without government interfer-ence, but with public funding.[9] *De Heraut* carried the mast-head, 'For a Free Church and a Free School in a Free Land'.

Groen van Prinsterer in 1847 had published *Unbelief and Revolution*, in which he exposed the secular humanism of the

French Revolution and summoned Christians to form a political philosophy and a political organization to combat it.[10] Since Kuyper's world-view demanded the recognition of Christ as King over all creation, implementing Groen's call became a vital part of Kuyper's cause. Groen composed a philosophic basis for government in opposition to the ideas of the French Revolution. He recognized the Reformed faith as the kingdom's greatest asset, a unifying influence that should be maintained in the face of secularism because there is an antithesis between Christianity and rationalism. Kuyper took up the theme of the antithesis and built a political following upon that basis.

Abraham Kuyper directed his political appeal to the lower middle class, which was very conservative in its views. As late as 1880, most of these people could not vote because they did not own property. Kuyper recruited them into the Anti-Revolutionary Party, which he promoted as the voice of the *kleine luyden* (common people). He had to convince these people to seek the franchise, for they had been apathetic towards politics. His quest for Christian schools aroused their interest.[11]

Groen van Prinsterer's slogan, 'The gospel versus the revolution,' asserted the radical antipathy between humanist politics and Christian faith, and that perceived incompatibility became the basis for the Anti-Revolutionary Party. Groen believed that the *philosophes* (radical French humanists of the eighteenth century) had promoted an anti-Christian political philosophy as part of their secularist world-view and that the consequence was despotism. In *Unbelief and Revolution* Groen argued against the anti-Christian character of politics without the sanction of God's law, and he showed that those rulers who had imbibed the principles of the *philosophes* exercised 'revolutionary omnipotence' unrestrained by historic liberties. They saw themselves as 'crowned deputies of the Sovereign People', and in the name of the 'people' they maintained despotic authority *over* the people.[12] The Anti-Revolutionary Party was Groen's alternative to Liberal and Conservative parties that had become infected with the ideas of revolutionary France.

Groen served in parliament at various times between 1840 and 1865. In 1848 he appealed for laws to protect children working in factories, but parliament did not enact such legislation until 1874. For a long time he thought of the Netherlands as a Protestant Christian state in which secularist politicians were out of place, but eventually he acknowledged that the influence of secularism had become so strong that his view was untenable. Secular humanism, the 'religion of unbelief', had come to dominate Dutch political life,[13] so he wanted a Christian political movement to combat it. He hailed the Protestant Reformation for bringing the true enlightenment of the gospel, and he advocated obedience to God's law as the basis for national life and government. He analysed European culture and called for a return to biblical norms, i.e., a recognition of divine sovereignty over all of life.[14]

Early in his public career Groen van Prinsterer supported the Conservative party, as did most Dutch Christians. His devotion to principle, however, offended many Conservatives and some of his fellow Christians. In 1871 he broke with the Conservatives, who did not accept his world-view, and began working with Abraham Kuyper. Groen's anti-revolutionary philosophy provided the ideological basis for a political movement, but he was not an effective leader, and even some believers opposed his efforts on behalf of Christian schools. His sole success in the matter of education was to gain permission from the government to operate private schools without public funds. The people who paid for such schools had to support state schools as well by their taxes.[15]

Like Groen van Prinsterer, Abraham Kuyper sought a Christian society through a progressive application of biblical principles to current problems. Kuyper was the most vigorous and effective advocate of Groen's ideas, which he developed into a working political movement — the Anti-Revolutionary Party — with a policy based upon principles rather than pragmatic political objectives. This was the first truly national political organization in the Netherlands. Organized at Utrecht in April 1879, it affirmed God's authority over the entire creation, including civil government. It did not seek a theocracy, but a separation of church and state into distinct, but not alien, spheres of authority. The Anti-Revolutionary Party promoted reforms within the parliamentary structure and respected the civil rights of non-Christians. It insisted nevertheless that God's moral laws must be the basis for the government of the nation.[16] When Kuyper entered parliament in 1874, he became the leader of the Anti-Revolutionary forces in that body, and he brought to that position great ability to communicate the concerns of his party to the common people, which Groen had not been able to do.

The campaign for Christian schools

When Groen first demanded state approval for Protestant schools, Roman Catholics became alarmed because they too wanted their own schools. Reformed Protestants and Catholics at that time had little political leverage. Kuyper saw the necessity for Protestant-Catholic collaboration to obtain freedom for parents to choose who would educate their children without the burden of paying taxes for a state system that inculcated within students the values of secular humanism. Both Reformed and Catholic leaders had to appeal for support to common people who did not yet have the right to vote, and they had to obtain that support while those people were still disposed towards a religious world-view. Herman Schaepman (1844-1903), a priest and church historian, became leader of the Catholic movement, and he and Kuyper joined forces to pursue their mutual goals in education. In order to succeed with their plans, Protestants and Roman Catholics had to secure the franchise for their constituents. In 1870, when the Dutch population was about 3,500,000, only 12% of adult males could vote. Laws in 1887 and 1896 would enlarge that to 49%.[17]

When Kuyper decided to accept a seat in the Second Chamber of Parliament, he had to resign as a minister of his church, for the constitution did not allow clergymen to serve in the Second Chamber. However, he remained an elder in the Amsterdam church and never ceased to promote its purity in doctrine and practice.

Secularist parliamentarians expressed much dismay at the election of Kuyper, and some of them greeted his arrival in the Second Chamber with scorn. They soon realized, however, that they had to deal with him, and he proved to be a tough-minded, able adversary who refused to compromise his Christian principles. The debate about Christian schools engaged Kuyper's attention almost as soon as he took his seat. In order to facilitate an understanding of what the struggle for Christian schools entailed, some consideration of the state of education in the Netherlands is appropriate.

During the era of Napoleonic rule a law of 1806 allowed for both public and private elementary schools, but private ones received no state aid. State schools had to teach a form of Christianity without doctrine, and religious exercises included prayer and Bible reading. Students who desired catechetical instruction were granted time off in school hours to obtain it. This was a major change from the policy prior to 1795, when state schools taught pupils the *Heidelberg Catechism*. The alteration that French rule introduced greatly diminished the influence of the Reformed faith in the schools.

The law of 1806 promoted a form of civil religion on the grounds that it was necessary for the moral and educational health of society, which was one of Napoleon's firm beliefs. By the mid-nineteenth century secularism was permeating Dutch schools, and it is evident that the government wanted this situation to continue. Some teachers lost their positions because of their overtly Christian practices in the schools, and some believers began their own schools to protect children from the alien philosophies to which public institutions were exposing them.

In 1878 Kappeyne van de Coppello, a liberal member of parliament, initiated legislation to cripple Christian schools by forcing them to meet standards that entailed expenses they could not afford. Despite opposition from the Anti-Revolutionary Party and the Roman Catholics, the law took effect. This convinced Dr Kuyper to lead the fight for equality and public funding of private schools. The law, nevertheless, remained in force until 1889.[18]

Kuyper went beyond Groen's criticisms of Dutch political parties and offered alternatives to the liberal-secularist policies of the state. He devised a dynamic programme for Christian political reforms, for his concept of an antithesis between Christianity and humanism featured much more than assaults upon the latter. He recognized plurality and diversity as facts of life, so he sought an arrangement in which Protestant, Catholics and humanists could pursue their own interests and maintain their own cultures within one state which would subsidize the schools of each group. The Anti-Revolutionary Party led the way towards these objectives and in the process presented the first national political programme in Dutch history based upon agreed principles.[19] That programme could not have succeeded without the support of Roman Catholics, which proved to be decisively important.

The proposal for a Protestant-Catholic coalition actually originated with Herman Schaepman, who believed it would aid in developing a Catholic political party to promote the aims of his own church. In 1880 Schaepman won a seat in the Second

Chamber, the first priest to do so. He gradually accepted more and more of Kuyper's ideas about social reforms and the extension of the franchise, but Schaepman encountered stiff opposition from some wealthy Catholics who feared his efforts would provoke a backlash against Catholicism in the kingdom. He persisted, however, and established his leadership of the Roman Catholic party.

In 1889 the Protestant-Catholic coalition government secured passage of an Education Act which allowed private schools to obtain one-third of their expenses from public funds. This major victory assured the financial viability of private schools, and it hindered the secularists' quest for a monopoly over education. Opponents of the law grudgingly accepted it rather than resume a bitter struggle about education. The coalition government scored another triumph in the Labour Act (1889), which protected women and children from exploitation in factories.[20] Full funding for private schools did not come until a revision of the constitution in 1917.

From 1888 to 1938 the Reformed-Catholic coalition won most of the elections, although by small margins. It never drew more than 55% of the vote. The coalition acquired control of the government because of changes in electoral laws that occurred in 1887. The death of Prince Alexander in 1884 had left a female heiress to the throne, but her succession required a change in the Fundamental Law which governed this matter. Queen Emma became regent for her daughter Wilhelmina, who was too young to reign. Reforms in 1887 provided for her eventual succession and for an enlargement in the electorate. The First Chamber of Parliament was to have fifty seats and the Second Chamber 100. Provincial legislatures continued to choose members of the First Chamber, but the electorate chose the Second Chamber, whose members served four-year terms. At that point males over the age of twenty-three, who were householders, or who paid a stipulated amount of tax, were eligible to vote, and the electorate increased from about 100,000 to about 350,000. The Reformed-Catholic coalition won the first election under the new system, and Baron Aeneas Mackay became prime minister in 1888. The new government and its supporters in parliament then enacted the law to benefit private schools.[21]

Despite the disdain of the humanists, Kuyper's leadership in pursuing equality for private and state schools has earned him appropriate tributes, as, for example, that of historian Bernard H. M. Vlekke, who asserted that Kuyper 'rendered immeasurable service to the nation in general. He ... brought the strictly orthodox Calvinist peasants and fishermen out of the cultural isolation into which they had withdrawn as a mistaken defence against modern trends of thought. He ... brought the people of the remotest sections to participation in national political and cultural life... He ... helped to do away with one of the most disastrous divisions in the Netherlands, the antagonism of Calvinists and Catholics based on events that happened three hundred years before.'[22]

Higher education and the Free University

A potent opposition to the Anti-Revolutionary – Roman Catholic programme for schools came from liberal university professors who wanted to preserve the secular character of education. Dr Kuyper knew, from experience at the University of Leiden and from familiarity with the works of professors at other universities, that the Dutch institutions of higher learning were strongholds of modernist theology and vigorous advocates of an anti-Christian world-view. He therefore proposed to create a Christian university in which the biblical theology of Reformed orthodoxy would be the foundation and its implications would inform the teaching of all subjects in the curriculum. From a human perspective this seemed to be an impossible dream, but Kuyper refused to be deterred by obstacles or by predictions of failure. The Free University of Amsterdam opened for classes in 1880.

While soliciting funds for the Christian school movement, Abraham Kuyper had to rely upon the people of the labouring and lower middle classes, because they were the ones oppressed by the school law which forced them to pay taxes for the state system. He appealed to his beloved *kleine luyden*, and they responded sacrificially. He likened their gifts to the 'widow's mite' that Jesus commended (Mark 12:42-44).[23] His plan for a Christian university meant that he would have to find more money from private sources already paying for both state and private schools, but Kuyper would not allow that problem to stop the project. He believed that all institutions in society are to be autonomous; that is, they do not derive their authority from the state. Christian schools and a Christian university were therefore necessary demonstrations of freedom from state control. Critics claimed that this philosophy of education was subversive of loyalty to the nation.[24]

In 1875 Kuyper spoke in the Second Chamber in support of the right of private organizations to maintain universities independent of government control. All three Dutch universities, those at Leiden, Utrecht and Groningen, were public institutions, and so they had a vested interest in preserving their monopoly over higher education. Kuyper's proposal seemed threatening, so many leaders in education and politics opposed it. He nevertheless formed a committee of interested Christians, and its deliberations led to the formation of the Association for Higher Education on Reformed Principles, which the crown recognized in 1879 as a legal corporation entitled to proceed with its plan for a university. Kuyper defended the right of universities to freedom from state control by citing the history of higher education in Europe. He argued that institutions such as Paris and Bologna had once been private, and he blamed the

French Revolution for imposing government authority and ownership upon them and other universities.[25]

Support for the new Free University of Amsterdam came from a few major donors, but most contributions came from the *kleine luyden*, who filled coin banks they kept in their homes. They were the ones upon whom Kuyper hoped his university would confer particular benefits. His resurgent Calvinism might be considered a kind of 'emancipation theology' for them. [26]

The need for a Christian university became especially clear in 1877 with the passage of the Dutch Universities Act, which changed the theology curricula so that the Dutch Reformed Church no longer controlled them. Thereafter systematic and pastoral theology were not to be parts of the curriculum; churches could establish seminaries for such instruction. Graduate departments of theology became faculties for the scientific study of religion, which were to assume a position of 'neutrality' towards the claims of all religions, including Christianity.[27] When church leaders protested against this change, the state allowed them to fill two adjunct professorial positions at each university, as selected by the synod of the National Church. Orthodox scholars were thereby excluded.

Dr Kuyper and his associates might have responded to the challenge coming from the state policy towards university education by founding a theological seminary, as the Christian Reformed Church had done earlier at Kampen. This course of action, Kuyper believed, would subvert a genuinely Christian world-view. Although providing orthodox theological instruction was the most pressing immediate need, Kuyper held that believers must reject isolation from the world, as Anabaptists have done; they must pursue all the arts and sciences and thereby appreciate the contributions to knowledge that come from unbelievers as well as from Christians. Nothing less than a full-orbed university could arrest the spiritual decay in the Netherlands. All Christian professors must begin with faith and present all disciplines from the perspective of a biblical world-view.[28] The Free University would have faculties of arts, sciences, law, medicine and theology, but when it opened for classes in 1880, there were only five students and five professors, and Kuyper himself taught theology, Hebrew, aesthetics and literature.

Although Christians had gained the right to operate their own university, the state had not granted that institution the power of *effectus civilis;* that is, degrees from the Free University would not be valid unless its graduates passed qualifying examinations at a state university. The Dutch Reformed Church refused to ordain Free University graduates as pastors, even when they validated their degrees as required.[29]

Abraham Kuyper was a professor at the Free University of Amsterdam from 1880-1901, and for part of that period he was the university's rector. During that time he was unable to obtain state agreement to recognize the inherent validity of the degrees awarded by his institution. In 1901, however, he became prime minister of the nation at the head of another Reformed-Catholic coalition government, so he possessed the authority to fulfil his cherished desire. He introduced a bill in 1903 which became a law in 1905, and it granted full legal standing for private universities, technical schools and schools preparing students for higher education. The Free University was the only private institution of higher learning at the time, but the Catholic University of Nijmegen opened in 1923 with the same rights as those enjoyed by the Free University of Amsterdam.

The Higher Education Law of 1905 not only ratified the equality of public and private institutions; it provided for private professorial chairs at state universities. It did not disturb the process of academic appointments that came from the Crown and involved the government and the universities themselves in the selection. Kuyper knew he was not prime minister of a Christian nation, and he did not seek to make it a theocracy. He believed sincerely in freedom for all schools of thought to contend with one another. He cited the Catholic University of Louvain and the Free University of Brussels in Belgium, and Johns Hopkins University, Harvard University and the University of Pennsylvania in America, as examples of outstanding private institutions, so he argued that there should be many comparable universities in Europe.

In justifying the particular character of the Free University of Amsterdam, Kuyper compared two educational models. The first, he argued, is indifferent towards objective truth, for there is no subscription there to a defined world-view. The second model is a confessional institution that fosters learning within a framework of accepted principles. He argued that government should not favour one type only. He asked for academic pluralism, in contrast to those 'liberals' who intolerantly demanded a state monopoly over education, one that excluded the possibility of grasping absolute, revealed truth.[30] In this way Kuyper tried to rebut complaints of professors at public institutions who argued that universities must be neutral towards God and the claims of religion. Since a Christian university demands that teaching be subject to the dogmas of the faith, it could not, in their view, be a true university. Kuyper responded by denying that neutrality is possible, and he showed that all learning begins with assumptions of faith that cannot be verified. He contended that secular scholars should admit that, like Christians, they too are dogmatists. Where Christians begin with a commitment to the sovereignty of God, secularists assume the autonomy of man.[31]

In Kuyper's view a Christian university must adhere to a biblical world-view, and only the Reformed faith promotes this consistently. Calvinism alone features the proper faith-assumptions that are necessary to pursue truth in all domains of learning and to contend with opposing non-Christian world-views. To accomplish this task a Christian university must be free from both state and church control. It operates in a sphere of authority separate from church and state and is therefore directly responsible to God for its teachings. Kuyper maintained that the principles of theocentricity (God-centredness) and anthropocentricity (man-centredness) are antithetical and in head-on collision with each other. Nowhere is this more evident than in higher education. Christ is both personal Saviour of believing sinners and Lord of the universe, so he must be Lord of the university as well. God has enjoined human beings to enact his cultural mandate (Genesis 1:27-28), so believers must not retreat from society, and they must not ignore any academic subject as unworthy of Christian study.[32] The Free University implemented this dictum.

By the time the Free University opened in 1880, Kuyper had established his reputation as the nation's leading exponent of reformation through journalism, education and political action. The philosophic basis for his political actions is the subject of the next chapter.

6.

The authority of the spheres

Throughout his public career Abraham Kuyper appealed vigorously for Christian action on the basis of principles, for he regarded Christianity as far more than a doctrine of personal salvation from sin. He maintained a strictly biblical view of sin and salvation, and he defended that teaching often. Kuyper understood, however, that Christianity is an entire *Weltanschauung*, or world-view, so believers must adhere to and espouse scriptural principles in every domain of life. He made this dictum patently and emphatically clear in the speech he delivered at the opening of the Free University of Amsterdam. There he asserted that the Christian world-view encompasses all academic fields and it conditions how professors and students pursue their learning. This is because it makes an enormous difference whether one regards man 'as a fallen sinner [or] … as a self-developed product of nature'.[1] In terms that leave no doubt about his conviction Kuyper declared: 'There is not one part of our world of thought that can be hermetically separated from the other parts, and there is not an inch in the entire area of our human life of which Christ, who is sovereign of all, does not cry "Mine!"'[2]

Because he viewed God as sovereign over everyone and everything, and man as a fallen creature corrupted by sin, Kuyper contended that all earthly officials, whatever the nature of their positions, possess only a derived authority which is limited to the sphere God has allotted to them. No one is entitled to rule absolutely, for that is a divine prerogative alone. God delegates authority to human agents in family, church, school and state, and those who govern in such spheres are accountable to God in the discharge of their duties and in the exercise of their limited authority. This means, for example, that neither the state nor the church is to intrude upon the other spheres but rather should protect their rights to operate freely.[3]

Humanist theories of authority rejected

His firm belief in the doctrines of creation and divine sovereignty led Kuyper into a protracted controversy with secular humanists, who regarded civil government as the product of a contract between rulers and subjects. The contract theory of government had received eloquent expression in the writings of John Locke (1632-1704) and Jean-Jacques Rousseau (1712-78), and by Kuyper's day it enjoyed almost universal acceptance in Europe and North America.[4] Kuyper, however, found the doctrine of popular sovereignty and the closely connected concept of state sovereignty objectionable because they ignore the biblical teachings about creation and the spheres of authority God has ordained for his own glory and for the benefit of mankind. Popular sovereignty and state sovereignty violate God's law in the interests of human autonomy. The French Revolution promoted this rebellion, and German idealist philosophers have encouraged it.

In an essay entitled 'False Theories of Sovereignty', Dr Kuyper cited the slogan popular in the French Revolution, *'Ni dieu, ni maître'* ('Neither god nor master'), as evidence that the humanists were in revolt against divine law. He agreed that the French monarchy prior to the revolution of 1789 had been authoritarian and oppressive, and he commended those who protested against the abuses of its rule. However, he believed the revolutionaries committed sin when they demanded freedom on the basis of human autonomy. The French rage for liberty brought tyranny to that nation and to those it conquered in revolutionary imperialism. Under the banner of popular sovereignty, the people of France had to endure military despotism under Napoleon, whose armies imposed his rule upon most of Europe.

Germans reacted to the French Revolution by promoting state sovereignty, which, Kuyper argued, was 'a product of Germanic philosophical pantheism'.[5] According to this theory, the will of the state is supreme, whether the particular form of government be monarchy, republic, or despotism. That is, the law proceeds from the will of the state without regard for eternal moral principles. Reformed Christianity must protest against both of these humanist theories of authority. As Kuyper expressed the matter, 'In opposition to both the atheistic popular sovereignty of the Encyclopaedians [French *philosophes*] and the pantheistic state sovereignty of German philosophers, the Calvinist maintains the sovereignty of God as the source of all authority among men... It teaches us to look upward from the existing law to the source of the eternal Right, in God; and it creates in us the indomitable courage to protest against the unrighteousness of the [earthly] law in the name of this highest Right.'[6]

The influence of Burke

Kuyper's entire career shows that he was never a mere reactionary trying to prevent changes of which he disapproved. His attitude towards the French Revolution was practically the same as that of his friend Groen van Prinsterer, although he was more eager to effect changes of a democratic character than his mentor had been. Both Groen and Kuyper acknowledged a debt to Edmund Burke (1729-97), an eloquent defender of constitutional government in Britain and perhaps the most perceptive critic of the French Revolution before Groen.[7] Like Burke, they viewed civil government as a historical, organic development based upon divine ordination. As Burke did, they denounced the French Revolutionaries for seeking to emancipate creatures from their dependence upon their Creator, although Burke argued as much from natural law as from Scripture, while for Groen and Kuyper the Bible was a sufficient authority.[8] Groen argued that revolution violates the order of nature because revolutionaries seek to rupture the necessary continuity of history. In so expressing his view Groen almost paraphrased Burke.[9]

Burke, Groen and Kuyper all attacked the *philosophes* as progenitors of a rebellion against the authority of God in order to exalt autonomous reason. This, they held, led to atheism and radical politics. They denied that existing social and political institutions were the sole causes of evil that revolution must destroy. Groen argued that popular sovereignty leads to statism in the form of absolute government which will not tolerate a religion that refuses to submit to it.[10] True freedom prevails where people submit to the laws of God. If law is merely the will of the majority, as Rousseau contended, socialism will be the inevitable result, and it will lead to despotism.[11] Groen lamented that the eighteenth century had witnessed the rejection of the Christian providential view of history in favour of a theory of progress based on presumed human perfectibility.[12] 'To deny God is [however] not to destroy him, and to deny human depravity is not to achieve human perfection.'[13]

Reform, not revolution

Many of Europe's conservatives reacted to rationalism and revolution by adopting romanticism as their world-view, but Groen and Kuyper refused to regard that as a healthy development. The spirit of romanticism sometimes fostered an excessive veneration for the past, which, Groen and Kuyper contended, ought not to occur. A conservatism that wants to restore the past is unacceptable because it ignores the need for growth and the inevitability of change. Progress has occurred despite the French Revolution, and Christians must recognize it. They should not desire 'a counter-revolution but the opposite of revolution'.[14] That is, Christians should strive to reform society in harmony with God's laws, which would thereby reduce the appeal of revolution.

Kuyper did not consider romanticism as a genuine opponent of rationalism, but as a necessary consequence of its predecessor's excesses. Both world-views regard man as autonomous, and romanticism makes emotion and intuition superior to reason, which is an unchristian point of view. He categorically denied the claim of some romantics that nature is an adequate guide to proper morality. Both rationalism, with its idea of 'progress', and romanticism, with its concept of *process*, deny humanity's sinful condition and thereby encourage people to seek utopia.[15]

Neither Burke, nor Groen, nor Kuyper defended the pre-1789 status quo. All were reformers seeking change. Although they rejected the anti-Christian principles of the French Revolution, they acknowledged that *some* complaints the revolutionaries brought against the old regime were legitimate, and *some* results of the revolution were beneficial. Burke, for example, denounced revolution, but he worked relentlessly to obtain reforms to alleviate suffering and to end harsh discrimination against Roman Catholics in Ireland and against the indigenous peoples of British India. He sympathized with the grievances of Americans and urged Britain to conciliate the colonies with compromises that might have averted the American war for independence. Kuyper hailed Burke as a true Christian liberal, but he misunderstood Burke's opposition in principle to revolution as such. Kuyper said Burke 'defended America's insurrection with loud enthusiasm',[16] and he seemed to imply that Burke was a Calvinist, which he was not.

Admiration for Gladstone and the American model

Abraham Kuyper contended that he was a genuine liberal, for true liberals would not coerce people, but would promote equality before the law, as the Anti-Revolutionary Party desired. He criticized the illiberality of the Dutch Liberal Party because it forced Christians to pay for the cost of secular education.[17] He likened the Anti-Revolutionary Party to the British Liberal Party, which encouraged progressive reforms consistent with the heritage of the nation. He cited prime minister William E. Gladstone (1809-98) as a fine example of a Christian liberal whose views were compatible with those of the Anti-Revolutionaries in the Netherlands. In this case, as in his appraisal of Burke, Kuyper was mistaken in regarding Gladstone as sharing his own Calvinist theology. The British statesman was actually an Anglo-Catholic who accepted Darwin's theory of evolution and found numerous errors in the Bible. Gladstone deplored the Reformed doctrine of sin and salvation.[18] In his eagerness to find support for his political views, Kuyper sometimes cited thinkers who did not endorse the world-view that comprised the foundation for those beliefs.

At times Dr Kuyper appears to have been naïve in his fervour to find other political leaders who shared his Christian philosophy of government. This is evident from his enthusiasm for developments in America. He thought most Americans were genuine Christians and their 'scholars and statesmen are positive believers, Christian in a definite sense, what we call orthodox'. 'When emigrants from Europe go to America,' he said,

they often abandon scepticism and 'adopt America's supernatural life-view'. Whereas in Europe people think they must
destroy faith in order to have freedom, in the United States
they regard faith as 'the surest safeguard for the continual possession of those liberties'. American leaders invoke divine blessing upon matters of state. Americans observe the Sabbath, and
a state school 'without the Bible would be unthinkable in
America'. The United States maintains its Pilgrim-Puritan
heritage.[19]

Although Kuyper wrote this glowing appraisal of the United
States in 1895, when secular humanism was much less evident
than it is now, his judgement about the spiritual condition of
America was a major exaggeration even then. He did not perceive that much of the public religiosity in the United States
towards the end of the nineteenth century was in the nature of
civil religion and did not reflect broad and deep commitment to
the principles about which he was writing in the essay 'Calvinism: the Origin and Safeguard of our Constitutional Liberties'.

Kuyper and the relationship between church and state

In believing that civil government must confine its operations
to the sphere of authority God has prescribed, Kuyper favoured
constitutional restraints upon its powers. He approved of mixed
government, in which aristocracy and democracy are function-
ing elements, as in the British monarchy, or in a genuine republic. He maintained that the sinfulness of mankind does less damage when many people share ruling authority. He showed that
liberty prospered most in countries such as Britain and the United
States, where the influence of the Protestant Reformation was
strong. Despotism flourished where it was not — for example,
in France and Russia.[20]

Kuyper's desire for the Netherlands was that the nation would
revive and preserve its Calvinistic heritage, with its doctrine of

limited government that respects the autonomy of all spheres of authority and thereby guarantees the freedom of its citizens. He lamented deeply the trends towards statism that had come with the French Revolution, and he, through the Anti-Revolutionary Party, proceeded to combat them. In this endeavour he extolled the rule of law and the equality of all citizens before the law. He explained: 'If God alone is sovereign, then we are all, the king included, creatures dependent upon him, and adoration of royalty and esteem of princes as being of a higher sort are heinous offences committed against the glory of his name.'[21]

As a Reformed Christian thinker, Abraham Kuyper knew that sinful people are always liable to abuse authority. Neither king nor parliament is supreme, regardless of the form of government, and Christians must disobey any civil rulers who command them to act contrary to God's Word.[22] The Dutch did so, he believed, when they resisted Spain's efforts to impose Roman Catholicism upon them in the Eighty Years' War (1568-1648). When they chose to disobey and to resist the Spanish king Philip II, Dutch Christians followed the directives of their provincial princes and assemblies, who defended liberty against oppression. This was in accord with Calvin's teaching about the role of *magistratus inferiores*. Calvin had taught that, when a conflict arises between authorities and one demands an evil course of action, while the other calls for resistance to that action, Christians must obey the one that orders resistance. Therefore, when the princes and assemblies of the Low Countries fought against Spain and its policy of imposing oppression, they were entitled to the loyalty and support of Christian people.[23] Kuyper said that all authority comes from God, and those upon whom he confers it must exercise it for his glory. No earthly regime is literally sovereign, and God accomplishes his purposes by a variety of political forms. American republicanism and the despotism of Russia can both serve his plan.[24]

Kuyper often referred to himself as a Christian Democrat. Since he lived in the Kingdom of the Netherlands, it would not have been appropriate for him to adopt the label 'republican', but he was not an advocate of democracy in a literal sense, in which the ultimate source of authority is the will of the majority, as his criticisms of Rousseau show clearly. As a believer in divinely revealed absolutes, he would not endorse the utilitarian morality-by-consensus that democracy, understood literally, entails. He did, nevertheless, show resolute opposition to any type of social hierarchy that would exclude common people from participating in the political process. That is why he worked so long to enlarge the electorate.

At the base of Kuyper's political perspective lay his understanding of the Reformed doctrine of election and its implications for church and society. In church government, for example, he held that God's sovereign choice of those he saves is without regard to human merit or social standing. In the church, therefore, laymen are in no way inferior to clergymen. Both share equal authority, and where this view of the church prevails, there is a corresponding recognition of political equality.[25]

Although Kuyper believed that Calvinism is the source of constitutional government and the freedoms that it protects, he realized that adherents to the Reformed faith had not always respected the rights of others. He hailed Great Britain and the United States as salutary examples of societies where free churches flourished in free states. He was especially fond of the United States, where Calvinistic influence had led to the separation of church and state. Kuyper regretted developments in sixteenth- and seventeenth-century France, where Huguenot Protestants had obtained political rule in many areas and then tried to impose the union of church and state. Kuyper opposed the concept of a state church and demanded toleration for all religions, along with freedom of speech, press and assembly.[26] His belief in sphere authority required separation of church and state and promoted the civil liberties that relationship allows.

He knew that some orthodox congregations within the Dutch Reformed Church remained silent about the doctrinal and spiritual decline that had become obvious within it because they feared the loss of financial subsidies from the state if they protested. He urged such local churches to find ways to free themselves from financial dependence upon the government.[27]

While Kuyper and the Anti-Revolutionary Party recognized the legal rights of all citizens and sought separation of church and state as one means to preserve them, they did not desire a secular state. The concept of sphere authority teaches that church and state are both of divine origin, and both must obey God's laws. The state must not try to be neutral towards God, but must recognize his supremacy over the civil sphere of authority. Government policies and procedures must respect God's moral precepts, so they must uphold the sanctity of marriage and the family; they must restrain and punish evildoers; and they must encourage respect for the Sabbath. Christ possesses 'all authority in heaven and on earth', so he is Lord over the state as well as the church. The state has no role in the matter of salvation, and it must not use its power to enforce the dogmas of any particular church body.

The concept of church-state relations that Kuyper wanted is comparable to that of John Calvin, to whom Kuyper owed a large debt. Like his sixteenth-century predecessor, he denied that the Old Testament theocracy is applicable in the Christian era and, like Calvin, he believed that the state has a duty to promote public welfare in matters of health, social security and protection of workers who might suffer exploitation from their employers.[28]

In asking the Dutch kingdom to acknowledge God in its constitution and to set aside days for prayer, as well as observance of the Sabbath, Kuyper entangled himself in a dilemma of his own making. He taught that church and state are to operate as separate spheres, each directly responsible to God, not to each other. He held that the state lacks competence to judge theological questions, so it should not favour one religion over others. It should regard all denominations collectively as the church of Christ. He did not specify which god the state should honour. He wanted civil officials to follow Christian principles without ratifying the Christian faith as a matter of public policy. It appears that he was trying to keep the spheres separate without sacrificing the historic religious character of the nation, but he could not see that his proposals could achieve no more than state acceptance of a unitarian religion which is inherently anti-Christian.[29]

7.
Christians as social reformers

At the same time as the political influences of the French Revolution were spreading across Europe, an industrial revolution was occurring in several countries, including the Netherlands. This phenomenon, which effected a fundamental change in the economic structure of Europe, began in England in the eighteenth century, and by Kuyper's time it was producing serious social consequences for the growing class of unskilled workers, most of whom owned no real estate. Large numbers of people left rural areas to take jobs in factory towns, many of which could not comfortably accommodate the influx. Crowded, unsanitary living conditions and dangerous working conditions, with long hours and low pay, became the lot for most of the urban proletariat, as such people became known. Even though those who moved to the towns often increased their income and expended less physical energy in factories than they had done on farms, they were at the mercy of market factors they could neither control nor understand. They had to endure many hardships, as Europe tried to adjust to a radically different economic system. The spectre of unemployment in the boom-and-bust pattern of commerce and industry was perhaps the greatest hardship of all.

By the time of the Industrial Revolution, the economic philosophy of free-enterprise capitalism was bringing unprecedented wealth, first to Britain, and then to countries that followed her

example. The industrial workers whose labour produced that
wealth did not, especially at first, participate in the prosperity to
any conspicuous extent, so some critics blamed the system and
the economic philosophy of classical liberalism undergirding it.
Abraham Kuyper became one such critic.[1]

In line with his doctrine of the spheres, Kuyper analysed the
social problems of his country and proposed solutions. He believed that traditional liberalism and modern socialism both
proceeded from anti-Christian, and therefore false, world-views.
Both, he contended, are materialist beliefs. He criticized liberalism because its individualism regards man as an autonomous
being entitled to almost unrestrained freedom. He saw this belief as a product of the French Revolution, a philosophy that
relegates God to the realm of subjective religion and denies his
authority over all spheres of life. Classical liberals believed in
innate human goodness, so, in their view, man is a rational
being capable of creating the proper economic order by his
own efforts. Kuyper held that a deist view of God had encouraged this thinking about human potential.

Kuyper's objections to socialism

Through his wide reading of social philosophers in several countries, Kuyper became acquainted with the then current analyses of socio-economic problems, and he was dismayed by the
various schools of socialism, especially that of Karl Marx. Just
as he decried the deism at the root of classical liberalism, so he
objected strongly to the atheism of Marx and other socialists.[2]
He acknowledged, nevertheless, that financiers and industrial
magnates often exploited the proletariat, as Marx contended.
Kuyper believed that the *bourgeoisie* had become a new aristocracy of privilege made possible by wealth, and he was deeply
concerned about the inequitable distribution of wealth and the

hardships that created for workers. He maintained that a perverse concept of free enterprise encourages an irreligious view of life and a selfish individualism that Christians should reject, and he asserted that government would have to take steps to correct injustice and the social problems that had appeared as its consequences.[3] He and his supporters were anti-revolutionaries, but not counter-revolutionaries. While they rejected the ideology of the *philosophes* and the French Revolution, they insisted that government must submit to God and implement justice in terms of his commandments. God alone is absolute Ruler, and all human beings, including civil authorities, should function as stewards of his enterprises.

Kuyper contended for a biblical world-view and its concomitant demand for a just social order at a time when socialism was hailing the state as humanity's saviour and trying to subject the citizens to its authoritarian rule. Kuyper's concept of sphere authority contradicted the basic principle of socialism that would make the state omni-competent to regulate life in practically all of its aspects — economic, political and social.

Dutch socialism began among intellectuals and spread to industrial workers, but it had a considerable following among farmers of the northern provinces as well. F. Domela Nieuwenhuis (1846-1919), the first prominent exponent of socialism in the Netherlands, had been ordained to the ministry of the Lutheran Church, but his study of the German materialist philosopher Ludwig Feuerbach (1804-72) led him to abandon the Christian faith. At first he became a radical pastor who used the pulpit to promote his social agenda. In a sermon entitled 'The Coming Religion', which he delivered in 1877, he rejected credal Christianity and called for a religion of universal love for humanity. He left the Lutheran Church in 1879, when he declared that science had discredited religion altogether.

After abandoning the church, Nieuwenhuis founded *Recht voor Allen* (Justice for All) as an organ of socialism and the labour movement. He was the first socialist to sit in the Dutch parliament, but he held that seat for only one term. His radicalism had the effect of isolating him within parliament, and he eventually alienated some of his followers, who split from his movement to form the Social Democratic Workers' Party in 1894. This organization was officially Marxist in ideology, but it gradually discarded its fervour for revolution and became a participant in parliamentary politics, recruiting supporters outside of the proletariat. Nieuwenhuis continued his work for revolution and founded the Free Socialists as a movement to promote that objective. In an overture to religious people he published the booklet *Was Jesus in Favour of or Against Socialism?* In the Russo-Japanese War (1904-5) Nieuwenhuis supported Japan because he hoped her victory would lead to the overthrow of Russia's reactionary government.[4] The Social Democratic Workers' Party, under the leadership of P. J. Troelstra (1860-1930), meanwhile sought universal suffrage as the means to accomplish its goals by legislation. Its evolutionary approach angered radicals within its ranks, and in 1909 communists formed a separate party, after the socialists expelled them.[5]

Dr Kuyper despised socialism because it espoused an atheistic materialism and did not recognize spheres of authority separate from the state. However, he shared the socialists' concern to find ways to aid the poor. While a pastor in Beesd (1863-67), he became aware of the poverty of peasants who toiled for their landlords, and he knew they and all the *kleine luyden* had no voice in politics, and so could not employ that means to improve their condition. Eventually, as already noted, he sought a seat in parliament so he could represent the interests of such common people in the matters of the Christian education of their children and their material well-being. Due to poor health, however, he had to leave parliament in 1877 and did not return until 1894.

A call for reform on biblical principles

Soon after Kuyper became editor of *De Standaard* in 1872, he began to publish articles in which he contrasted his own political philosophy with those of liberals, Roman Catholics and other Protestants. In the course of his appeals for social and political reforms, he asserted that governments do not create justice, for it comes from God's ordinances. Human laws can only approximate justice, which has its standard in God himself.[6] In a nation where only 100,000 men could vote, he saw major obstacles to obtaining relief for the poor. He denied the socialist claim that humans could produce perfect justice and equity, because he believed that human sinfulness makes that impossible. Contrary to the socialists, whom he regarded as utopian thinkers, Kuyper hoped to achieve substantial but not perfect improvements in social justice. Whoever his opponents were, Kuyper engaged them on the basis of *principles* first, and only then did he attack their specific policies and programmes.[7]

The cardinal principle of Kuyper's belief was his commitment to the sovereign authority of God over the whole creation, God's right to reign and rule over all he has made. Therefore he called for reforms which would accord with God's ordinances revealed in creation and affirmed in Scripture. He held that the broad rejection of divine ordinances was due to the effects of sin that prevent people from perceiving the will of God in creation and in natural life. Christians know that redemption through Christ is the only solution to sin, and they do not naïvely expect social reforms to remedy humanity's fundamental moral problem, its alienation from God. They do, nevertheless, seek beneficial reforms as part of their moral duty as servants of God and of mankind.[8]

The 'Christian Socialists'

When Kuyper began addressing the need for social reform, he
was not alone, for noteworthy religious leaders outside the
Netherlands were doing likewise. One of them, England's
Frederick Denison Maurice (1805-72), especially aroused
Kuyper's admiration, even though Maurice was not entirely
orthodox in his doctrinal beliefs. Together with Charles Kingsley
(1819-75) and some others, Maurice had introduced so-called
Christian Socialism as an answer to the problems for which
they blamed free-market economic policy. These thinkers were
prominent in the Broad Church movement within the Church
of England, a school of opinion that assigned little importance
to Christian doctrine and did not hesitate to embrace critical
theories about the reliability of the Bible comparable to the
ones Kuyper had encountered from Dutch modernists. Kuyper's
knowledge of this may have been inadequate, but it is clear
that he appreciated the Christian Socialists' compassion and
their efforts to aid the poor. They operated shops to teach trades
to poor people, and Maurice became a professor at a Working
Man's College that he helped to organize.[9] Since these were
initiatives from the private sector of society, they did not reflect
Britain's endorsement of state socialism.

Kuyper, too, preferred private initiatives to aid poor people
to improve their lives. He argued that both private enterprise
and state authority must be subject to God's law. If common
people gained full political rights, their influence would promote a proper balance between the public and private sectors
in such matters.[10] It is evident that Kuyper did not foresee the
way in which democratic political reforms would actually encourage a materialist world-view, as they have done in almost
all Western countries in the twentieth century, where the rise
and growth of Social Democratic parties attest to this
development.

The Anti-Revolutionary manifesto

The Anti-Revolutionary Party participated in elections in 1879, when, in its *Programme of Principles*, it affirmed God's rule over all of life, including politics. It denied the contention of Liberals and Conservatives that popular sovereignty should determine values and policies. The Anti-Revolutionaries won nine seats in the Second Chamber. Their *Programme of Principles* proclaims twenty-one affirmations, the first five of which comprise the foundation and express the party's philosophy. These principles declare:

1. The Anti-Revolutionary Party and its allies represent the genuine historic tradition of the Netherlands since the Reformation. This requires the assertion that all authority comes from God and does not originate in human autonomy.
2. God is sovereign over all, and he has ordained earthly agents to rule for him in the constitutional state. This is the teaching of Romans 13:1-7.
3. The authority of government is subject to the laws of God, and civil rulers must employ those laws as their guidelines. The state is not subject to the church. The Anti-Revolutionaries desired to apply divine laws to national life outside the structure of the church so as to avoid creating a theocracy, or perhaps an ecclesiocracy.
4. The state must not hinder the expression of religion, and it must afford all churches equal treatment under the law. It must not interfere with freedom of conscience. Church and state must be separate, even though society be officially Christian.
5. The Anti-Revolutionary Party called for the state to uphold the sanctity of the Sabbath and to require oaths

> in courts of law. Government should respect the Lord's
> Day by refraining from civic functions on that day.[11]

The leader of the Anti-Revolutionaries believed that Christians who avoided political involvement were in dereliction of their duty and thereby conceded power to unbelievers, when they should strive for godliness in public life. As author of *Ons Program (Our Programme)*, Kuyper spoke for his party and asked for laws to protect workers' safety and to regulate wages and hours of toil. The Netherlands did not enact such legislation until soon before World War I. Kuyper called for social security insurance and workmen's compensation, and he supported the right of trade unions to organize for the protection of workers. He wanted Christian unions as alternatives to socialist ones, and he favoured giving the franchise to heads of households, unions and organizations, rather than to individuals *per se*.[12]

The state must repect sphere authority

Although Kuyper believed state intervention into social and economic affairs is sometimes necessary, he feared the unrestrained power of government and proposed his concept of sphere authority to prevent it. He said that the state must protect economic freedom and interfere only if it becomes anti-social. Society, like the church, is an organism, not just an aggregate of individuals; no person exists as an isolated individual. Man, as the divine image-bearer, must respect the spheres of authority God has ordained, and the state must assure the just operation of those spheres. It must administer justice, for example, by recognizing the right of the workforce to organize within its own sphere and the right of families to decide who would educate their children.

A Christian approach to social problems

Progress towards an industrial economy was somewhat slower in the Netherlands than in some other countries, so the social problems which came with it became pronounced only in the second half of the nineteenth century. The Anti-Revolutionary Party addressed this situation in its *Programme of Principles* in 1879, and the first Christian Social Congress convened at Amsterdam near the end of 1891 with Kuyper delivering the key-note address entitled 'The Social Problem and the Christian Religion'. In this speech he set forth what he believed to be a biblical alternative to both capitalism and socialism.[13]

In this address Dr Kuyper posed the question: 'What should we, as confessors of Christ, do about the social needs of our time?' He asked Dutch Christians to consider the efforts of Maurice, Kingsley and the Christian Socialists in England, Count von Waldersee in Berlin and the Swiss Society for Social Economy. He hailed Roman Catholic efforts, too, especially the papal encyclical *Rerum Novarum* of May 1891, in which Leo XIII affirmed the rights of workers and, while rejecting so-cialism, called for justice in socio-economic affairs.[14] Kuyper reminded members of his audience that Willem Bilderdijk, Isaak da Costa and Guillaume Groen van Prinsterer had earlier ap-pealed for their attention to the great social needs of the day. He showed that Groen, in particular, had aroused constern-ation within parliament by calling for the government to give serious attention to problems that the socialists had exposed. Groen had contended that Christianity alone has the answer to the social crisis.[15]

His biblical world-view required Kuyper to reject all versions of the sacred-secular dichotomy and to assert that all of life is religious, but not all of life is ecclesiastical. Spheres of authority denominate various activities (family, school, state, work, etc.) that are religious but not under church auspices. Kuyper acknowledged that Dutch society was pluralistic, but he nevertheless sought to reform it by the application of Christian principles. This quest reflects his firm commitment to fulfilling the cultural mandate to 'fill the earth and subdue it. Rule over the fish of the sea and the birds of the air and over every living creature' (Genesis 1:28). He understood this as a precept 'to preserve and cultivate the material world'; that is, to apply human abilities (art, craftsmanship) to nature, 'to work on nature through human art, to enable and perfect it'. Civil government must intervene at times in the course of nature to promote this development: 'It is nothing but primitive barbarism whenever human society, without higher supervision, is left to the course of nature.'[16] Kuyper argued that governments have always influenced 'the course of social life and its relationship to material wealth', which is their proper role.[17]

Government intervention, however, in Kuyper's view, has proceeded from false concepts and, therefore, it has increased human suffering. This has been due to the control that vested interests have gained over government and which has allowed them to exploit the poor and the weak. This occurred because people ignored man's role as God's image-bearer. As the book of Ecclesiastes states, 'I looked and saw all the oppression that was taking place under the sun; I saw the tears of the oppressed — and they have no comforter; power was on the side of their oppressors — and they have no comforter' (4:1).[18]

The French Revolution, Kuyper believed, was a consequence of prolonged exploitation and was therefore God's judgement on sinful society. Its principles were, however, humanistic in that they denied divine authority over life. Social problems are results of error and sin. People are alienated from one another because they are alienated from God. Jesus called both rich and poor to return to God, and he warned about the danger of wealth and the pursuit of material possessions. Christ stood with the poor when they suffered at the hands of the rich, but he never encouraged violent revolution.[19]

As Kuyper unfolded his presentation, he showed that Jesus not only denounced the worship of wealth and the exploitation of the poor; he organized his church as an instrument to witness to society with his Word. That Word contains an indictment of injustice, and it directs people to consider eternal riches and life with God in heaven. The church must minister through charity to alleviate suffering, and within its structure it must not recognize distinctions of social standing but promote brotherhood.[20] In Kuyper's words, 'The church forsakes its principle when it is concerned only with heaven and does not relieve earthly need.'[21]

Lessons from history

Church history provided Kuyper with an abundance of examples to illustrate his plea for Christian social action in the Netherlands. Although the church and society that survived the fall of the Roman Empire were far from the New Testament ideal, they did bring some great social improvements to Christendom, in that Christian moral influence greatly affected the practice of slavery, the church prohibited usury to protect the poor, and it taught people to regard life on earth as preparation for eternal life. When the church in the Middle Ages became a large landowner, corruption infected it and so diminished its proper role in society. The decline of the church as the moral teacher of Western civilization began when Emperor Constantine in 311 declared himself a Christian and subsequently used the strength of the state to support the church. Soon vast numbers of pagans were baptized but remained pagans at heart, and the church hierarchy succumbed to the worldliness that wealth made possible. The Protestant Reformation challenged that corruption but did not eliminate it, and in those countries still Roman Catholic, 'Royal absolutism and aristocratic pride created conditions for the ripening of an unbearable social tension that eventually brought forth the French Revolution,'[22] which extolled human autonomy and denied the sovereignty of God. The French Revolution encouraged a self-centred quest for material treasures, rather than compassion for human needs.

Kuyper believed that Christianity, when true to its mission, upholds human dignity within 'an organically integrated society', which the French Revolution, with its exaltation of individualism, has fractured, a fact to which the rise of modern liberalism and socialism bears witness. Revolutionary ideology has 'made the possession of money the highest good, and then, in the struggle for money, it set every man against every other'.[23] The triumph of *laissez-faire* capitalism has produced a situation in which 'a well-to-do *bourgeoisie* rules over an impoverished working class, which exists to increase the wealth of the ruling class and is doomed, when it can no longer serve that purpose, to sink away into the masses of the proletariat'. The slogan of the French Revolution, 'Liberty, Equality, Fraternity,' was, in Kuyper's opinion, a farce.[24]

The responsibilities of the state to aid the poor

Although Abraham Kuyper's indictment of the middle class appears surprisingly similar to those coming from the socialists, even the Marxists, he made it clear that he did not endorse their proposals for change. Even democratic socialism was unacceptable to him, because it sought a social structure based on the sovereignty of the people, which is a humanist, not a Christian, approach to society's problems. Kuyper concurred with Isaak da Costa's contention that the nation is 'not a heap of souls on a piece of ground', but rather 'a God-willed *community*, a living human organism'.[25] With Willem Bilderdijk he maintained that the state should provide employment if none is available in the private sector, for God does not want any person willing to work to die from hunger.[26]

In addressing the social problems of his nation, Dr Kuyper had to consider the matter of private property, a cherished tenet of liberalism, one that appeared to have biblical sanction in the commandment against stealing (Exodus 20:15). He argued that the holding of private property is not an absolute right, for humans are stewards of God's gifts. God owns all, and stewards must consider the welfare of their neighbours when they acquire, maintain and dispose of their property. Property rights must not impede society's obligation to care for the elderly folk who can no longer work, and employers must not consider their workers as property. To do so is to 'kill the worker socially', which is a violation of the Sixth Commandment (Exodus 20:13). Even though Kuyper agreed with the Reformed tradition in holding that the Old Testament theocracy is not an applicable political form any longer, he believed that Old Testament laws regarding the treatment of workers are still binding as moral precepts of enduring applicability.[27]

A call for Christian social action

His advocacy of state action to aid the helpless poor notwithstanding, Kuyper did not want to create a permanent welfare system. He believed that the state should aid the needy with funds only when necessary, and only in minimal amounts, because major subsidies would stifle initiative.[28] In promoting public assistance for the indigent, he implied that it had become necessary because the church was in dereliction of duty with regard to its responsibility to dispense charity. He urged Christians not to wait until legislation made provisions for reforms, but to take action immediately. He said, 'Never forget that all state relief is a blot on the honour of your Saviour.'[29]

Abraham Kuyper's appeal for Christian social action came at a time when orthodox churches gave scant attention to social questions. A bifurcated view of life stressed concern for eternal life in heaven, not for earthly responsibilities. There were then few organizations seeking to aid distressed people, so his call for employers and workers to co-operate with government in finding solutions to social problems was a bold initiative. As a member of parliament he worked for legislation to relieve the plight of impoverished people, but he realized no great success. During the administration of prime minister Aeneas Mackay (1888-91), when an Anti-Revolutionary – Roman Catholic coalition comprised the cabinet, the School Law (1889) introduced state inspections of factories to protect workers from harm and to regulate working hours for women and children. This was the first labour law in Dutch history, and it set a precedent for further improvements. Groen had largely failed to see the compelling nature of the social problems arising from the Industrial Revolution. Kuyper was not in parliament when these measures became law, but they reflect his influence and indicate success for the policies of his Anti-Revolutionary Party.[30]

8.
Doleantie: a sorrowful separation

While Abraham Kuyper and the Anti-Revolutionary Party were promoting their programme of social reforms congruent with their Christian faith, the spiritual condition of the Dutch Reformed Church continued to deteriorate. The *réveil* had brought a resurgence of Protestant piety earlier in the century, but at first its leaders had shown little interest in precise definitions of doctrine. A rather elastic Protestantism had developed that did not affirm allegiance to the historic standards of the Reformed faith *per se*. The challenge of the Groningen theology, however, forced the evangelicals to clarify their doctrinal position, and when they did so, they espoused historic Calvinism.

The spread of modernism in the National Church

Groningen scholars rejected the miraculous character of Christ as the God-man and contended that he had come to teach people how to be godlike. The church, in their view, must do the same. Liberal intellectuals found this teaching appealing, perhaps because it accorded well with the traditional Dutch attitude of tolerance towards diverse beliefs. Such people viewed Calvinism as an alien religion imported from Switzerland, one incompatible with their Dutch heritage.[1] Kuyper's efforts to combat such beliefs within the National Church, though vigorous and relentless, were not successful.

Soon after 1860 religious views more radical than those of the Groningen school gained a substantial following among leaders and pastors of the Dutch Reformed Church. A popular book entitled *Letters About the Bible*, the author of which was Busken Huet, had appeared in 1858, and it did much to spread critical ideas about the trustworthiness of the Scriptures. Huet eventually left the Dutch Reformed Church, but many who accepted his views remained within it, prominent among them Allard Pierson (1831-96), a brilliant spokesman for modernism, who, like other modernists, denied the possibility of divine intervention in history.[2]

Pierson grew up in a family that had embraced the *réveil*, and he became pastor of the French Reformed Church in Rotterdam. While in that position Pierson embraced the belief that faith is a religious feeling completely apart from reason, and that a feeling of dependence upon God leads believers to love their fellow humans. God's relationship to the world is an unfathomable mystery, for cause and effect operate throughout the universe, and God does not intervene. According to this view, the church must proclaim Jesus Christ as the example of divine love, even though legends surround him and obscure him to an uncertain extent.

Allard Pierson eventually concluded that his own conception of the Christian religion actually negated the faith, and he left the church to become a secular humanist. By then he had lost all confidence that it was possible to know the real Jesus and his teachings. Since Christ seems to have believed in a personal, transcendent God, Pierson decided he must be wrong, and Christianity false.[3]

Kuyper leads the fight against modernism

As early as 1865, opponents of modernism within the Dutch Reformed Church had organized a Confessional Union to uphold the historic teachings of their church. During the time of his pastorate in Utrecht (1867-70), Abraham Kuyper became the leader of the confessional party, and he continued in that role when he moved to Amsterdam in 1870.

Kuyper believed that modernism was the enemy of real Christianity and that Calvinism alone had the strength to combat it effectively. Modernism promoted a comprehensive world-view to which only the Reformed faith provided a sufficient rebuttal. Kuyper held that, while the church must promote evangelism and nurture the spiritual lives of her members, Christians must subject all of life to the authority of God's Word and seek to glorify God in all their activities. Modernism, on the contrary, made man his own authority and point of reference from which to judge life and the world, so Christians must resist it. He did not define modernism just as an anti-Christian system of theology, but as a godless world-view popularized by the French Revolution.

As evidence of the damage modernism was causing, Dr Kuyper cited the influence of the German philosophers Arthur Schopenhauer (1788-1860) and Friedrich Nietzsche (1844-1900), the rise of socialism and nihilism, plus a growing rejection of Christian moral values. He contended that the Darwinian concept of the survival of the fittest was eroding Christian morality. Because Calvinism affirms the total sovereignty of God and exposes human depravity, it has the principles needed to influence major developments in philosophy, law, literature, politics and the sciences and humanities.[4] No other school of Christianity was so well equipped to answer the challenge of modernism. Kuyper spoke to this issue with confidence and authority out of the well of his own experience: 'I was once a modernist myself and have dreamed its dreams and have called it slander when others said I did not see what I thought I saw. It was then that I saw the magical illusion of the Morgana, and its beautiful fabrics sank away from my sight into airy nothings, when a soft zephyr from above caused the horizon of my life to become tremulous, and before long in the rising glory of my Lord and King true reality appeared.'[5]

Kuyper contended that modernists had no real theology, that their belief was a philosophy of religion without revelation. As leader of the orthodox party in Amsterdam, he used his newspapers as vehicles through which he contended for the faith of his fathers, and from his pulpit and in official councils of his church he worked relentlessly in defence of historic Christianity. In the Dutch Reformed congregations of Amsterdam orthodox believers comprised a majority of the members, and many of them supported Kuyper's efforts. In 1874 he had to reduce his activities because overwork as a member of parliament had produced a nervous collapse. He then became elder emeritus to reduce his work further. Not until 1884 could he resume a leadership role in church affairs. However, he did what his strength would allow, and in 1882 he formed a body of pastors and elders who subscribed to the historic Reformed confessions of faith. Kuyper hoped to make this group the vanguard for a reformation of the National Church. While still a pastor in Utrecht he had said, 'The church I want is Reformed and democratic, free and independent, as well as fully organized in doctrine, teaching, formal worship, and the pastoral ministry of love.'[6] Dr Kuyper called believers to adhere to the principle of 'continuous purification and development. The Reformed Church is always reforming before God.'[7]

The *Doleantie*

Although Kuyper was for some time optimistic about restoring the historic character of the Dutch Reformed Church, by the 1880s the prospects for a successful internal reformation were not encouraging. By then the Free University of Amsterdam was educating candidates for the gospel ministry who were well prepared to expound and defend the orthodox faith, but the National Church refused to ordain them and the Dutch government required them to pass examinations at state institutions in order to validate their degrees. In 1883 the National Synod decided it would no longer require candidates for ordination to subscribe even in principle to the Three Forms of Unity — the *Belgic Confession of Faith*, the *Heidelberg Catechism* and the *Canons of Dort*. In other words, ministers of the church would not have to accept Reformed doctrine, even in a formal sense. Many orthodox believers construed this announcement as a call to battle, and Kuyper devised a strategy for the struggle in his *Tractaat van de Reformatie der Kerken (A Pamphlet on the Reformation of the Churches)*, which he had been preparing for ten years.

With zeal and determination, Kuyper and his followers committed themselves to defend their faith regardless of the cost, and thereby they declared themselves to be the *Doleantie,* a Latin term that means to sorrow, or to bear pain. Orthodox believers then expressed deep sorrow about the decadent condition of their church, and they resolved to take all measures necessary to preserve their spiritual heritage. When the National Synod rejected their pleas, they renounced the synod's authority and proposed to return to the historic pattern of church government as it had been before 1816, when King William I had imposed state control. The first Reformed congregations to disavow the synod were those under the leadership of pastors J. Van Den Bergh and J. Ploos van Amstel. Since the state supported the modernists, adherents to the *Doleantie* faced the animosity of the government as well as that of the National Church.[8]

The break with the national church

Kuyper's concept of church reform featured the belief that defenders of orthodoxy should stress their continuity with the Protestant Reformation of the sixteenth century and the historic creeds of their church. He did not advise secession, except as a last resort. Kuyper had criticized the *Afscheiding* (the secession of 1834) because its leaders had not pursued reform of the National Church long enough and had separated too soon. In his opinion the reform of the church meant the 'restoration of truth and holiness in the place of error and sin'.[9]

Like many theologians before him, Abraham Kuyper regarded the preaching of God's Word and the proper administration of the sacraments as the marks of the true church. Although no Christian body maintains these marks perfectly, false churches discard the Word, pervert the sacraments and oppose lovers of divinely revealed truth, as the National Synod had been doing. When ecclesiastical authorities demand that true Christians support sinfully false teachings, separation from the church over which they preside is necessary. Kuyper warned, 'Satan wants a church for Antichrist by subverting existing Christian churches.'[10]

When it becomes necessary for believers to leave an apostate church, they must try to persuade others to do the same. Godly pastors in particular have this obligation, and pastors and laymen must then form a faithful church, if one does not exist in their area.[11] Christians must not, however, leave a church just because it is imperfect: 'Just because your church is sick or crippled, you may not withhold from her your love. Just because she is sick, she has a greater claim on your compassion. Only when she is dead and has ceased to be your church, and when the poisonous gases of the false church threaten to kill you, do you flee from her touch and withdraw your love from her.'[12]

In Kuyper's view, 'One may not leave his church unless one is certain it has become a synagogue of Satan.'[13] Although, by his estimate, about five hundred Dutch Reformed congregations were still preaching God's Word and rightly administering the sacraments, he concluded by 1886 that the National Synod had become incurably corrupt, so loyalty to Christ demanded separation from it.[14]

One of the issues that propelled Kuyper towards separation pertained to the right of pastors and elders to deny the Lord's Supper to people who had embraced modernism and so did not offer a credible profession of faith. Those denied the sacrament appealed to ecclesiastical officials, and the Provincial Synod of North Holland ordered the Amsterdam congregations to admit the plaintiffs to the Eucharist. Kuyper led the effort to resist the synod, but that action led to the suspension of the dissident pastors and elders.

This dispute involved the control of church properties, as Dutch Reformed Church officials claimed the buildings in which unco-operative orthodox congregations met for worship. The provincial synod next moved to make the suspension of the orthodox leaders a permanent removal from the ministry. The orthodox believers had to move to rented halls to conduct church services, where they drew larger crowds than those who attended worship at the traditional buildings. A large majority of church-goers in Amsterdam supported the dissident movement.

When the synod deposed the Reformed leaders from the ministry of the National Church, Kuyper replied with 'A Last

Word to the Conscience of the Members of the Synod'. In this statement he accused the synod of defecting from the Scriptures and from the historic Reformed standards by denying the Trinity, Christ's atonement for sin, the eternal punishment of unbelievers, the bodily resurrection of Christ and other fundamental truths of genuine Christianity. He showed that the nature of the dispute between orthodox Christians and modernists was doctrinal, not just a matter of ecclesiastical procedure and synodal jurisdiction. The defenders of the Reformed faith insisted that they were preserving the essential character of the Dutch Reformation, which the modernists had betrayed.[15]

For almost twenty years Abraham Kuyper had led a vigorous effort to restore the historic character of the Dutch Reformed Church, but councils of that body had rebuffed all such endeavours and had dismissed seventy-five leaders of the Amsterdam church who refused to compromise their faith. As of 1886 it no longer seemed realistic to expect a restoration of confessional orthodoxy in the National Church, and the pastors, elders and deacons removed from office in that body became the nucleus of the *Doleantie* — a separate church that maintained the historic understanding of the Scriptures as affirmed in the traditional Reformed confessions of faith.

A new church established

As Kuyper led the way in forming the *Doleantie,* he contended that he and his comrades were not engaging in schism. They were preserving and continuing the actual Reformed faith as set forth at the Synod of Dort (1618-19). Therefore the churches of the *Doleantie* were entitled to retain their properties. The law courts, nevertheless, ruled against the orthodox movement.[16] The Dutch government and the National Synod seized the contested church buildings, sometimes by force.

Early in 1887 a conference of orthodox Reformed leaders convened in Amsterdam to plan a secession from the Dutch Reformed Church and to arrange for the formation of a continuing body to be genuinely Reformed in belief and in church order. About 1500 people attended, approximately 1200 of them from outside the Amsterdam church, a clear evidence that a national movement was underway. Soon about 200 congregations with about 170,000 members withdrew from the National Church, and in rapid order they formed synods in almost all the Dutch provinces. Very quickly the *Doleerende Kerk* (the Sorrowing Church) became a nationwide religious body.

The rupture between the *Doleantie* and the Dutch Reformed Church of course caused much contention and division. Since the National Church enjoyed state support, it could and did employ agencies of the civil government to protect its own interests and to persecute people who joined the secession. In addition to seizing church buildings, National Synod officials took cruel reprisals against orthodox believers, some of whom lived in houses owned by the church and administered by its diaconate. Such people suffered eviction from their homes, even though they paid their rent, and on occasions church officials ransacked their houses in search of books, documents and other items they claimed were church property. Leaders of the *Doleantie* sometimes fell victims to violence at the hands of their opponents. Kuyper, as leader of the secession, was often the object of scornful abuse, and there were a few threats to kill him, threats he ignored.[17]

Reformed Christians outside the *Doleantie*

The organization of the *Doleerende Kerk* could not be all-inclusive of Reformed believers in the Netherlands. Many loyal

Calvinists remained within the Dutch Reformed Church, convinced that Kuyper's action was rash and therefore unwarranted.
Since the National Synod did not often interfere with what its
pastors chose to preach, it was still possible to maintain a Reformed witness within it, but the synod did require obedience
to all of its directives. To some extent, therefore, people could
keep their orthodox convictions while remaining inside an evi-
dently heterodox church.

Not all genuinely Reformed believers outside the National
Church rallied to the standard of the *Doleantie.* The Christian
Reformed Church had been separate since 1834, and some of
its leaders were hesitant to join with Kuyper, even though both
groups subscribed to the same doctrinal standards, and both
endorsed the structure of church order adopted at Dort in 1618.
Neither the Christian Reformed Church nor the *Doleerende Kerk*
enjoyed recognition from the state, but in 1888 Baron Aeneas
Mackay of the Anti-Revolutionary Party became prime minister
at the head of a Christian coalition cabinet that granted legal
recognition to the two dissident church bodies.

The 'Reformed Churches in the Netherlands' established

Although the two Reformed groups had good reason to merge
and thereby to strengthen their position in national life, there
were impediments, especially from the Christian Reformed point
of view. That church had its own theological seminary at
Kampen, and its supporters did not respond enthusiastically to
Kuyper's Free University of Amsterdam. He argued that education, even theological education, is in a sphere by itself, separate from church ownership and operation. The Kampen Seminary was, however, a denominational institution that most Christian Reformed people wanted to preserve. There were some
fine points of doctrine to be clarified as well, and some mem-

bers of the Christian Reformed Church feared that Kuyper would dominate a merged church by the force of his personality and because of his prestige as a scholar and his reputation as a defender of the faith. Some adherents to the Christian Reformed Church disliked Kuyper because he had criticized the *Afscheiding* of 1834.

These obstacles notwithstanding, a merger occurred in 1892, although some Christian Reformed congregations did not participate in it. The product of the union became known as the *Gereformeerde Kerken in Nederland,* the Reformed Churches in the Netherlands,* and the new body restored traditional church polity and affirmed allegiance to the *Belgic Confession,* the *Heidelberg Catechism,* and the *Canons of Dort.* The reformation of 1886-92 had involved some painful experiences that were unavoidable. It marked the final frustration of Kuyper's hopes to purify the Dutch Reformed Church, but it considerably strengthened the witness of the Reformed faith. Kuyper portrayed the whole matter as a warfare with Satan, who 'sets himself over against God and imitates, in the desperation of his impotence, all that God does, to see if he is able to succeed in destroying God's kingdom with God's own instruments'.[18]

The newly established Reformed Churches in the Netherlands were dynamic in their assertion of the distinctively Calvinistic doctrines and in missionary and evangelistic outreach, and Dr Kuyper, by careful, conciliatory measures, gradually acquired acceptance from most of those Christian Reformed people who had reservations about his leadership. Many orthodox believers who remained within the Dutch Reformed Church continued to admire him, and some of them voted for the Anti-Revolutionary Party in parliamentary elections.

*In Dutch there are two words for 'Reformed'. The *Hervormde Kerk* is the former National Church; the merged bodies still bear the name given above.

9.
Abraham Kuyper's theology (I): The triune God

Since the church union of 1892 was accomplished despite some concern about specific points of doctrine in Kuyper's understanding of the Christian faith, it is appropriate at this point to examine his theology. Dr Kuyper believed that all Christians should study the Bible so as to comprehend its teachings and to apply them to all of life. He criticized the Roman Catholic Church for maintaining an intricate system of dogmas while not encouraging laymen to study that system. He held that the Roman church expected laymen to be satisfied with an 'implicit faith', in which obedience to the church is sufficient without clear understanding of the doctrines which that church propounds.[1]

Symbolism versus revelation

One of Kuyper's great laments was the popularity of symbolism in ceremonial worship which, in some churches, often eclipsed personal study of the Bible and expository sermons based upon it. He complained that people who want symbolism for their religion desire short sermons and elaborate sensual ceremonies and music. They want to 'enjoy fully the mystical titillations of a delightful religious feeling',[2] but they do not aspire to know

God as he has revealed himself in Scripture. Kuyper attributed this development in modern times to the influence of German philosophers who encouraged the growth of a romantic world-view, and he indicted the Church of England for making the performance of prescribed rituals its chief concern in worship services. He cited Freemasonry as a religion that denies divine revelation and promotes a religious feeling directed towards symbols. In this religion people do not relate to God in faith but by 'sensation'. Kuyper argued that the logical consequence of such belief is pantheism. Symbolism regards as poetry what historic Christianity proclaims as literal truth.[3]

In Kuyper's view, the Protestant Reformation was a power-ful protest against symbolic, ceremonial religion. The Reformed churches 'stressed *understanding* of the revelation and its per-sonal application to the soul. They denied absolutely the ne-cessity of connecting the Infinite with the finite by symbols.' Protestant churches published the Bible in vernacular languages and distributed it widely, and they proclaimed their dogmas in clear statements of faith. 'Standing before the dilemma of feel-ing or faith, they chose for *faith*,' and for revelation over symbolism.[4]

God's self-revelation in Scripture as the basis for theology

In 1881, upon the occasion of his inauguration as rector of the Free University of Amsterdam, Kuyper delivered an address entitled 'The Biblical Criticism of the Present Day', in which he affirmed clearly and unequivocally, 'The self-disclosing God is the origin of theology, and he determines its directions.'[5] He had no doubts that the Bible is the Word of God, and he held that the Holy Spirit reveals Christ by that Word and impresses the Word upon human minds. He thereby affirmed *Sola Scriptura*, the formal principle of the Protestant Reformation.

He argued that people who claimed to receive post-biblical special revelations denied the sole authority of Scripture.[6]

Kuyper's love for the Bible led him to establish the Free University of Amsterdam because the 'science of religion' had replaced theology in the curricula of the state universities. Not only did he object to the teachings of modernist scholars in those institutions, he contended that they had no actual theology at all. A humanist philosophy of religion there had supplanted the study of God as God has revealed himself. Abraham Kuyper expressed anger because the modernists misled people about the Scriptures. He said, 'It makes the blood rush to the face to see how mercilessly and unpardonably cruelly these vivisectors of the Holy Scriptures deal with the souls of our children.'[7] The only proper attitude towards Scripture, he contended, is one of awe and unreserved belief, for 'When in private or at the family altar, I read the Holy Scriptures, neither Moses nor John addresses me, but the Lord my God.'[8]

The authority and inspiration of Scripture

Kuyper's confidence in the trustworthiness of the Bible was boundless. With exuberance he declared, 'It is the same Holy Spirit who spoke through the prophets and inspired the apostles, it is the same primary author [of Scripture] who by the apostles *quotes himself…*'[9] In lectures to students at the Free University he said, 'If God himself had come and dictated the Bible … it would not look different than it now does.'[10] To question the inspiration of the writers of the Bible is, according to Kuyper, to deny its authority. He believed that all error, even unintentional error, is due to sin. Since Scripture is the Word of the immaculately holy God, it cannot be mistaken. To deny the historicity of an event in the Bible is to call God a liar.[11]

In affirming the verbal inspiration of the Bible writers and the infallible truth of their compositions, Kuyper did not hold that all of them received revelation by means of dictation. He believed that the mode of the Holy Spirit's direction of the human authors varied from dictation in a few cases to influences of which the writers were not cognizant.[12] The inspiration of the authors entailed 'the entering in of the Spirit into the centrum of the personality of the writers and an absolute subjection of what was in and belonged to them to the sovereignty of the Holy Spirit'.[13] Inspiration, then, was the work of the Holy Spirit, and he alone can persuade people to acquiesce in the authority of the Bible.

Although he contended vigorously for the inspiration and authority of Scripture, Kuyper did not oppose historical-critical studies of the sacred text. He believed such studies were valid, but he lamented that most of them were the work of unbelievers. He wanted professors at the Free University to deal with this matter from a Christian perspective, and he denounced as arrogance the attitude that assumes any human is entitled to judge God's Word. As he expressed it, 'The Holy Spirit condemns the world and the spirit that governs it… Either it must bend before the Scripture, or the Scripture must bend before it, and it cannot be otherwise than that the spirit which inspires the world must wage inexorable war against the Spirit that inspired the Scripture.'[14]

Kuyper attacked modernists and so-called 'Ethical theologians' for rejecting the infallible truth of the Bible while extolling its value for spiritual guidance. He had no patience with people who cited 'pious frauds' in Scripture, for the existence of such things would mean the Holy Spirit had contradicted himself. Kuyper contended that humans must believe what 'the Holy Spirit asserts in Scripture concerning Scripture'.[15]

Closely connected with the role of the Holy Spirit in the inspiration of Scripture is his work in convincing people to believe its message. Like earlier Reformed theologians, Dr Kuyper assigned crucial importance to the witness of the Holy Spirit that instils in believers confidence in divine revelation. To Kuyper this ministry of the Spirit is indispensable, and he disliked efforts on the part of some Christian scholars to prove the claims of Scripture by appeals to unaided human reason, for to do that usurps the Spirit's witness: 'If human reason were ever able to demonstrate the divine [truth], then reason would stand superior to the divine [revelation], and thus, *eo ipso,* the divine character of the divine Word would be destroyed.'[16]

When Abraham Kuyper attributed infallible inspiration and supreme authority to the Bible, he meant the sacred text as originally composed by prophets and apostles. He believed nevertheless that God had protected the transmission of that text so that modern versions convey his Word accurately. He denied that the human authors of the Bible were theologians. They were recipients of truth which theologians must expound and apply to themselves and to others. The age of direct revelation ended with the passing of the apostles, so Christians must not seek God's Word through extra-biblical means. Were they to do this, they would be claiming equality with the authors of Scripture. Since the completion of the New Testament, believers must be content with the Bible as their sole source for the knowledge of God and his will.[17]

A God-centred theology

By extolling the supreme authority of Scripture, Kuyper believed he was glorifying God, the ultimate Author of the Bible. Kuyper's intention in all he espoused and advocated was to promote theocentricity — a God-centred world-view. He expressed this in a majestic fashion: 'The greatest religious height will be reached by him who, at every point of his horizon, views God as God, by honouring him in all things as the almighty Creator who has made all things for his own sake, who, as God, is not bound by anything but himself and determines for every creature both its being and the law thereof, now and for evermore. Not only *Deo Gloria*, but *Soli Deo Gloria*, and before his adorable majesty let every creature, prince or pauper, be as the small dust of the balance, a drop of a bucket, nay, be counted less than nothing.'[18]

Kuyper believed theocentricity to be the bedrock of the Reformed faith on which all its doctrines depend. He rejected the view that theology should be concerned chiefly with religious feelings, as the so-called 'science of religion' contended. The object of theological study, Kuyper maintained, is not religion but God.[19] Obtaining the knowledge of God through a believing study of Scripture is the proper occupation of all Christians, not only of theological scholars. His own pursuit of this knowledge was not merely a formal academic enterprise. As he exclaimed, 'My soul pants, yea *thirsts* after the living God, not after an idea about God, not after a remembrance of God, not after a divine majesty ... but after God himself ... the *living* God.'[20]

Rejection of pantheism and evolution

Dr Kuyper's quest for God led him into militant opposition against all modern teachings that deny the personhood of God revealed in Scripture as the Trinity. He found rationalistic approaches to the Godhead deplorable, and he denounced all efforts to make Christianity more 'reasonable' by adjusting its claims so as to satisfy radical philosophers who wished to make the human mind the sole judge of truth.[21] Kuyper showed particular disdain, therefore, for pantheism, a view of God that denies his personal, transcendent independence and thereby obliterates the Creator-creature distinction of historic Christianity.

In his rebuttal of pantheism Dr Kuyper asserted that it denies the antithesis between God and nature, God and man, by removing all distinctions or boundaries. He showed that the biblical doctrine of creation avows that God is separate from the world he has made, but in pantheistic belief, 'Every boundary is taken away between God and the world, between time and eternity, between the here and the hereafter.'[22] Nowhere was this more evident than in the growing popularity of Charles Darwin's theory of evolution, for which Kuyper expressed great dislike. He contended that the theory of evolution is really an application of pantheism to the study of the material world, an expression 'of the human heart to rid itself of God'.[23] The Creator-creature distinction is the pre-eminent boundary, and to deny this boundary is to reject God. In unequivocal terms Kuyper declared: 'The whole pantheistic stream has left a poisonous slime upon the shore, and it is in Darwin's evolution theory that this slime reveals its power.'[24]

Not only did Kuyper object to evolution as an explanation for life in the universe, he assailed it because its proponents made it the basis for an anti-Christian world-view. They argued that they had found an absolute, all-embracing principle that is applicable to all of life and to every discipline of study, including religion. As Kuyper watched the ascendancy of the Darwinian hypothesis in academic circles, he responded with an address at the Free University of Amsterdam in October 1899. In attacking the theory of evolution he was quick to cite the problems that this world-view poses in the realm of ethics. Political leaders, by adopting Darwin's concept of the survival of the fittest species, could justify brutal aggression and imperialism on the part of powerful nations over weak ones. He pointed to Britain's conquest of South Africa in the Anglo-Boer War (1899-1902), to the United States' policy towards the Philippine Islands about the same time, and to the meteoric rise of Prussia to dominance in Germany by her military victories over Austria (1866) and France (1871).[25]

Kuyper argued that belief in evolution leads to a materialist view of life in which people demand *panem et circenses* ('bread and circuses', i.e., sustenance and entertainment), and they forsake the moral obligations entailed in their marriage vows. He cited the German philosopher Friedrich Nietzsche's categorical rejection of Christian ethics, which the latter dismissed as a servile morality, as being the consequence of Nietzsche's evolutionary world-view.[26] Kuyper realized that the biblical teaching and Darwin's contentions are incompatible because they are antithetical. He called them 'mutually exclusive systems', and his personal lamentation about the matter makes this clear: 'If the theory of evolution ... should triumph, the days of freedom of conscience, of tolerance and forbearance are past, and there will be a return to a rigid, violent persecution of all that is called Christian. For the dogma of evolution not only *condones* the violent eradication of the weak but makes it the *duty* of the strong.'[27]

In the pantheist-evolutionary world-view autonomous people determine their own morality.[28] Kuyper perceived that, if all human behaviour is explicable in terms of evolution, then all disciplines of learning must proceed upon that basis. History, for example, must be understood as the 'action of mechanical factors'.[29] It would be absurd to pass moral judgement upon actions, past or present, because pantheism-evolutionism removes the distinction between good and evil: 'Nero and Jesus are merely different manifestations of the same divine impulsive power... What we call Satan is but another name for the Holy One of Israel.'[30] There can, therefore, be no personal responsibility for one's moral actions.

Kuyper knew that Christianity must maintain the doctrine of creation, with the transcendence of God the Creator, for the antithesis between good and evil is foundational to everything Christians believe.

The political implications of believing in evolution caused
Kuyper particular concern, for as leader of the Anti-Revolutionary Party, he sought to prevent the growth of governmental
authority at the expense of personal freedoms. He held that
acceptance of the evolutionary world-view could lead the state
to assume that it is qualified to establish public morality. By
ignoring the true God, civil rulers could make themselves the
authoritarian arbiters of right and wrong. They could become
the personifications of G. W. F. Hegel's dictum: 'The state is the
divine idea as it exists on earth.' Were the state to assume such
divinity, it would have no absolute basis for its authority, so it
could rule tyrannically, and its subjects would not have a moral
reason to prevent them from disobeying their rulers or revolting
against them.[31] Jurists who adopted the evolutionary philosophy would have no absolute standard of judgement, and so
could ignore the laws of God and render their decisions solely
in accord with their own aspirations for society.[32] Kuyper realized that acceptance of a materialist world-view had prepared
his homeland for socialism.

The person and work of Christ

Like all orthodox Christians before him, Abraham Kuyper was
a strict Trinitarian in his view of God. He knew that creatures
cannot comprehend their Creator, but they may obtain reliable
information about God because of divine revelation. The general revelation of the created world testifies to the reality of
God's being; the special revelation of Scripture discloses that
God is a tri-unity, one God in three equally divine persons.
Jesus Christ is therefore the perfect revelation of God in human
form, God's supreme self-disclosure. He expressed this exuber-
antly: 'The Son is not to be excluded from anything. You cannot

point to any natural realm or star or comet, or even descent into the depth of the earth, but it is related to Christ, not in some unimportant tangential way, but directly. There is no force in nature, [there are] no laws that control those forces that do not have their origin in that eternal Word [Christ]. For this reason it is totally false to restrict Christ to spiritual affairs and to assert that there is no point of contact between him and the natural sciences. Rather, every deeper penetration into nature must lead to the greater glory of the majesty of the eternal Word.'[33]

With Martin Luther and the sixteenth-century Reformers, Kuyper held that believers must seek God in Christ and not speculate about the hidden, unknowable aspects of the Deity. The Son reveals the Father, and 'Outside of Christ it is all darkness and hiddenness, but in Christ … the crystalline window is opened, through which the liberated soul gazes into the depth of the Divine Being.'[34]

By means of a literal incarnation God became man in Jesus Christ. As theologians have said, Christ humiliated himself by coming to earth in human flesh in order to redeem lost sinners. Kuyper likened Christ's sojourn on earth to a healthy person residing in a hospital for contagious diseases, or to a civilized European living among barbarous primitive peoples. Christ had daily contact with selfish, God-rejecting sinners.[35] In a Christmas meditation he admonished his readers to remember that Christ is precious, not because he stirs the emotions, but because he saves from sin. The manger of Bethlehem 'begins our exaltation but his [Christ's] humiliation'.[36] Although the Old Testament is God's revelation, 'Until the birth in Bethlehem, God spoke … in *human words*, but in Christ God appears … in *human nature.*'[37] While his liberal contemporaries were trying to find the 'historical Jesus', Dr Kuyper had no doubts that the real Christ had become man, as the Creed of Nicaea (A.D. 325) affirms, 'for us men and for our salvation'.

The work of the Holy Spirit

Kuyper's Trinitarian belief required him to give considerable attention to pneumatology, the study of the Holy Spirit. This led him to publish a series of articles in *De Heraut* that appeared in book form in 1888, a work now available in English. As in all areas of doctrine, he insisted that the sole source of knowledge about the Holy Spirit is the Bible. Repeatedly and emphatically, he cited the Holy Spirit as the primary author of Scripture: 'Among the divine works of art produced by the Holy Spirit, the sacred Scripture stands first.' It is the means by which 'the triune God prepares men's souls for higher glory'.[38]

Kuyper was convinced that God the Holy Spirit had inspired the writers of the Bible and that the Spirit ceased to grant such inspiration at the completion of the New Testament. The Holy Spirit, he said, 'has bestowed on the church a complete and infallible Scripture'.[39] The written Word of God has superseded the direct inspiration of prophets and apostles. God has not spoken directly since the apostolic age, and he 'is silent now that we may honour Scripture'.[40]

The same Holy Spirit who inspired the writing of the Bible persuades and enables people to believe its message and to submit to its authority. The sinful condition of fallen human beings makes them, however, naturally hostile to God and rebellious against his revelation. Kuyper maintained that only the Holy Spirit can change sinful human nature and convince human minds to accept the truth of Scripture. This begins with the Spirit's work of regeneration, when God sovereignly imparts spiritual life to people 'dead in transgressions and sins' (Ephesians 2:1). Only after receiving this life from God can people believe the Bible, because the Holy Spirit enables them to do so; he illumines their minds to understand it.[41]

The self-authenticating Word of God

Kuyper's confidence in the regenerating, persuading and illu-
minating work of the Holy Spirit led him to disapprove of all
efforts to prove the claims of Scripture by appeals to extra-
biblical evidences or rationalistic arguments. In Kuyper's understanding, 'The revelation of the Holy Spirit granted to the
apostles was of such a nature that it could not be perceived by
others. Hence the impossibility to prove its genuineness by
notarial evidence. He that insists upon it ought to know that the
church cannot furnish it… Hence it is evident that every effort
to prove the contents of the New Testament by external evidence only condemns itself in the absolute rejection of the authority of the Holy Scripture.'[42]

As a recipient of the Holy Spirit's regeneration and illumination, Abraham Kuyper believed the Bible is self-authenticat-
ing because it is the Word of God. To subject Scripture to the
judgement of unbelievers who demand proof would be to denigrate God's Word and thereby to concede that it is not the
highest authority. Kuyper contended that all demands for proof
are actually evidences of human sinfulness and rebellion against
God, which only God himself, by regeneration, can suppress.
'God's elect obtain a firm assurance concerning the Word of
God that nothing can shake, of which no learning can rob
them.'[43] Certainty regarding the truth of Scripture is a fruit of
faith, and faith is a gift from God. The Holy Spirit creates faith
in the Word of God and in the God of the Word.[44] It is the
Spirit's work 'to enter man's heart and in its recesses to proclaim God's grace until he believes'.[45]

Contending for the faith

There was nothing unique or innovative in Abraham Kuyper's
understanding of God. He subscribed heartily to the historic

creeds of the ancient church, and he aligned himself with the Protestant Reformers of the sixteenth century who had done the same. His objective was to uphold orthodox teachings that contemporary liberals and modernists denied. In doing so he clarified the issues of debate for the benefit of Reformed believers and thereby promoted a powerful resurgence of theocentricity, which he regarded as the greatest distinctive of the Reformed faith.

IO.

Abraham Kuyper's theology (II): Sin and salvation

The theocentricity of Abraham Kuyper's world-view permeated every area of his beliefs, as his understanding of sin and salvation exhibits. Like his forefathers of the Protestant Reformation, he held firmly to a belief in human sinfulness and depravity that rendered mankind subject to the wrath of the holy God, who might have condemned the entire race to perdition with no provision for redemption. Kuyper based this belief upon his conviction that the fall of Adam and Eve, as recorded in Genesis 3, was a literal, historical event, and he subscribed to the New Testament explanation that the original sin has contaminated all of Adam's natural descendants.[1] Since the Fall all sins come from a single source — original sin, and all guilt (liability to punishment) comes from that first guilt.[2] 'This was the fall in paradise, that the woman made peace with Satan and hence came to stand in enmity with God.'[3] All of her descendants, with the exception of Jesus Christ, are, like their mother, in a state of enmity towards God.

The tragic condition of sinful humanity means that people do not naturally love God and therefore do not desire to obey his will. Every aspect of the human personality experiences the effects of sin, and those effects make people insensitive towards God, a condition the apostle Paul described as spiritual death (Ephesians 2:1). In their depraved state humans possess neither the will nor the ability to please their Creator, and God might have left them in eternal alienation from himself. The fact that he did not do so brought great delight to Kuyper and caused him to expound enthusiastically upon soteriology, the doctrine of salvation.

Salvation is the work of God

Kuyper explained from Scripture that God in Christ came to rescue lost sinners. He did so as an act of grace, a compassionate undertaking without regard for human merit or the lack of it. Dr Kuyper cautioned his readers to understand that God came to their aid primarily to glorify himself, for Christ does not exist for men; they exist for him. His sacrifice accomplished the redemption of sinners, but 'The real objective was the restoration of the justice and glory of God... When we read, "God so loved the world that he gave his only begotten Son" [John 3:16], we may not conclude that our intrinsic value motivated God to be merciful to us. It means that God would not allow his handiwork to be for ever despoiled by Satan, but [he] intervened with the ultimate means to restore his power on earth and thereby [to] rescue the world from eternal perdition.'4 In this way Kuyper affirmed the theocentric character of salvation.

As a Reformed theologian, Dr Kuyper asserted that salvation is entirely the work of God. Man's only contribution is his sins. In order to maintain his own holiness and justice, God had to punish sin. Either sinners must pay for their own offences, or they must have an acceptable substitute to pay on their behalf. Christ, the sinless Son of God, is the only acceptable substitute. 'Christ stood there [at Calvary] to face the *unbroken power* of the curse of sin and Satan. He had no saviour to shield him, no saviour to draw near and comfort [him] in the trying hour. He was himself the Saviour.'5

What death on the cross entailed for Christ, Kuyper explained in vivid terms when he wrote that Jesus went to Calvary as 'the covenant head of the redeemed; the concentrated sin of our whole race was laid on him... Going in against this, the absolute wrath of God's holy majesty worked upon his soul with an eternal death-breathing curse ... a travail that was more than pain, never less than the sum total of all the terror of hell.'[6]

Although Kuyper wrote much about the proper human response to Christ's sacrifice, he was careful to explain that salvation began in the mind of God in eternity past. Since all people are sinners, undeserving of divine favour, salvation must come from God, who bestows it sovereignly as he wills. To a world that was imbibing Darwin's theory of *natural selection*, Dr Kuyper proclaimed the doctrine of *divine election*. He affirmed God's full control over all he has made, and he declared categorically that, by predestination, God determined to save only his chosen people. In taking this position Kuyper demonstrated his allegiance to orthodox Protestant teaching as it had appeared in the works of Luther, Calvin and the Puritans and in all the Reformed confessions of faith.[7] He did not make predestination the principal distinction of the Reformed faith, but he viewed it as a necessary expression of theocentricity. All grace flows from the sovereign will of God without regard for human merit. Man must be subject to God in everything and therefore completely dependent upon the Creator for salvation.[8] Commenting upon Roman Catholic veneration of the Virgin Mary, Kuyper contended that she was merely a recipient of undeserved divine favour. In Kuyper's words, 'There is no reason to praise her... Grace bars the possibility of credit and pride.'[9]

Salvation by grace alone

Kuyper was especially vigorous in asserting that salvation is *sola gratia*, by grace alone, and he cited from the Bible numerous illustrations of grace at work. One example is Rahab, a woman who appears in the book of Joshua (2:1-24) as a pagan prostitute in Canaan who protected the Hebrew spies who had sneaked into the country to reconnoitre in preparation for Israel's conquest of the land. The New Testament hails Rahab as a woman of great faith in the true God (Hebrews 11:31). Where did she obtain such faith? Kuyper had no doubt that God had chosen her for salvation. God had granted her faith while she was still a pagan and a prostitute, and she abandoned her trade as a consequence of God's gift. God accepted Rahab 'to teach us that his grace is omnipotent and that he is able and willing to redeem even the most profoundly sinful [people]'.[10]

In the period between the death of Joshua and the establishment of a monarchy in Israel (c. 1390-1050 B.C.) judges governed the Hebrew nation during a time of apostasy, warfare and civil strife. God punished the unfaithful Hebrews by sending famine that caused Naomi and her family to flee to Moab in search of food. One of her sons married Ruth, a Moabite pagan, who had no knowledge of the true God. After her husband died, Ruth embraced her mother-in-law's religion and declared her faith in Naomi's God (Ruth 1:1-22). This same Ruth appears in the genealogy of Jesus Christ (Matthew 1:5) along with Rahab. Kuyper explained this remarkable occurrence as due to divine providence working sovereignly to draw Ruth to salvation: 'Men hungered for bread in Bethlehem that Ruth might hunger for the bread of life.'[11]

Among women of the New Testament Dr Kuyper cited Lydia, a merchant from Thyatira, who responded believingly to the preaching of the apostle Paul (Acts 16:11-15). Lydia believed because 'the Lord opened her heart'. Likewise, the grandmother and mother of Paul's companion Timothy were recipients of the gift of saving faith because God had chosen them.[12]

In all the biblical examples Kuyper mentioned he showed that salvation is always the work of God on behalf of sinners who do not deserve his mercy. As Kuyper explained the matter, 'The work of grace does not begin with faith or with repentance or with contrition, but ... all these are preceded by God's act of giving power to the powerless, hearing to the deaf, and life to the dead.'[13]

Abraham Kuyper agreed with John Calvin's assertion that the doctrine of election is the *cor ecclesiae* (heart of the church), and he insisted that the public proclamation of this truth is a solemn duty for all pastors. Failure to do so would mean they were not preaching the 'whole counsel of God' (Acts 20:27, NKJV). Kuyper was particularly chagrined because so many ministers of the former National Church had abandoned the Reformed faith and therefore espoused a man-centred view of salvation.[14]

Divine sovereignty and human responsibility

Although the doctrine of election means that God saves chosen sinners by the sovereign exercise of his will, Kuyper was quick to affirm the correlative truth of human responsibility in salvation, as in all areas of belief and behaviour. He wrote, 'We dare not forget, that while God, according to the secret of his counsel, elects those who are to be saved ... this same omnipotent God has made us morally responsible, so that we are lost, not because we could not be saved, but because we would not.'[15]

Kuyper realized that the precise relationship between divine sovereignty and human responsibility is a mystery and that Scripture does not offer a full explanation of this matter. He refused to speculate about it, and he discouraged all efforts at harmonizing these truths for the satisfaction of inquisitive minds. He was content to leave the matter unresolved, but he contended that God's sovereignty and man's responsibility 'must be maintained in all their completeness and fulness and strength'.[16] He was sensitive about the implication that predestination makes God the author of sin. He denied this, and he rejected the belief that God created people only so that he might condemn them. Kuyper saw the apparent tension between predestination and the New Testament portrayal of God's love and grace, and he advised his readers to be content with the amount of knowledge God has revealed in his Word, for 'The Scriptures do not permit us to minimize God's omnipotence nor the extent of our guilt. Therefore it behoves us to bow solemnly before this mystery and [to] confess wholeheartedly both God's omnipotence and our guilt, since the Scriptures do not reveal the connection between the two.'[17] He went on to say, 'The lost will have to confess throughout eternity: "I have rejected God, and therefore he rejects me." '[18]

The new birth

The concomitance between salvation by predestinating grace alone and belief in human depravity has always been a major emphasis in Lutheran and Reformed theology. If humans since the Fall are truly 'dead in transgressions and sins' (Ephesians 2:1), their spiritual condition makes it impossible for them to seek God, or to do anything that would merit his favour. God, nevertheless, has shown pity for his elect creatures by imparting spiritual life to them through a new birth (John 3:1-15) that theologians call regeneration. To this teaching Kuyper assigned enormous importance. He maintained that God alone gives 'birth to his elect again, and in that rebirth ... plant[s] *faith* in them'.[19]

In defining the doctrine of regeneration Dr Kuyper clearly and emphatically denied synergism, the belief that God and man work together to effect rebirth for sinful human nature. Kuyper was a monergist, that is, one who regarded regeneration as a sovereign act of God the Holy Spirit prior to any human response or decision. Any human contribution to re-birth is impossible because, prior to regeneration, a sinner has 'all the passive properties belonging to a corpse ... [so] every effort to claim for the sinner the minutest co-operation in this first grace destroys the gospel, severs the artery of the Christian confession and is anti-scriptural in the highest degree'.[20]

As Kuyper understood this matter, the impartation of spiritual life by regeneration enables recipients of this grace to respond obediently to the divine call to believe the gospel, to embrace Christ and to repent of sin. Conversion from unbelief to faith is then the fruit of regeneration. It is the proper human response to the gospel made possible by the new birth. Saving faith expresses confidence in Scripture, takes refuge in Christ, enjoys the assurance of salvation in love for the Saviour.[21] All true believers are born-again Christians (John 3:3), for apart from regeneration, people remain dead in sin and do not believe Christ's message.

Two contrasting world-views

Kuyper's view of sin and salvation, of course, provoked objections from religious people who did not accept his theocentric world-view. Some of them contended that Reformed orthodoxy contradicts the love of God for all mankind by restricting saving grace to the elect. Kuyper responded to this argument by insisting that God alone is competent to define his own love. There is no reason to be surprised that the revelation of God's love in Scripture offends sinners and contradicts their conceptions of what that love should be and how it should operate. Kuyper explained: 'We absolutely deny our own hearts and feelings the right to decide this matter or even to have any voice in it, and [we] claim that we ... should unreservedly submit to all that God has revealed in this respect.'[22]

For Abraham Kuyper the issue of predestination is just one more example of the inevitable antithesis between biblical Christianity and religious humanism. As in all other points of contention between opposing world-views, the root of the matter is the question of authority. Insisting upon *Sola Scriptura*, Kuyper decried any objection that preceded from an assumed human autonomy as the work of 'a meddlesome spirit or unhallowed curiosity',[23] and he concluded, 'Divine wisdom does not compromise with the speculations and delusions of worldly wisdom but calls them folly and demands their surrender.'[24]

The effects of sin on all human thinking

The relevance of regeneration for life and work in the academic world was patently clear to Dr Kuyper. He attributed all arguments against biblical teachings in all areas of learning to the unregenerate condition of the minds in which those contentions arose. He had a keen perception of what theologians call 'the noetic effects of sin', the consequences of sin for the human mind. Although the Fall did not rob man of his humanity, it did impair his mental faculties and make him think in a way that is contrary to God's truth and to his own interests. Prior to the Fall Adam and Eve did not err, but were flawless in thinking about God and his will. After the Fall, however, they could no longer maintain full correctness in the exercise of their intellects, for sin had distorted the image of God in which the Lord created them. That is why sinful minds regard some of God's claims as absurd and unreasonable. They are not actually unreasonable, but sin has so marred the human mind that people think completely reasonable truths are absurd.

Kuyper believed that sin impairs learning and teaching in all disciplines of study. He cited Ephesians 4:17-18, which exposes unbelievers for 'the futility of their thinking' and their 'darkened ... understanding' because they are 'separated from ...

God'. The noetic effects of sin appear in all falsehood, both deliberate and unintentional, in all deceptions and delusions. The common inability to distinguish between reality and imagination is, for example, an effect of sin.[25] Sin has disrupted mankind's harmony with nature, and it has ruined the inner harmony that Adam and Eve enjoyed before the Fall. Therefore the human 'sense of what is the good, the true, the beautiful, of what is right, of what is holy, has ceased to operate with accuracy'.[26] Lacking the proper knowledge of God, people cannot understand themselves and the world adequately. This condition renders sinful minds incompetent to appreciate divine revelation and to accept its claims upon them. Unregenerate people continue to bear the image of God in which he created them, but sin has distorted it badly, so 'All kinds of religious emotions go hand-in-hand with hatred for God.'[27]

As he realized the implications of his belief about human depravity, Abraham Kuyper concluded that it would be futile to argue with unbelievers in the hope of persuading them with evidence to accept the teachings of Scripture. Satan introduced falsehood by calling God a liar and by presenting himself as a herald of truth (Genesis 3:1-4). Falsehood, then, is due not only to human error, for demonic activity lies at it root. Christ alone has evaded its influence, so he is 'the truth' incarnate (John 14:6). To be apart from Christ is be without the ability to perceive truth as he had revealed it. In Kuyper's words, 'Ignorance wrought by sin is the most difficult obstacle in the way of all true science.'[28]

The implications for scholarship

People at all levels of education and learning need the new birth (regeneration), which the Holy Spirit alone can accomplish, for that divine action makes them alive in their relationship to God and thereby enables them to grasp his truth. The effect of regeneration appears in the academic world when believing scholars extol Jesus Christ and reject those teachings that oppose his claims. Kuyper believed the antithesis between Christian and humanist scholarship would continue until the return of Christ. While believers await their Lord's advent, they must interpret all of life within the framework of the biblical worldview. At the Free University of Amsterdam that meant every department had to teach from a distinctively Christian point of view on its particular discipline. The theology faculty would thereby combat evil in the human heart (soul), the faculty of medicine in the human body and the faculty of law in human legal relationships. In each of them God's moral precepts must govern the teaching. Theology, for example, must not be a comparative study of religions, but an exposition of biblical truth. The law faculty must not become a department of sociology that decides issues in terms of the current preferences of society. It must judge on the basis of God's eternal standard of right and wrong.[29]

Kuyper believed a Christian university is necessary because only regenerate scholars possess an adequate perception of truth. For them the existence of God is not an intellectual problem. In all fields of study they experience the effects of grace upon their intellectual labours.[30] Since theology is the study of God's self-disclosure, it is a pursuit that requires entire dependence upon God and submission to 'the object of [the scholar's] investigation'. In other disciplines Christian scholars stand 'above the object to be studied'. Nevertheless, in all learning Scripture has the last word, for it is the standard of truth across the whole curriculum.[31]

Justification by faith

Whether Christians engage in scholarship or not, Dr Kuyper called them to appreciate the benefits of regeneration, without which no one can receive faith and turn to Christ. Kuyper, like all orthodox Protestants, affirmed that regeneration produces faith that justifies believing sinners. That is, saving faith, as the *Heidelberg Catechism* defines it, is 'not only a certain knowledge whereby I hold for truth all that God has revealed to us in his Word, but also a hearty trust which the Holy Spirit works in me by the gospel, that not only to others, but to me also, forgiveness of sins, everlasting righteousness and salvation, are freely given by God, merely by grace, only for the sake of Christ's merits'.

Martin Luther regarded the doctrine of justification *sola fide* (through faith alone) as the article on which the church would stand or fall, and Kuyper agreed. He understood that there is a factual reality in saving faith without which it could not exist. That is, one must believe the content of the Scripture and its declarations about the person and work of Christ, but intellectual acceptance of the historical facts of Christianity is not sufficient. Justification means acceptance by God on the basis of Christ's merits and his righteousness imputed to sinners who have nothing meritorious of their own to present to God. It requires perfect righteousness, something sinners cannot achieve. When a sinner, exercising the gift of faith, realizes his depravity and inability to please God, the Lord 'not only manifests his mercy but also the omnipotence of the mercy by declaring that entirely lost soul completely justified' (righteous).[32]

Sanctification

In Kuyper's understanding, regeneration plants the seed of faith; grace enables it to grow and to produce conscious conversion; conversion then leads to the performance of good works. Works contribute nothing to justification, but they are fruits of saving faith.[33] If good works do not appear, there is reason to question the validity of one's faith. Kuyper warned about 'temporary faith' that does not endure, even though for a while it seems to express belief in Christ and love for his Word.[34] Genuine faith seeks holiness throughout a believer's life.

The quest for personal holiness is the subject of sanctification, to which Kuyper devoted much attention. He was an academic theologian with a pastor's heart, so he strove ceaselessly to minister to his beloved *kleine luyden* as well as to his students and university colleagues. He believed a clear understanding of sanctification is vital for all Christians without regard to the level of their formal education.

Although Dr Kuyper insisted that regeneration is the work of the Holy Spirit alone, a work to which humans make no contribution, he held that regenerate sinners, justified through faith alone in Christ alone, must co-operate with God in their sanctification. He admonished readers of his book *Keep thy Solemn Feasts* (1903) that love for Jesus Christ is not a mere emotional experience. He wrote, 'Love for the Babe of Bethlehem is at the same time *hatred* for sin, *hatred* of Satan, and *hatred* of the unrighteousness which … Satan supports.'[35] He urged parents to inculcate this hatred in their children.

Kuyper rejected the view that sanctification is only 'a human effort to make oneself holy or holier',[36] because he knew that the Holy Spirit brings the disposition of regenerate and converted people into harmony and compliance with God's will. Where regeneration is an instantaneous impartation of spiritual life, sanctification is a progressive experience of grace that gradually restores 'the holiness of Adam before he had performed any holy work'. Holiness entails the believer's desire to obey God's laws and to perform good — the good works it requires.[37] Sanctification does not mean that human works supplement Christ's work on the cross. It proceeds from grace, as the Holy Spirit creates a holy disposition within believers. Good works are the fruits of the Spirit's gracious gift. Sanctification does not occur contrary to the believer's will, because regeneration has produced a 'new heart' that loves God and his laws. Conversion leads to mortification of the sinful nature and cultivation of the new nature with its holy desires and inclinations.[38] Kuyper explained that Christians are saved from the guilt, penalty and stain of sin: 'From the penalty by Christ's *atonement*, from the guilt by his *satisfaction*, from the stain by *sanctification*.'[39] To show that believers are not passive in sanctification, Kuyper urged them to understand that the Holy Spirit employs means to effect their growth in holiness, and they must avail themselves of those means of grace.[40] He urged them to pray for sanctifying grace to enable them to love God's law and to perform good works for God's glory. He said that God uses people to exhort one another to good works, so humans become instruments as they co-operate with God in sanctification.[41]

The Christian's response to suffering and temptation

The pursuit of holiness, as Dr Kuyper understood it, involves a lifelong struggle against temptation. On Calvary Christ defeated the kingdom of Satan 'in principle', but the final destruction of diabolical evil will occur at the return of Christ. While Christians await that triumph, they must pray, 'Deliver us from the evil one' (Matthew 6:13). As Kuyper stated the matter, 'We are still subject to his [Satan's] attacks and deceptions; he injects his parsimonious profanities even into our … prayers.'[42] Satan, however, is subject to God's control. Reason fails believers when they try to comprehend God's purpose in allowing Satan to molest them, but satanic attacks do not occur randomly by chance. Christians should rejoice because they know that 'Whatever threat or destruction may come upon [them], … [they] must accept it as coming from God, directed towards [them] and inflicted upon [them] by him. There cannot be any exception, not even the smallest.'[43]

The assurance that Satan is subject to God and is actually his unwilling accomplice should encourage disciples of Christ who suffer diabolical assaults. They should realize that toil and pain are also necessary parts of their growth in holiness. Believers, Kuyper insisted, must not become fatalists who resign themselves to the inevitability of evil. God has called them to exercise dominion over creation as his vicegerents, and that requires struggle against destructive forces. The Fall has made working conditions difficult (Genesis 3:17-19), but the mandate to work remains in effect. People should not assume they are entitled to exemption from toil and pain, 'as if sorrow and trouble were an offence against [their] innocence'. Submission to suffering, not resentment against it, is the Christian's duty.[44] Christ demands that his disciples deny themselves and 'take up the cross' (Matthew 16:24). This, Kuyper contended, means enduring all hardships that faithfulness to Christ entails. Anything that threatens to undermine one's faith is a 'cross'. Bearing that cross means that troubled disciples may always know they are 'more than conquerors' through Christ who loves them. They 'live in the consciousness that Jesus may come tomorrow or may appear upon the clouds even tonight'.[45]

Abraham Kuyper believed in God's sovereignty over everybody and everything, everywhere, all the time. Yet, as his dynamic career shows, he held with equal fervour to his belief in human responsibility. He bowed reverently before this mystery of divine revelation without diminishing either biblical truth. He disavowed all efforts to explain it, and he called on Christians to rejoice in divine sovereignty while fully accepting their obligations to serve him, for 'Even the cleverest among ... men stand speechless before this wondrous mystery.'[46]

The assurance of ultimate victory

With theologians across the centuries, Dr Kuyper believed that the completion of the believer's sanctification awaits the return of Christ, who will destroy the power of evil for ever. To satisfy God's justice and to display his mercy, Christ, on the cross, 'descended into hell' as a substitute for sinners and then rose triumphant over sin and death. He ascended into heaven and there intercedes for his chosen people: 'Jesus' ascension declares ... that this battle shall never be resumed, that it is impossible for Satan and death to get the upper hand again; and that, thanks to the glory to which Immanuel arose ... salvation is for ever sure.'[47]

The ascended Christ, then, is now in heaven with the souls of his redeemed people, and he is poised to return to earth as the climax of redemption which will bring the final vindication of his covenant people. When he was seventy-six years old Kuyper wrote about the second advent of Christ in a series of articles published in *De Heraut*. This material appeared in book form in 1920 and is now available in English under the title *The Revelation of St John*. In this exposition of the last New Testament book Kuyper explained that it predicts a series of events that will occur near the end of time, events connected with Christ's return. Kuyper lamented the general lack of interest in biblical prophecies apparent in his day, and he urged believers to seek comfort and assurance of complete victory over sin by meditating upon the certainty of the Saviour's return. He regarded Revelation 4-22 as prophetic Scripture that points to the *parousia,* Christ's Second Coming. Believing that the climax of the ages could be very near, Dr Kuyper asserted that, for the believer, 'Morning by morning, and evening by evening, his expectation is the appearing of his Saviour.'[48] The antithesis between God and Satan, Christ and Antichrist, Christianity and humanism, will reach its finale when God defeats all evil forces for ever.[49] Christians struggling with temptation and lapses into sin should take heart as the day of complete salvation draws nearer.

Abraham Kuyper's theology (III): The church

Writing in a book of a devotional nature entitled *Asleep in Jesus*, Abraham Kuyper expressed deep dismay about the condition of Christendom: 'All that is called "modern Christendom", one part faith mingled with nine parts philosophy, is nothing but the old heathen nature, which, in the name of Christ, is brought into the church of Christ and destroys her.'[1]

Kuyper's lamentation was due to the defection of the Dutch Reformed Church from its historic roots as expressed in its official confessions of faith and, as earlier chapters of this book have shown, his efforts to reverse the tide of infidelity failed. Kuyper's thinking about ecclesiology, the doctrine of the church, went through several stages of development. His first study of the subject was an academic essay about papal authority during the pontificate of Nicholas I (858-67), and his last written work also dealt with the church. He made the concept of the church as an organism the basis of his ecclesiology. Kuyper held that the true church is the body of Christ into which the Holy Spirit incorporates all God's chosen people.[2] He viewed divine election as the source of the church. As a person's soul is his or her real essence, so the elect comprise the true church, which subsists within the visible religious organization known as the church. The actual church is present, however, only because the elect are there. The organized, institutional church is important, so Kuyper devoted his life to serving as one of its officers, but he insisted that the institution is not identical with the real body of Christ. The marks of the true church are the preaching of God's Word and the administration of the sacraments; that is, implementing the means of grace. Kuyper regarded the discipline of church members as an important function of the church, but not as one of its essential marks. He knew that no church maintains the marks perfectly, but he contended that false churches discard God's Word, pervert the sacraments and oppose those who love divine truth.[3]

Church government

Kuyper's deep love for the family of God caused him much concern about the order and government of the church. He disapproved strongly of the concept of the *Volkskerk*, which was the belief that all people of a particular state are to be members of the state church and are therefore within the kingdom of God. At the same time, however, he disliked the view that makes the church exclusively a society of individuals who have declared faith in Jesus Christ, for this view does not allow for the inclusion of believers' children within the community with which God has established his covenant of grace. Kuyper pointed to Timothy, one of the apostle Paul's converts, as an example of how the covenant of grace operates. Timothy's grandmother Lois and his mother Eunice were early believers who created a Christian family into which Timothy was born. Being part of that family placed him in a position to receive the saving grace of God, a grace that God has promised to believers and to their children (2 Timothy 1:3-5; Acts 2:38-39).[4]

Kuyper encouraged a pattern of church government which made the local congregation central, and he believed that no organic connections between or among local congregations are necessary or desirable. He did not want local churches to be subservient to higher ecclesiastical bodies, as had become the pattern in the former National Church because King William I had imposed his will upon it in 1816. In Kuyper's view, church agencies such as synods should be servants of the local congregations with which such congregations affiliate voluntarily. In taking this position Kuyper deviated from the Reformed tradition, as he admitted.[5] He maintained that local churches are God's primary instruments to accomplish his work through the ministry of the Word and the sacraments.

Just as he denied popular sovereignty as the basis for civil government, so Dr Kuyper rejected utilitarian thinking about church order. He believed the church must 'conform itself to that form ordained by God. Not by the will of believers, but God's will; not human choice, but God's Word must be the formative power which controls its origin.'[6]

Kuyper argued that the belief that members of the church have sovereign authority over its affairs was due to the evil influence of the French Revolution and its doctrine of popular sovereignty.[7] He asserted, 'The church is a strictly spiritual monarchy, a kingdom under the absolute kingship of Christ.'[8]

Although he considered the church a spiritual monarchy, Kuyper recognized that Christ governs his church on earth through officers he has created for that purpose. Such leaders are not ecclesiastical magistrates, but servants of the body. Believers should unite in a Presbyterian structure in which elected elders exercise authority and discipline over them.[9] Pastors are teaching elders, and laymen with gifts for leadership are ruling elders, but there must be no gradations of rank; all are equal, and Christ alone is head of the church.[10] Deacons have responsibility for ministry to the believers' material needs, but they are not inferior to elders. They perform a service of love that follows Christ's example.[11] In the true church there is no place for priestcraft and a clerical hierarchy. Believers must not accept their pastors' teachings casually, for each Christian is a priest before God and must exercise spiritual discernment. Believers, therefore, must rebuke negligent or apostate pastors.[12]

The faithful proclamation of God's Word

The first mark of the true church, as Kuyper contended, is the faithful proclamation of God's Word, for the true church is 'confessing, professing, and propagating … sharply defined principles, ideas, and notions of truth, not to be sought, but already found, because revealed'.[13]

The church, then, is not searching for truth, but labouring to understand, clarify and proclaim truth already in her possession by means of divine revelation. This commitment to Scripture distinguishes the true church from religious bodies that have succumbed to the allure of humanism-modernism. The true church stands in resolute opposition to modernist churches. The impasse between them is 'nothing less than the antithesis between deifying man and humanizing the Almighty'.[14] That is, Kuyper argued that modernists had exalted man to such an eminence that they made him his own god. They, likewise, portrayed God as though he were subject to the limitations of humanity.

Kuyper knew that the proper form of church government would not guarantee the purity of the church, but he argued that the wrong polity prevented Christians from taking steps to prevent the spiritual decay of the church, as had happened in the Dutch Reformed Church. In churches that fail to practise discipline, ungodly people intimidate the godly and, in effect, impose discipline upon them.[15] Kuyper saw this development in the German Lutheran churches and in the Church of England, where civil rulers controlled ecclesiastical affairs and prevented the reform and cleansing of the churches.[16] He believed the degeneration of churches begins with laxity about doctrine and proceeds to the evil behaviour of church members, so maintaining the confessional position of the church is essential. The church, therefore, must not tolerate officers who deviate from her confession, for that inevitably leads to profaning the sacraments, as well as to diluting the preaching of God's Word. When that happens, the church has renounced the kingship of Christ.[17] As indicated in chapter 8, by 1886 Kuyper and a large number of orthodox believers within the former National Church had decided that they had to separate from it, and they formed the *Gereformeerde Kerken in Nederland*, the Reformed Churches in the Netherlands, on the basis of the historic Three Forms of Unity.

Although Abraham Kuyper adhered zealously to the Reformed faith, he did not maintain a narrow, sectarian view of the church. The true church, as he understood it, is catholic in that it transcends denominational and confessional lines, so he readily acknowledged the genuine faith and the contributions of believers in other confessional bodies.[18] He often grieved over his own sins and those of fellow believers, for he realized that their sins and his marred the church and weakened her ministry. He once wrote to his supporters with much dismay, 'You have no right to or claim to a model church. You acknowledge yourselves humble sinners whose imperfections add to the corruption of the church.'[19] The church is holy only because Christ, its head, is complete holiness. Its members remain soiled by sin, even though Christ has saved them.

The proper administration of the sacraments

In accord with traditional Reformed theology, Kuyper cited the proper administration of the sacraments as the second mark of the church. Since the Protestant Reformation of the sixteenth century, all major Protestant bodies had recognized only baptism and the Lord's Supper as sacraments, but there were important differences among those churches over the significance of the sacraments. The term 'sacrament' comes from the Latin word *sacramentum*, which originally meant something set apart because it was sacred. When a Roman soldier joined the army, he swore an oath of obedience to his emperor and to his military superiors. The sacrament was a pledge, a commitment from a man who was set apart for military service. The early church used this term for baptism and the Eucharist (the Lord's Supper) as a Latin translation of the Greek term *mysterion*, 'mystery', which in the New Testament identifies the kingdom of God (Matthew 13:1-23; Mark 4:11). Preaching the *kerygma* (the gospel) is the primary means of conveying the grace of forgiveness to sinners. It is an oral declaration of God's promise and pledge to forgive all who come to Christ in penitent faith.

The sacraments, too, proclaim the gospel of forgiveness, but in a visible manner by means of outward signs — water in baptism, bread and wine in the Eucharist. Augustine defined the sacraments as the 'visible Word', or 'outward and visible signs of an inward spiritual grace'. That is, he held that these signs convey what they signify; they are means and channels of grace. Augustine's definition left a lasting impression upon the Protestant Reformers, especially upon Martin Luther, for, like Augustine, Luther affirmed the inseparability of Word and sacraments, as did John Calvin and the branch of the Reformation that developed through his influence. Unlike the Roman Catholic Church, which in the Middle Ages, came to view the sacraments as the primary means of grace, Protestants maintained the New Testament and Augustinian priority of God's Word. Reformed theologians since Calvin have not bound the saving work of God exclusively to the sacraments, but they have, nevertheless, rejected the view that the sacraments are peripheral symbols that Christians may neglect without harm to their spiritual lives. The historic Reformed confessions categorically deny that the sacraments are mere symbols devoid of the grace they depict. The *Belgic Confession* (1561 revised 1619) affirms in articles XXXIII and XXXIV:

> We believe that our gracious God ... has ordained the sacraments for us, thereby to seal unto us his promises and to be pledges of the good will and grace of God toward us and to nourish and strengthen our faith, which he has joined to the Word of the Gospel, the better to present to our senses, both that which he signifies to us by his Word and that which he works inwardly in our hearts, thereby assuring and confirming in us the salvation which he imparts to us. For they are visible signs and seals of an inward and invisible thing by means whereof God works in us by the power of the Holy Spirit. Therefore the signs are not in vain or insignificant, so as to deceive us...
>
> The ministers ... administer the Sacrament and that which is visible, but our Lord gives that which is signified by the Sacrament, namely, the gifts and the invisible grace; washing, cleansing, and purging our souls of all filth and unrighteousness; renewing our hearts and filling them with all comfort; giving to us a true assurance of his fatherly goodness...[20]

Kuyper's teaching on baptism

As a loyal minister of the Reformed faith, Abraham Kuyper concurred readily with the historic teachings about the sacraments, but he added a view about baptism that caused considerable debate among fellow adherents to the Three Forms of Unity. Kuyper held firmly to the traditional belief in the validity of infant baptism as the New Testament successor to circumcision in the Old Testament; that is, as the Hebrew children received circumcision as an outward sign of their inclusion within the covenant community of God's people, so the children of New Testament believers should receive baptism to show that they stand within the New Covenant community. The *Heidelberg Catechism*, in questions 69-74, explains the meaning of baptism and it states clearly that it is the 'washing of regeneration and the washing away of sins'. This, however, does not invest the water of baptism with miraculous power, 'for only the blood of Jesus Christ and the Holy Spirit cleanse us from all sin'. Baptism is a 'divine pledge and token' of what God has done for his people by the atoning sacrifice of his Son. Divine grace 'is not inherent in the means as a divine deposit, but [it] accompanies the use of these'.[21]

As he studied the matter of baptism and reflected upon the declarations about it in the historic confessions, Kuyper agreed that it is a seal of God's grace and that the water of the sacrament does not regenerate sinners, but he contended that most children of believers already possess spiritual life when they are baptized.[22] He believed that God, in regeneration, works apart from means, immediately, so infants may be regenerated without the Word of God as the means of grace. Regeneration implants faith that infants cannot exercise, but that will become active later in their lives.[23]

To this point in his doctrine of baptism Kuyper displayed no essential disharmony with the historic Reformed position, but he aroused controversy by asserting a concept that has become known as 'presumed regeneration'. In an essay he directed to Presbyterians in the United States in 1891, he stated, 'Baptism should be administered on the presumption that regeneration has preceded [it].' He argued that, in the case of infants, regeneration has occurred, and baptism is the covenant seal that attests to it. Only God knows his elect, so the church should not 'issue dogmatic pronouncements about absence of spiritual life in infants'.[24]

Kuyper was careful to distinguish between the presence of regeneration and conversion, and he did not assume that all baptized people would be saved. He knew that vast numbers of circumcised people in the Old Testament perished in unbelief, so he entertained no delusion that a comparable situation did not exist within the visible church. Regeneration and conversion are not the same, and they seldom occur together. The former usually happens in the life of an elect person when he or she is an infant, and 'The glorious assumption that secret regeneration does take place is the sole and conclusive ground upon which the Reformed churches base their demand that every baptized person must repent and turn to God, if he would sit at the Lord's holy table [the Eucharist]'.[25]

In other words, Reformed churches are to assume that baptized persons have been regenerated, for otherwise they would not be able to repent. The presumed regeneration of baptized infants is, in Kuyper's view, the basis for believing that those who die in infancy are saved, and belief in infant regeneration gives Christian parents the right to demand repentance from their children.[26] Since the Holy Spirit produces faith, a child who dies in infancy can be saved even though he or she cannot understand God's Word.[27] This applies only to children, as the *Canons of Dort* declare.[28]

The necessary distinction between regeneration and conversion, Kuyper maintained, means that pastors must preach evangelistically so as to call baptized, regenerate people to repentance and to public confession of their faith in Christ. Pastors must address this call to their entire congregations, knowing that the non-elect within them will not respond. The church must exhort everyone to come to Christ in repentance.[29] Kuyper did not believe that the doctrine of presumed regeneration should, or would, discourage evangelism, and in his own ministry he relentlessly sought the conversion of sinners. Another implication of presumed regeneration, as Kuyper regarded it, is the responsibility of Christian parents and churches to provide for the spiritual care of their covenant children. They should urge children to confess faith in Christ, for such a confession is not a mere ecclesiastical formality. It is a personal affirmation that must entail resolute allegiance to the Son of God. Parents must impress this upon their baptized children. As Kuyper said to parents, 'You must not permit your child to grow accustomed to indifference or to passivity, but [you] must teach him to sing his Saviour's praise and to rise to his Lord's defence at every occasion.'[30] The age at which a person becomes personally responsible for confessing faith appears to have produced some uncertainty in Kuyper's thinking. In one essay he suggested it is at seven years old, but in another of his writings he mentioned the ages of sixteen to twenty-three.[31]

Kuyper claimed to have substantial support for the concept of presumed regeneration from historic Reformed authors. He cited the work of the Dutch theologian Gisbert Voetius (1589-1677), who had contended that children of the covenant community possess the Holy Spirit and enjoy the forgiveness of sins as do adult members, so they should be baptized. Kuyper thought that Calvin, too, had taught this view, so he pointed to the *Institutes of the Christian Religion* (IV, XVI, 17-20), but a careful reading of this passage in Calvin's great work shows that he did not presume that baptized infants are regenerate. Unlike Kuyper, who believed that the Holy Spirit works immediately without means in regeneration, Calvin regarded the Word of God as the means God employs to effect the new birth.

Despite his conviction that he represented the orthodox Reformed view concerning presumed regeneration, many of his fellow Calvinists disagreed with Kuyper's teaching. He

maintained that the church should regard the children of believers as regenerate unless they renounce God's covenant with
his people, but other Reformed theologians have not endorsed
this argument.[32] The Christian Reformed Church, created by
the secession from the National Church in 1834, had rejected
presumed regeneration long before Abraham Kuyper became
a church leader. The synod of that body in 1846 declared: '...
all the children of those who have joined the congregation ought
to be baptized; this, however, imparts no internal holiness to
the children, and when these children, in coming to maturity,
give no evidence of godliness, they must, without exception,
be dealt with as children of wrath.'[33]

Soon after the separation of the *Doleantie* from the Dutch
Reformed Church, leaders of the *Doleantie* and some from the
Christian Reformed Church began talking about a merger of
the two movements which had so much in common. As we
noted in chapter 8, union between these churches became a
reality in 1892, but some Christian Reformed congregations
chose to remain separate. One of the reasons for their decision
was their opposition to Kuyper's teaching about baptism.
Doleantie leaders maintained that Kuyper's belief was only his
personal opinion and would not become the doctrine of the
merged churches, but critics of his view feared Kuyper's
powerful influence, and they thought his teaching would diminish evangelistic zeal. A synod of the Christian Reformed
Church in 1894 resolutely rejected presumed regeneration
as a non-Reformed doctrine, and it cited Kuyper's belief as
a reason for remaining apart from the Reformed Churches
in the Netherlands, the newly formed body produced by the
merger. A synod of the Reformed Churches in the Netherlands adopted Kuyper's position in 1905, and this action
seemed to confirm the concerns of the Christian Reformed
Church, a body which today has about 185 congregations
with about 75,000 members.[34]

Not everyone even within the *Doleantie* agreed with Kuyper's doctrine of baptism, and some Reformed thinkers then and now have argued that it depreciates the need for conversion, even though Dr Kuyper himself emphatically emphasized that need.[35] Some regard presumed regeneration as a presumptuous belief in that it purports to know the secret (i.e., unrevealed) will of God.[36] Many Reformed believers contend that regeneration occurs through the Holy Spirit working in conjunction with God's Word (1 Peter 1:23), the Word the church must proclaim. Covenant children need faith and conversion, but they are not children of wrath prior to conversion. Their holiness is not natural, but is bestowed upon them by grace because of the covenant God has made with his elect. Churches that maintain this position do not presume that the children they baptize are regenerate.[37]

The Lord's Supper and public confession of faith

As baptism is the divinely appointed means of grace to proclaim the forgiveness of sins and the washing of purification that Christ's blood has accomplished, the Eucharist is, as Kuyper understood it, the 'sacrament of nourishment'. With much delight he cited Article XXX of the *Belgic Confession*, which affirms:

> Christ, that he might represent to us this heavenly bread, has instituted an earthly and visible bread as a Sacrament of his body, and wine as a Sacrament of his blood, to testify by them … that, as certainly as we receive and hold this Sacrament in our hands and drink the same with our mouths, by which our life is afterward nourished, we also do as certainly receive by faith … the true body and blood of Christ, our only Saviour, in our souls for the support of our spiritual life.[38]

Since the Protestant Reformation of the sixteenth century, there has been much debate about the nature of Christ's presence in the Eucharist. All Protestants rejected transubstantiation, the belief that the bread and wine of the sacrament become the body, blood, soul and divinity of Christ when a priest consecrates them on an altar. The Reformers realized that this belief denies the sufficiency of Christ's atoning sacrifice on the cross, and so they decried the concept of the mass as a sacrifice. The Protestants could not, however, agree among themselves about the relationship between that sacrament and what it signifies. Martin Luther held that Christ is really and truly present in, with and under the forms of bread and wine, so that all who receive the elements from the eucharistic table receive also the body and blood of Christ.[39] Ulrich Zwingli (1484-1531), chief Reformer in German Switzerland, rejected Luther's teaching and held that the bread and wine are merely symbols of Christ's body and blood. John Calvin affirmed the real but spiritual presence of Christ in the sacrament, and the Reformed churches followed him in this teaching.

The Greek term *eucharistia* means 'thanksgiving', and the verb-form 'to give thanks' appears in the Gospel record when Jesus instituted the Lord's Supper (Matthew 26:27). The New Testament indicates that the Eucharist is the successor rite to the Jewish *seder*, the Passover meal in which bread and wine are essential elements. Various beliefs about the presence of Christ in this sacrament were current across the centuries until the Fourth Lateran Council in 1215 decreed transubstantiation a dogma of the Roman Catholic Church. The Protestants of the sixteenth century all contradicted that belief, and Calvin's concept of a spiritual presence became the accepted understanding in Reformed churches, including those in the Netherlands. Abraham Kuyper heartily endorsed Calvin's position, as his subscription to the *Belgic Confession* attests. He believed that baptism opens the way to the Eucharist and to the 'mystical communion with our Lord that it provides'. He warned, 'It is a terrible sin to ignore the holy supper after one has been baptized,'[40] and he asserted that one's public confession of faith in Christ must occur at some point after infant baptism and before one's first reception of the Eucharist. That confession before the church must not be the end, but only the beginning of standing in public to affirm faith in the Saviour. Believers must confess Christ regularly in the face of evil and opposition to his cause. Kuyper admonished Christians to remember the dictum of Ezra to Israel: 'Make confession unto the LORD God of your fathers, and do his pleasure, and separate yourselves from the people of the land' (Ezra 10:11, AV).[41]

Kuyper regarded public confession before the church body in preparation for receiving the Lord's Supper as the perfect opportunity to demonstrate the reality of saving faith. He believed that true confession of Christ is not merely adherence to sound doctrine. It is both an intellectual and an emotional embrace of Christ that necessarily entails admission of one's sins. As he expressed the matter, 'Your confession of your Saviour and Lord before the congregation must include a confession of your personal wretchedness. A confession which desires Jesus but is not characterized by a profound conviction of personal sin and guilt is false... He who confesses his Saviour must confess his [own] wretchedness too. He must ... sense that he is lost and that therefore he, together with all God's children, is taking refuge under the Saviour's wings.'[42]

The responsibility of Christians to the church

Because he believed that God has entered into covenant with his chosen people, Kuyper attached great importance to the role of the church in the lives of Christians. The ministry of the Word and the sacraments is the work of the church, so all believers must loyally support the church and attend to the means of grace that she employs. Kuyper explained: 'Every child of God is, by his confession, obliged to join the true Church of God. The trueness of the church can be determined from the purity of her confession, by her purged administration of the Word and of the sacraments, and by her maintenance of Christian discipline...The body has room only for active members. Hence, he who is passive and indolent in the affairs of the church is courting a lie and raises reasons to suspect that he is not a member of the body, even though his name is enrolled on the records.'[43]

Dr Kuyper always regarded himself as a servant of God's church, and he expected others to be the same, for, as he believed, 'No saint can see his Saviour fight and remain neutral. No, the love of God is so deep, stirring, and captivating that he cannot but enter the conflict.'[44]

To all Christians this committed churchman declared: 'Your heart is God's; your soul is God's; and all your powers are God's property. Hence you bring God nothing. You merely return to him that of which you had robbed him.'[45]

12.

Antithesis and common grace

One of the most prominent themes in the theology of Abraham Kuyper is the distinction he made between common grace and special grace. He held that divine grace combats the effects of human sinfulness in two principal ways. Common grace restrains the human tendency towards destructive evil and encourages people to perform actions that are beneficial to the human race as a whole. Special grace transforms the sinful nature of God's elect so that they renounce unbelief and sinful behaviour to serve the God who has redeemed them. Both kinds of grace are unmerited gifts from God.

The origins of the antithesis

Although unbelieving sinners enjoy the effects of common grace, they remain spiritually dead and hostile towards God. They abuse this grace and resist the kingdom of God, and thereby they demonstrate the reality of an antithesis that has divided humanity since the fall of Adam and Eve. In Genesis 3:15 the Bible states that an angry God responded to Satan's temptation of humankind and their subsequent disobedience with a declaration of divine displeasure. God said to Satan:

I will put enmity
>between you and the woman,
>and between your offspring and hers;
he will crush your head,
>and you will strike his heel.

Following his pronouncement of judgement upon the first sinners, God expelled Adam and Eve from his presence and barred the entrance to the Garden of Eden (Genesis 3:24). The fallen sinners did not leave God's presence voluntarily; he drove them from it. At that point God himself declared the antithesis by creating hostility between two lines of human development, the offspring of Eve and the offspring of Satan. This became the conflict between believers and unbelievers. Since God's special grace is the only power that can persuade sinners to believe and to accept his laws, it is clear that God, not man, initiated the antithesis that has continued since the Fall.[1]

Two mutually exclusive world-views

At the time when modernists were promoting a theology of synthesis, Kuyper emphasized the antithesis that posits an impassable gap between God and Satan, between Christ and Anti-Christ, a conflict of cosmic dimensions, and he called Christians to wage a struggle against all compromises of truth in every area of life and learning. He summoned them to become part of a counter-offensive against all forms of falsehood and in so doing to confront evil with the gospel of divine mercy and grace, which Christ bestows on all who leave the kingdom of Satan and enter the diametrically opposed kingdom of God.[2] Kuyper held that Christ spoke of this antithesis when he said, 'I did not come to bring peace' upon earth 'but a sword' (Matthew 10:34), and he reminded his readers that the prophets and apostles declared that unbelievers would regard Jesus as a 'stone of stumbling and a rock of offence' (1 Peter 2:8, NKJV).[3]

Kuyper explained his understanding of the antithesis in an article that appeared in *De Standaard* on 7 June 1873. There he wrote, 'God has spoken. There is a revelation of his will. We possess this revelation in God's Word. On this basis we demand that the pronouncements of God's Word be obeyed in each clash of principles. Human discernment (or inference) is to be decisive where God's Word is unclear. Everyone agrees that human insight must yield to God's pronouncements. The disagreement begins because our opponents do not believe that God himself has spoken, while we *confess* that he has spoken.'[4]

In a speech to parliament which he delivered in March 1904, while he was prime minister, Kuyper said, '… the modern world-view and its idea of scholarship as defended by the parliamentary Left, takes a position affirming that scholarship is the judge over divinely given revelation. This brings us to the general question strongly affirmed in varying degrees by the parliamentary Right, which asserts the opposite: from revelation a Christian world-view is derived, antithetical in character to the new world-view. We are firmly convinced that this antithesis is permanent and extends to every branch of scholarship… The Left wants Christian scholarship to be kept in bondage, while its own brand of scholarship retains the privilege it presently enjoys … to ensure its final triumph.'[5]

In his numerous assertions of the antithesis, Dr Kuyper contended that the Christian and non-Christian world-views begin with mutually exclusive assumptions which lead necessarily to a contest for dominion in all areas of life. Each seeks to destroy the other, so no science or discipline of learning is actually impartial.[6] This is why, although Christians and non-Christians hold *some* theoretical ideas in common, disagreements about the interpretation of facts is inevitable. In the physical sciences, once scholars move beyond material factors, division between believers and unbelievers is unavoidable. Subjective judgements occur, especially when scientists deal with the origin and end of phenomena.

Common grace at work in the arts and sciences

Since the antithesis is evident in all disciplines, one might think that unbelievers would be incapable of discovering and appropriating truth, but that is not so. God bestows common grace upon humanity without regard to a person's spiritual condition, so even militant atheists may possess and employ scientific acumen or amazing artistic talent. Empirical research is the same for all investigators, regardless of their attitude towards God, and weights, measures and numbers are their common property. Christians and non-Christians conduct the same activities in the sciences because common grace enables them to do so for the benefit of the whole race. Common grace prevents science from becoming entirely false, and sometimes it enables scholars opposed to God to make marvellous discoveries and to advance profound theories. 'Sin continues spreading decay, but common grace has entered in, binding, slowing sin's operations.'[7]

Dr Kuyper maintained that all scientific enquiries begin with axioms of faith that scholars choose to believe are true. All people exercise a type of faith, even though it is not that saving faith that God imparts to his chosen people by special grace. One effect of such faith is to convince scientists that they possess certainty, and without that faith they could not be sure about the accuracy of their observations. Thanks to common grace, even anti-Christian researchers are able to discover very useful truths, but the noetic effects of sin (that is, its detrimental influences upon the mind which impair human ability to think correctly about God) prevent them from grasping the proper conception of reality as a whole.[8]

There is no actual conflict, Kuyper contended, between faith and science. Genuine faith encourages science, but conflict arises because one group of enquirers affirms God's sovereign decrees as the basis for science, while the other explains the world in terms of deism, pantheism, or naturalism. Christians believe that the world is now in an abnormal condition because of sin, but non-Christians argue that its present state is normal. Christians see a need for cosmic regeneration (Revelation 21), while unbelievers expect evolution to produce improvement. Since the two communities of scholars view reality from radically different points of view based upon their conflicting faith assumptions (axioms), they cannot agree about ultimate questions.[9] Agreements about other questions occur because common grace leads unbelievers to some truths, and Christians are still subject in some degree to the noetic effects of sin.[10]

Since the noetic effects of sin cloud human minds, no area of learning has escaped their influence. Art, as well as science, reflects the consequences of the Fall. Roman Catholics have at times accused Calvinists of denigrating art, but Kuyper showed that the charge was not just. Reformed churches have stressed the spiritual character of worship as the highest expression of a believer's relationship with God, so they have not found the sensual artistic emphasis of much popular religion to be attractive. Calvinists, therefore, have not developed a distinctive style of church architecture. The Reformed faith 'abandoned the symbolical form of worship and refused, at the demand of art, to embody its religious spirit in monuments of splendour'.[11]

Kuyper explained that, although Calvinism has not produced an art style of its own, it does offer an interpretation of art. Calvin and the Reformers encouraged the proper employment of the arts. As Calvin said, 'All the arts come from God and are to be respected as divine inventions.'[12] In agreement with Calvin, Kuyper believed that all the arts should seek to glorify God, but sin has perverted the human sense of beauty. For this reason artists often copy marred nature and present it as though it were good and normal. This is a major error of the pantheists. Reformed Christians see in art both the consequences of sin and hope for the restoration of true beauty. Christians, therefore, are to participate in the arts and to enjoy them with a view towards the coming restoration of the creation to its pristine state.[13] Since God created beauty, he must enjoy it, and man's appreciation for beauty is part of the image of God. Although sin has marred the creation, much beauty remains, though its lustre is diminished. The survival of such beauty is due to common grace, which prevents sin from making the world completely desolate, but beauty and ugliness stand side by side in this world, and they will do so until divine intervention brings the 'new heaven and new earth', when Christ triumphs finally over all evil.[14]

Common grace, Kuyper asserted, works as God 'inspires … geniuses in the field of art… He allows them to see beauty and to experience it in their spirits … which enriches the world, when, carried beyond their imaginations, [they] … add something to human life which it would never have possessed without … art.'[15] He believed that Calvinism had prompted the development of the celebrated school of Dutch painters, who portrayed 'upon canvas the ordinary life, and as [though] by magic, made it expressive of rich satisfaction and inward delight'.[16]

The role of the musical arts in Christian worship was a matter of considerable interest for Abraham Kuyper, as he expounded the subject of common grace. He called upon Christian musicians to regard their talents as gifts from God to use in their Creator's service. He wrote, 'There is no worship service without adoration, and adoration requires the best song and the purest accompaniment. For our God, we may not be satisfied with less than the best.'[17]

In appealing for musicians to render the best of their art to God, Kuyper was careful to admonish them not to seek personal glory in performing, for 'An organist who makes himself heard has misunderstood his calling, and … he who leads the song does not sanctify, but sins when he is aroused by letting people hear his voice.'[18]

Kuyper was deeply concerned about the abuse of the arts in churches, and he sternly rejected the demand of some that art should be exempt from divine moral law. He warned believers against lapsing into an idolatrous love for art. 'Art for art's sake' has no place in a godly life. As sin leads people to conduct scientific endeavours apart from God, so, likewise, it promotes perversion of the arts, because scientists and artists alike labour under the noetic effects of sin. They have 'lost the gift to comprehend the true context, the proper coherence, the system of the unity of things'.[19] Therefore even the brightest and most skilful people see only portions of knowledge and do not understand their connection with the whole of creation. Regeneration equips believers for the task of pursuing the unity of truth, and they should avail themselves of whatever truth unbelievers, by common grace, have discovered. Ultimate meaning is, nevertheless, accessible to regenerate minds alone.[20]

In his book *Pro Rege* ('For the King'), published in 1911, Abraham Kuyper affirmed that Christ has freed redeemed people from some of the disabilities that were due to the Fall. This enables them to investigate the powers of nature and to regain some mastery over them. In the Western world, where the influence of Christianity has been the greatest, progress of this kind has been most advanced. As believers use this ability, they implement the requirements of God's cultural mandate for them to 'fill the earth and subdue it' (Genesis 1:28).[21] Dr Kuyper summarized this matter when he wrote, 'It is time we broaden our spiritual horizon and recognize that Jesus as King has sovereignty over the totality of human culture. Once that is realized, it becomes inevitable that both our spiritual development unto eternal life and our general cultural development, that has led to such an amazing increase in our knowledge and control over nature, are placed under his rule.'[22]

Common grace and civil government

In addition to the effects of common grace upon the arts and sciences, Kuyper cited civil government as one of its great benefits, because it works to control the sinfulness of humanity and thereby to limit the destructive forces of evil. Kuyper maintained that the Reformed faith offers not only a system of doctrine different from that of Roman Catholicism, but that it promotes a different view of life in all its religious and political aspects. He steadfastly insisted that all of life is religion, and people must not confine their Christianity to formal church services in which they participate on Sundays. It is therefore foolish to debate about the role of religion in public life, since public life is part of religion. The only question is, to which religion will public figures adhere?[23] Christians must assert the claims of Christ over all of creation, no matter how evil society may become, and through common grace God enables his people to uphold his rights and to battle on behalf of his sovereignty. This means that they must be God's instruments as the antithesis appears in political matters, as in other realms of life.[24]

If society were truly Christian, civil government would operate self-consciously as a divine instrument to retard evil and to encourage righteousness. It would rule as an agency of common grace for God's glory and for the benefit of mankind. This, in fact, is its solemn duty, but sin infects the halls of government, and public officials more often than not ignore this responsibility. When they do this, they stand on the wrong side of the antithesis, but God does not permit them to achieve their full potential for wickedness. In most political structures he, by his common grace, requires civil rulers to govern in a manner that, to a degree at least, does prevent evil people from bringing their society to ruin. Without common grace God's will for his creation could not proceed. Common grace makes civil life possible, as it enables sinful people to retain some concept of God and some correct moral principles.[25]

The operations of common grace are entirely earthly. By reducing the effects of sin, common grace allows fallen beings to develop their talents in pursuit of socially beneficial ends. All real progress on earth is due to common grace, and Christians must be active in political affairs — not in revolutionary ways, but as influences to develop and improve life. They will be the best citizens when they work to maintain God's structures for society, which means they will strive to confine civil government to the sphere of authority God has allotted to it. When this occurs, it assists the church because it assures a stable society within which the church can conduct her ministry. If political forces work against the church, Christians should form their own political party to protect it. As the church spreads Christian teachings, those teachings enhance the effects of common grace. That is, the more influential special grace becomes, the more common grace will affect society. In this way saving grace, although it reaches only the elect, promotes the development of true culture through common grace. The church should encourage such cultural growth without trying to rule in the domain of common grace.[26] *De Gemeene Gratie* (Common Grace) contains Kuyper's arguments for Christian action in all areas of life — church, state, art, science, literature, philosophy, etc. The doctrine of common grace he espoused in this extended treatise, which extends to three large volumes, provided the motivation for his Anti-Revolutionary Party. In *Pro Rege* he presented his call for specific actions as Christians live and work in the domain of common grace.[27]

The doctrine as a feature of the Reformed faith

In Kuyper's opinion, the doctrine of common grace is fundamentally important for the maintenance and survival of a humane society, and it is no coincidence that Calvinists have been its most vigorous exponents. John Calvin was the first theologian to make a clear distinction between common grace and special grace, and Kuyper developed Calvin's position and showed how it is a vital feature of the Reformed faith. For the most part, only Reformed believers have shown serious interest in common grace, and this is because they alone, among all Christian groups, have appreciated sufficiently the implications of God's sovereignty. Their understanding of this matter means that Calvinists do not become concerned with personal salvation to the point where they have little interest in mundane affairs that lie outside the realm of saving grace. Because of the influence of Reformed theology, 'Cosmic life has regained its worth, not at the expense of things eternal, but by virtue of its capacity as God's handiwork and as a revelation of God's attributes.'[28]

Calvinists therefore applaud the humanist desire to explore and to develop the resources of the earth, while they reject the humanist claim that this world is ultimate. As Kuyper stated the matter, 'A Calvinist who seeks God does not ... think of limiting himself to theology and contemplation, leaving the other sciences ... in the hands of unbelievers; but, on the contrary, [he looks] upon it as his task to know God in all his works; he is conscious of having been called to fathom, with all the energy of his intellect, things *terrestrial* as well as things *celestial.*'[29]

A Reformed world-view rejects the sacred/secular dichotomy of medieval Catholicism, and it denies to the church the right to control spheres to which God has granted autonomy. During the Middle Ages the Roman Catholic Church intruded itself into the sphere of higher education and sought to control the universities. The Holy Roman Emperors sometimes contested papal authority over such institutions and tried to subject them to imperial control. In that way both church and state exceeded their God-given bounds. The medieval universities were not sufficiently assertive of their rights and so fell under the domination of one or the other of these powers. The Reformation reversed that pattern, especially in lands where Calvinism became the major expression of Protestant belief. Reformed believers, because of common grace, have respected the independence of academic scholarship and have encouraged it to develop outside of any ecclesiastical institutions. The Netherlands consequently became a cradle of free enquiry as, for example, when René Descartes (1596-1650) fled there from France. Some Calvinists opposed Descartes' philosophy, but they allowed him freedom to express his ideas. William of Orange (1533-84), leader of the Dutch resistance to Spain in the early part of the Eighty Years' War (1568-1648), founded the University of Leiden as a Christian institution in opposition to the University of Louvain, to promote believing scholarship. By Kuyper's day Leiden had become a stronghold of unbelief, so he established the Free University of Amsterdam to operate in its own sphere, separate from church and state, to explore the truths of common grace and special grace.[30]

Abraham Kuyper, in his 1898 lectures at Princeton Theological Seminary, explained that the purpose of his presentations was to 'eradicate the wrong idea that Calvinism represents an exclusively dogmatical and ecclesiastical movement'.[31] In the course of doing this he tried to combat the claim that modern people have outgrown Christianity. He decried the French Revolution and the deism that was characteristic belief among eighteenth-century *philosophes*, and he blamed that ideology and the revolution it spawned for plunging Europe into wars of aggression and the establishment of tyrannical governments. He lamented that the nineteenth century brought the Darwinian hypothesis of evolution expressed as the survival of the fittest. This, Kuyper argued, had led to the moral justification of the claim that powerful states are entitled to rule weaker ones in the fashion of Bismarck's unification of Germany under Prussian rule. Dr Kuyper believed that Calvinism alone could provide the philosophic base and the world-view that could combat the pernicious ideologies of modern times that threaten Christendom. As he perceived the situation, the battle was between the Reformed doctrine of *election* and the Darwinian concept of natural *selection* by blind, impersonal fate.[32]

In his zeal to promote the crown rights of King Jesus, Kuyper called his Reformed brethren to stand resolutely committed to the Saviour and opposed to his enemies. He wrote, 'He only is a real Calvinist who, in his own soul, personally has been struck by the majesty of the Almighty, and yielding to the overpowering might of his eternal love, has dared to proclaim this majestic love over against Satan and the world and the worldliness of his own heart in the personal conviction of being chosen by God himself, and therefore of having to thank him alone for every grace everlasting.'[33] This standard that he set forth for others was the same one by which Kuyper lived and worked.

Was Kuyper teaching a new doctrine?

As John Calvin deserves recognition as the theologian of the Holy Spirit, so Abraham Kuyper was the theologian of the antithesis and common grace. In a manner more thorough and systematic than any other Christian thinker before him, he formulated, expounded and applied these concepts to show that they are essential principles of the Reformed faith. Since he was a pioneer in this endeavour, he did not say the last word on the subject, nor did he profess to have done so. Since so few Christian thinkers had given serious consideration to these concepts prior to his doing so, there were some who found his ideas objectionable, at least in part. Critics of Kuyper remain outspoken in opposition, especially to his doctrine of common grace. It is easy to establish a biblical basis for the antithesis, as Augustine had applied it to the interpretation of history in his book *The City of God* (*c.* 426). The doctrine of common grace was, however, new to most Christian scholars of the nineteenth century, and to some it appeared to be a radical innovation.

Kuyper always said that he had not devised the concept of common grace, but that he had found it in the writings of Calvin and had developed it and applied it to the situation confronting Christians in modern times. In taking this position he was rejecting the nature/grace dichotomy that had become traditional in Roman Catholicism and which many Protestants had imbibed, some of them without realizing its source. Thomas Aquinas (c. 1225-74), the foremost philosopher-theologian in Catholic history, had taught that Christians live in two realms, nature and grace. Areas such as politics, science and philosophy belong to the domain of nature, in which reason is supreme. There Christians and unbelievers stand on common ground. In the domain of grace, where divine revelation is supreme, believers stand alone, but the church must control culture, and art and science must serve her interests.

The effect of Thomism, as the teaching of Aquinas has come to be called, was to denigrate culture as being inferior to grace and to demand that it be in subjection to the church, which is the fountain of grace. Some medieval thinkers, for example Thomas à Kempis (d. 1471), the most prominent figure in the movement known as the Brethren of the Common Life, disavowed culture, regarding it as part of sinful 'nature'. He thought the site of sin is within matter, so he rejected culture as evil. The logical conclusion of such thinking is that Christians should renounce the world and pursue lives of asceticism.

John Calvin, in a chapter of his *Institutes of the Christian Religion* entitled 'Christian Liberty', rejected the nature/grace division.[34] He stressed instead that the spheres of life are autonomous in relation to one another, but are all subject to the laws of God. Church and state operate in distinct spheres of authority, and each supports the other in the execution of its God-given tasks. There is a sphere of life in which there are no biblical mandates, and there the human conscience must decide. Culture is part of this sphere, and Christians must apply the antithesis within culture to distinguish their education and art from those of unbelievers. Church and state must not rule over culture. Calvin was not consistent about this, however, for in Geneva education was subject to both church and state.

Abraham Kuyper amplified Calvin's teaching about the spheres of authority and applied it vigorously so as to present a consistent structure in which all spheres could function autonomously. He insisted on the separation of the spheres so as to free culture from the dictates of church and state. He showed that sin does not inhere within matter but in human nature, so believers should approve the cultural arts and enjoy the provisions of common grace, and thereby implement the requirements of the cultural mandate.[35]

A lack of clarity in definition

One criticism of Kuyper's position pertains to his failure to clarify the tension between, on the one hand, the co-operation of believers with unbelievers, made possible in various academic pursuits by common grace, and, on the other, the antithesis which he asserted dogmatically to exist in all of learning. He divided academic disciplines into the natural sciences and the humanities. In the first category objective standards of measurement often enable Christians and non-Christians to reach the same conclusions. In the humanities, however, subjective decisions are more frequent and more significant. These disciplines deal with philosophic concerns, such as the origin and purpose of created phenomena, so scientific procedures cannot answer ultimate questions. Kuyper maintained that science would fail without common grace. At times he said that regenerate and unregenerate people could work together to fulfil the cultural mandate, but at other times he stressed the antithesis with such vigour that he made such co-operation appear unlikely, if not impossible. His lack of clarity here has confused some of his readers and has led to continuing debates about his meaning.[36]

Opposition to Kuyper's doctrine of common grace

An example of his strident affirmation of the antithesis appears in a statement in which he said it 'operates in every sphere and in every sensation of the heart, in every tissue of our thinking, in our antipathies and sympathies, in our entire world-and-life view, in the whole of our conception of the personal, familial, social, and political existence... It exists in our jurisprudence and in our pedagogy.'[37] He made this remark in 1909 in an essay in which he cited co-operation between the Anti-Revolutionary and the Roman Catholic parties as an expression of the antithesis. Some of his fellow Calvinists disagreed.

When Kuyper became leader of the orthodox party within the Dutch Reformed Church, many of his adherents were poorly educated people who were suspicious of the learned pastors of the National Church. They practised their piety in the form of a personal faith and an anti-cultural attitude. They had, therefore, very little influence in society, and to them the concept of common grace seemed strange and somewhat threatening. Because of his love for these *kleine luyden*, Kuyper taught them patiently, and he gradually persuaded most of them to accept his doctrine. Among fellow scholars, however, he encountered some stiff opposition, in some cases because they denied the validity of common grace as a concept.

When the Free University of Amsterdam opened in 1880, it required all professors to subscribe to 'Reformed principles', which meant mainly the doctrines of creation and common grace. This seemed to be an adequate procedure at the time, but soon uncertainty about the proper application of those principles produced controversy between Abraham Kuyper and A. F. De Savornin Lohman, professor of law. The latter resigned in 1896, after Kuyper accused him of departing from the Reformed standards. The two were not reconciled until shortly before they died.

Lohman was a disciple of the *réveil*, an aristocrat, who opposed Kuyper's democratic political ideas and his strict adherence to his understanding of Reformed theology. Lohman believed that Christians should influence public policy through their moral example by personal participation, but at first he argued that a Christian political party as an instrument of God's sovereignty was not appropriate. He denied that the Bible reveals principles, and he preferred not to be called a Calvinist. It is evident that he did not share Kuyper's view of common grace and the antithesis. Lohman did nevertheless help to create the Christian Historical Union as an alternative to the Anti-Revolutionary Party.

The Kuyper-Lohman dispute led the faculty of the Free University to adopt a statement of principles that affirmed historic Reformed theology as the basis for a Christian world-view. All subjects must, therefore, be studied on the basis of creation and divine sovereignty.[38]

The cultural mandate and evangelism

Some Reformed leaders came to fear that Kuyper's enthusiasm for the concept of common grace would lead Christians to emphasize the cultural mandate and to neglect the evangelistic mandate (Matthew 28:16-19); that is, they thought that zealous efforts to reform society would distract believers from seeking the salvation of souls. Kuyper stressed the role of Christ as mediator of creation as well as mediator of redemption, and he emphasized the cultural mandate and the doctrine of general revelation more than previous Reformed thinkers had done, and some Calvinists were concerned that this would lead to giving priority to social action which might diminish zeal for personal spirituality.

After Kuyper's death in 1920, a number of Reformed scholars issued criticisms of his position on common grace, and some argued that his ideas about the antithesis and common grace were contradictory. They lamented that fascination with the idea of common grace was obscuring the need to maintain the antithesis.[39] His critics did not always realize that the life of Abraham Kuyper showed clearly that one could espouse the doctrine of common grace without losing one's evangelistic zeal and aspiration for personal godliness, as his numerous devotional writings demonstrate.[40] Although some deviants from Reformed orthodoxy appealed to the principles of common grace and sphere authority to justify their rejection of the antithesis, they did so by using Kuyper's teachings wrongly. It is not appropriate to blame him for their misuse of his doctrines.[41]

13.
Church and state

In 1897, on the twenty-fifth anniversary of his editorship of *De Standaard*, Abraham Kuyper explained his supreme purpose: 'One desire has been the ruling passion of my life. One high motive has acted like a spur upon my mind and soul, and sooner than that I should escape from the sacred necessity that is laid upon me, let the breath of life fail me. It is this: that, in spite of all worldly opposition, God's holy ordinances shall be established again in the throne, in the school, and in the state for the good of the people; to carve, as it were, into the conscience of the nation the ordinances of the Lord, to which Bible and creation bear witness; until the nation pays homage again to God.'[1]

Chapter 6 of this book makes reference to Kuyper's thinking about church and state in connection with his concept of sphere authority. It is appropriate at this point to consider the matter more thoroughly, because his position has been misunderstood.

God's sovereignty over every area of life

Dr Kuyper's world-view had no place for dichotomy where divine sovereignty is concerned. To deny God's comprehensive authority over everything he has made, Kuyper believed, is infidelity.[2] God's Word must therefore be paramount in politics, both in theory and in practice. The revival of Calvinism that Groen van Prinsterer and Kuyper promoted challenged secular humanism by asserting that true freedom prevails only when people submit to God's ordinances, since human life is *heteronomous*, that is, it comes from God and depends upon him. This contrasts sharply with the liberal political philosophy spread by the French Revolution, a view which holds that humans are *autonomous*. Belief in man's freedom to govern himself as he deems fitting has become the basis for political theory in Western civilization as a necessary development from a world-view in which man is supreme.[3] Groen and Kuyper called upon Christians to obey God in the application of his laws to civil society and public policy. All believers, in all callings of life, must discharge their duties as members of the body of Christ, even when they perform those duties in the political sphere apart from the church as an institution.[4]

Kuyper delivered the Stone Lectures at Princeton Theological Seminary in 1898, and in his presentation entitled 'Calvinism and Politics', he cited the 'root principle' of his beliefs as being 'the *sovereignty* of the Triune God *over the whole cosmos*, in all its spheres and kingdoms, visible and invisible'.[5] Declarations such as this could be construed to mean that Kuyper desired a theocratic union of church and state, but such an arrangement would have contradicted his belief in sphere authority. He argued that every government has its base in a philosophic belief, either Christian or anti-Christian. A neutral state is not possible. The New Testament denominates civil rulers as agents of God (Romans 13:1-7), and although government has a constitutional-contractual relationship with the citizens, its origin and its responsibilities are due to divine ordination. God, not the state, is the supreme judge of good and evil; his laws must be the basis for public as well as private morality. Any denial of God's authority over the state is anti-Christian.

Disagreement with the Reformers over the separation of church and state

Although he emphasized the divine right of government, Kuyper insisted that civil rulers remain within the sphere of authority God has designated for them. They must not rule the church, nor may the church dictate to the state. When Groen and Kuyper wanted to exert Christian influence upon political affairs, they founded the Anti-Revolutionary Party, a political movement separate from any ecclesiastical body. They knew that the Reformed faith had not achieved a perfect understanding and application of divine revelation, so they advocated continuing reformation. In particular, they believed that Calvin and the sixteenth-century Reformers had not understood adequately the need for separation of church and state, but conditions in the nineteenth century made the need for such understanding clear. Theocracy was appropriate for Old Testament Israel because God spoke directly by his prophets and gave specific directions for conducting civic affairs.[6]

In the sixteenth century Protestant Geneva became the scene of a tragedy, the implications of which continue to stir up controversy. The event was the burning of the Spanish physician and amateur theologian Michael Servetus (1511-53). Servetus had denied the Trinity and the eternal, essential deity of Christ, and the Roman Catholic authorities in the Habsburg Empire had condemned him to death for heresy. He escaped and, after a period of wandering, arrived in Geneva, where he had good reason to expect a hostile reception. Shortly before going to Geneva, Servetus had published the *Restitutes of the Christian Religion*, an obvious attack upon Calvin's *Institutes of the Christian Religion*, and it appears that Calvin's enemies in Geneva hoped to humiliate and discredit him by provoking a confrontation between him and Servetus, who called on the city government to expel Calvin and to award the Reformer's property to him.

Calvin accused Servetus of heresy, and a trial in a civil court condemned the Spaniard to death by burning, a decision with which Roman Catholic and Protestant leaders across Europe concurred. Calvin asked the court to execute the heretic by decapitation, but the magistrates proceeded with the burning. Although Calvin was not yet a citizen of Geneva at that time, and though he held no civil office and had no authority to execute anyone, he did initiate the proceedings against Servetus, and he agreed with the sentence of capital punishment.

Abraham Kuyper deplored the execution of Servetus, which he attributed to an inadequate grasp of the New Testament teaching about church and state, even though there was no legal union of the two in Geneva. He regarded the whole affair with Servetus as a failure in church-state relations, an aberration of the Reformed faith, one compounded by the *Belgic Confession of Faith*. Article XXXVI of that historic document declares that the magistrates must 'protect the sacred ministry and thus may remove and prevent all idolatry and false worship'. Kuyper concluded that this is a serious error, and he criticized Calvin and Theodore Beza, Calvin's successor in Geneva, for subscribing to the concept that the confession asserts. 'We do not hide the fact that we disagree with Calvin, our confession, and our Reformed theologians,' he wrote. Since the Old Testament theocracy is no longer extant, and the age of direct revelation is past, church and state must be separate.[7] As Kuyper commented, 'The church never sank away more deeply than when she went back to the inn and sought to become a national or state church; neither did she revive again in spiritual vigour, except when the Lord drove her out of the inn and pointed her back to the stable.'[8]

Kuyper's ambitions for the Netherlands

A free church in a free state was Kuyper's aspiration for the Netherlands, and he greatly admired the United States for achieving it. In remarks to American Presbyterians, he exulted, 'The free life of free citizens as it ... flourishes in America, and is making its way into states of Europe, is not the fruit of the bloody orgies of the French Revolution, but of that energetic earnestness which Calvinism has infused into its adherents.'[9]

In order to obtain their desired church-state relationship, Groen and Kuyper and their supporters promoted 'principled pluralism' as their alternative to traditional Dutch Liberalism and Conservatism, both of which they found to be humanistic because they denied God's authority over civic institutions and public policy.[10] Kuyper realized, of course, that Reformed believers had, in the past, often failed to maintain the catholicity of the true church by seeking and obtaining the status of the established religion, as had happened in his own country. He lamented such failures of Calvinists to be true to their own principles, and he especially regretted the slow progress of freedom of religion in Dutch history, even though the Netherlands was far ahead of many other nations in this regard.[11]

The Netherlands, despite the violence through which she gained freedom from Roman Catholic Spain (1568-1648), eventually became Europe's most tolerant society, a refuge for persecuted Jews, various Protestant groups, Anabaptists and Catholics. This, Kuyper believed, was because the dominant Calvinists gradually abandoned the intolerance they had inherited from the Middle Ages. In allowing liberty in religion, they discarded the belief that absolute unity is an essential mark of the true church. Visible unity, as in Roman Catholicism, they deemed unnecessary because it could not be maintained without the use of force.[12]

The responsibilities of the magistrate

In accord with his concept of the spheres, Kuyper contended that civil magistrates have no legitimate authority over church affairs. They are not competent to judge the claims of competing churches to be the true church, or to be true to God's requirements. If government had such authority, it would be an absolute regime. Churches must determine their own understanding of divine revelation and issue their own confessions of faith, and civil rulers must not favour one church over others. In Kuyper's words, 'The government bears the sword which wounds, not the sword of the Spirit, which decides in spiritual questions... The government ... must ... allow to each and every citizen liberty of conscience, as the primordial and inalienable right of all men.'[13]

Calvinism recognizes the world as God's creation and man as God's image-bearer, so it rightly restricts the church to its God-given sphere. Kuyper showed, therefore, that commerce, science, art and politics are outside that sphere, so the church must not try to dominate them. Christians must serve God within the world, and not flee into seclusion, as monks and some Anabaptists have done. When Christians obtain positions of civil authority, they must operate in obedience to God, since the Lord has ordained their authority (Romans 13:1-7). This, Kuyper argued, means that civil government must 'restrain blasphemy, where it directly assumes the character of an affront to the Divine Majesty'. The constitution of the state should acknowledge God as supreme ruler, and government should set aside its regular activities on Sunday and protect it as a day of worship. Magistrates should not be under the authority of any particular church, but they should regard themselves as responsible to God in the discharge of their duties. They should punish public attacks upon God as crimes against civil law, which acknowledges God as the source of the state's authority.[14]

Although Kuyper was sincere and fervent in his advocacy of freedom for all religions, his reliance upon civil rulers to protect God's name from blasphemy and to punish offenders seems inconsistent with his contention that magistrates are not competent to judge spiritual questions, and he did not specify in exactly what way the state should punish offenders. He knew the state would not become Christian, and many public officials would not be believers. How to entrust them with the power to punish blasphemy is a matter Kuyper seems to have left unresolved. If, for example, atheism, the denial of God's existence, is the ultimate blasphemy, should the state imprison those who advocate it? Kuyper did not say it should do so. His expectation for government seems, at least in this case, unrealistic, even though the general Christian consensus at that time disdained public expressions of blasphemy.

Rendering to Caesar...

Whatever vagueness may have occurred in Kuyper's thinking about the role of magistrates in religious matters, it is patently clear that he strove for genuine pluralism as the best means to assure maximum freedom for all the Dutch people. By insisting that absolute sovereignty belongs to God alone, he argued that the authority of every earthly sphere must be limited, and the state should protect the rights of those spheres to assure that justice prevails. Sphere authority, when implemented faithfully, protects liberty by denying the state, the church, or any other authority, the right to rule absolutely. As one of Kuyper's recent interpreters has expressed it, 'Rendering to Caesar the things that are Caesar's and to God the things that are God's is clearly interpreted throughout the biblical texts to mean that everything (even Caesar) belongs to God, while only a few things belong to Caesar under God's dominion.'[15]

In his inaugural address at the opening of the Free University of Amsterdam in 1880, Abraham Kuyper explained the concept of sphere authority and made specific applications to several areas of life. He affirmed the independence of the churches from state control, and he categorically denied the contention of some humanists that the state is the supreme authority which grants or permits some freedoms to its subjects. Kuyper held that Christ fought against the principle of 'caesarism', and thousands of Christ's early disciples lost their lives because they disputed Caesar's claim to complete dominion when they refused to acknowledge him as lord over their faith. It was a contest between *Deus Christus* and *Divus Augustus*. The collapse of the Roman Empire, Kuyper claimed, brought a return to divided authority, as in the medieval distribution of power among princes, guilds, estates and various orders, ecclesiastical and political.

Denying sphere authority leads to oppression

In early modern times the Dutch Republic successfully resisted Spanish tyranny — a tyranny which was one consequence of rejecting sphere authority. Kuyper, with much dismay, admitted, however, that the Dutch did not long preserve their liberty, for their nation 'sank away into sin, and the last strong bulwark of freedom remaining on Europe's mainland succumbed with [the demise of] our Republic'.[16] He saw the Anti-Revolutionary Party as an instrument to restore the rightful authority of the spheres, for that party rejected both popular sovereignty and state sovereignty. He warned, 'Do not forget that every state power is inclined to look upon freedom with suspicion.'[17] Without respect for the authority of the separate spheres, Kuyper was convinced, a free church in a free state could not endure.

Kuyper believed that the arrangements of sphere authority come from God, and those who ignore or transgress upon them sin against their Creator and inflict oppression upon fellow human beings. Throughout history governments have violated the rights of other spheres, as the cruelties of Philip II (1556-98), Louis XIV (1643-1715) and Napoleon I (1804-14), and others illustrate. When a state decrees that humans exist for the sake of the community, rather than to serve God, it expresses a totalitarian ideology that will not tolerate an independent church operating within its own sphere of authority. The church must inform the state about the requirements of God's Word. It must do so for its own protection and for that of other spheres the state might abuse. The struggle to defend sphere authority is, therefore, the crucial battle against totalitarianism, whether it be that of an autocratic church, as in the Roman Catholicism of the late Middle Ages, or modern socialist political structures. Without respect for sphere authority, it is impossible to prevent oppressive rule.[18]

Kuyper knew that modern secular society fears pluralism because, if implemented in accord with sphere authority, it would undermine the state's conception of unity. Secularists therefore want people to regard religion as an exclusively private matter without relevance for public life. Kuyper understood this, so he contended that no compromise between the secular individualism of the traditional liberals and the secular collectivism of the socialists would be acceptable. Christians must demand pluralism to preserve their own freedom and the freedom of those who do not espouse their faith. They must resolutely refuse to restrict the practice of their faith to the confines of church buildings, because, as Kuyper said, 'There is not an inch in the entire domain of our human life of which Christ, who is sovereign of all, does not proclaim "Mine!"'[19]

14
Kuyper and America

As Abraham Kuyper thought and wrote about the concept of sphere authority, and as he strove to achieve freedom for each of the spheres in Dutch society, he cited the United States as an example of pluralism for which Calvinist influences had laid the foundation. Kuyper was, at times, almost ecstatic in his praises for America, which he visited in 1898. In that year Princeton Theological Seminary invited him to deliver its annual Stone Lectures, and Princeton University conferred the honorary degree of Doctor of Laws upon him at the same time.

The Stone Lectures

Kuyper chose Calvinism as the topic for the lectures. In his presentation 'Calvinism and Politics', he hailed the Dutch resistance against Spain (1568-1648), England's Glorious Revolution (1688-89) and the American Revolution (1775-81) as just defences of freedom against tyranny 'undertaken with praying lips and with trust in the help of God'.[1] He argued that informed historians must concur with the judgement of George Bancroft (1800-91), author of a massive history of the United States that exudes its author's romantic patriotism. Bancroft wrote, 'The fanatic for Calvinism was a fanatic for liberty, for in the moral warfare for freedom, his creed was a part of his army and his most faithful ally in the battle.'[2]

In his euphoric expressions about the United States, Kuyper asserted that its constitution shows no trace of influence from the radical Jean-Jacques Rousseau. He likened the supreme law of the land rather to the French Huguenot constitution of 1573, and he compared American rebels against King George III to the English Independents under Oliver Cromwell, as they overthrew Charles I in 1649.[3]

Thoughts of emigration

Kuyper's interest in America was so great that in 1886, in the midst of the troubles that agitated the Reformed movement in his homeland, he considered leading a migration of orthodox believers to the United States, and his son Frederick went to Michigan, where he attended Hope College and later became a dentist who practised in the East Indies. His father was concerned because Frederick was not a Christian.

It seems that Dr Kuyper decided against the migration when he received a discouraging report from N. M. Steffans, a teacher at Hope Academy in Holland, Michigan. Steffans related that the religious climate in the United States was becoming hostile to the Reformed faith, and that defection from orthodoxy was spreading, even within officially Reformed and Presbyterian denominations. He told Kuyper that the prospects for the Reformed faith were better in the Netherlands.[4]

Kuyper's tour of America

Despite Steffans' discouraging account of spiritual conditions in America, Kuyper sailed for the New World in August 1898, delighted by the opportunity to tour and lecture. He met President William McKinley, Secretary of Labour Carroll D. Wright, the Mayor of Baltimore and other dignitaries of state. He lectured in Rochester, New York, Philadelphia, Chicago, Cleveland and Grand Rapids, and he drew large crowds wherever he appeared. Dutch Americans in particular hailed him as the champion of Calvinism, and Kuyper became impressed that the Reformed community was healthy and vigorous in America, at least in the Midwest. He did, however, note with regret that the Calvinist witness had declined on the East Coast.[5]

In preparation for Kuyper's appearance at Princeton, the local newspaper described him as 'an eminent divine of the Calvinistic type, of which he is a leader, and which he is labouring to make once more regnant over Dutchmen in the fatherland and elsewhere, and in which he has the sanction, authority, and aid of young Queen Wilhelmina, recently crowned. Dr Kuyper is said to be, if not the ablest, yet the "cleverest, staunchest, and most convincing defender of the creed of the Reformation, developed by Augustine and carried forward and perfected by … Calvin." '[6]

Kuyper delivered the Stone Lectures at Princeton Theological Seminary from 10 to 21 October 1898, and he brought to the task the credentials of a renowned theologian and a respected member of the Dutch parliament. Princeton University celebrated its Commemoration Day on 22 October, and Kuyper was awarded his honorary degree at that ceremony.[7]

The lectures at the seminary were supposed to be one hour each in length, but Kuyper insisted that he needed ninety minutes. He actually took two hours for each presentation, but he kept the attention of his audience with no difficulty, despite his Dutch accent. Numerous professors from the university and the seminary attended, and publication of Kuyper's *Encyclopaedia of Sacred Theology* in English appeared soon after his visit. He addressed the Presbyterian Historical Society in Philadelphia

Kuyper receiving the honorary doctorate in law at Princeton

the week after his lectures at Princeton, and his topic on that occasion was *The Antithesis Between Symbolism and Revelation*, which was a powerful assault on modernist theology and a pantheist world-view.[8]

Kuyper's views on America

Abraham Kuyper approved of the separation of church and state in America, which was consistent with his conviction that no churches should receive public funds. His opinion of church life in the New World was, however, not entirely positive. He perceived that, in their efforts to lure people to their services, many churches were resorting to entertainment at the expense of preaching. He lamented, too, that some of the numerous denominational divisions were due to ethnic factors and had little to do with doctrine.[9]

The American political scene, of course, engaged his attention. He considered the Republican Party more worthy of support from Christians than the Democrat Party, but he feared that the Republicans had been drifting from their historic principles. He knew about corruption in American politics, especially because of patronage and the 'spoils system' that was entrenched in some political jurisdictions. He thought that would lead to the creation of a 'bureaucratic proletariat' of people who depended upon the patronage of political leaders to earn their living.

Kuyper disapproved of United States' imperialism in the Pacific region, and he blamed the influence of East Coast manufacturers who wanted Asian markets. He saw a growing materialism among capitalists and workers as evidence that Christian influence was declining, but he supported protective tariffs to preserve jobs for Americans.[10]

Reactions to Kuyper's visit to America

Because of his reputation as a political and religious leader in
the Netherlands, Dutch Americans were especially pleased by
Kuyper's visit to their country. Many immigrants from Kuyper's
homeland came to the New World in the nineteenth century,
and some of them had participated in the revival of Calvinism
in their native land. They had already conveyed Kuyper's influence to Reformed believers in America some time before he
toured their new country. By the time of his arrival in 1898, the
Reformed Church in America and the Christian Reformed
Church were the two major denominations with Dutch roots,
and Kuyper had difficulty understanding why they maintained
separate identities. The Christian Reformed Church began officially in the United States in 1857 and was in fellowship with
the Christian Reformed Church *(Afscheiding)* in the Netherlands,
so it had a reputation for a rigorous adherence to Calvinism
long before Kuyper's début in the New World. The older Reformed Church in America had been moving slowly away from
its Calvinistic heritage for some time. Kuyper did what he could
to encourage his American brethren to remain faithful to their
doctrinal legacy from the Reformation, and he urged them to
preserve their ethnic connection as well.

In order to motivate Dutch Americans to retain their cultural
and historical identity with the Netherlands, Kuyper initiated
the formation of the General Netherlands Union, an organization he hoped would attract people of Dutch extraction throughout the world to its membership. During the Anglo-Boer War
(1899-1902), the union was strongly pro-Boer.[11]

Although there was broad acclaim for Kuyper in America,
not all church leaders who shared his theological persuasion
agreed with his emphases. As was the case among some members of the *Afscheiding* in his homeland, some of his American
colleagues criticized him. They contended that he was more

concerned about what he perceived to be Reformed principles than about the exegesis of the Bible. They charged him with elevating these principles to such a height that, in practice, he had made them superior to Scripture and the historic confessions of the Faith.[12] It is evident that some Calvinists in America did not understand that the Reformed faith is not only a system of doctrine, but an entire world-view which that system of doctrine requires.

A large majority of Reformed believers in the United States received Kuyper's concepts gratefully and began to implement them, in some cases, even before his visit to America. Members of the Christian Reformed Church became zealous advocates of Christian schools organized and controlled by parents, and Calvin College and Calvin Theological Seminary became academic centres of Reformed thinking. For some of those parents, however, the maintenance of private schools was as much a way of preserving Dutch ethnic solidarity in a pluralist society as it was a means to educate children in biblical truth. In 1921 some Dutch American Christians began publishing the *Christian Standard*, a daily newspaper, but the project failed after only two months because of inadequate funds and small circulation. Efforts to maintain a Christian political party comparable to the Anti-Revolutionary Party were also not successful.[13]

The proposed revision of the *Westminster Confession*

Long after his visit to the United States, Dr Kuyper continued to maintain a keen interest in that country, especially with regard to developments in its church life. As in Europe, so in America, departures from historic Christian beliefs became frequent as the nineteenth century ended and the next century began. Nowhere was this more evident than in Presbyterian circles, where there were efforts to revise the *Westminster*

Confession of Faith. In 1889 fifteen presbyteries appealed to
the General Assembly, and by the next year 134 presbyteries
across the nation had indicated support for some revisions. Firm
opposition came from professors at Princeton Theological Seminary, and there occurred concurrently the dramatic heresy trial
of Charles A. Briggs, an Old Testament scholar at Union Theological Seminary in New York. The General Assembly of 1893
suspended Briggs for denying the infallibility of Scripture, and
Union Theological Seminary responded by severing its ties with
the Presbyterian Church and proceeded to espouse modernis-
tic views of Christianity. This explosive incident blunted the
movement for revision of the *Westminster Confession*, but only
temporarily.

By 1903 demands for some revisions of the confession had
gained enough support to win approval. The General Assembly and a sufficient number of presbyteries ratified changes that
diluted the strongly Calvinistic character of Presbyterian teaching about sin, human depravity and salvation by grace alone.
Arminian influences within the Presbyterian Church in the USA
were leading it away from historic Reformed beliefs.[14]

When Abraham Kuyper learned about proposals to revise
the Westminster Standards, he wrote an article to encourage
resistance to that effort because he saw it as a threat to biblical
Christianity. His first attempt to help American Presbyterians
was published in 1891 in the *Presbyterian and Reformed Review*, an essay entitled 'Calvinism and Confessional Revision'.[15]
In 1898 the Stone Lectures gave him an opportunity to rein-
force his earlier appeal and to do so at Presbyterianism's most
distinguished school of theology in America.

Kuyper's overall assessment of America

Even though his efforts on behalf of the Reformed faith had
not turned the tide against modernism in America, Kuyper did

not relent. In 1906 he wrote 'The True Genius of Presbyterianism', in which he related that Dutch Calvinists continued to admire their brethren in the New World, and he hailed Presbyterian theology and polity for extolling Christ's kingship. He rejoiced over the freedom that Americans enjoyed because they had no state church, but he lamented that denominations there, as in Europe, sometimes identified themselves by the names of their founders. He disliked labels such as 'Lutheran' and 'Mennonite' for that reason, and he disapproved of national religious designations such as 'Church of *England*' and '*Dutch* Reformed Church'. He held that the true church is catholic, and that the term 'Presbyterian' is appropriate because it signifies a biblically correct form of government, one that acknowledges and magnifies Christ's full authority over his church. It shows that God's people are not coextensive with a nation, and civil officials have no right to rule the church. Kuyper admitted that early leaders of the Reformation had failed to separate church and state adequately, and he regretted that the consequences of that error remained in several European countries which would do well, he thought, to follow the example of the United States.[16]

It is evident that Dr Kuyper thoroughly enjoyed his visit to America, and his writings about that country showed his continued admiration and concern for her spiritual well-being. He made a lasting impression upon Reformed believers in the New World, and a Kuyperian legacy remains with them until the present. Kuyper's enthusiasm for the United States was, however, somewhat excessive. He had a tendency to assign to Calvinist influences developments that, in some cases, had diverse origins. Although he might not have been aware of it, Kuyper's political ideas had much in common with those of John Locke (1632-1704) and the Baron de Montesquieu (1689-1755), both of whom espoused constitutional government with a system of checks and balances and civil liberties guaranteed by law. Kuyper failed to understand the extent of deism-rationalism as an influence in the formative period of the American nation, and as a consequence, he maintained a somewhat romantic view of that country. This perspective is especially prominent in his essay 'Calvinism: the Origin and Safeguard of our Constitutional Liberties', which he wrote in 1874 and which appeared in English in 1895. By the time he went to lecture at Princeton, he had read widely and deeply in all of the works of Edmund Burke and had come to share Burke's fondness for America. Like Burke, he despised the radical political ideas of the French *philosophes*, but he did not realize the extent to which some of the founders of the American republic admired them. Kuyper chose to believe that the influence of Calvinistic Puritanism was decisive in the thinking of American political leaders of the eighteenth century.[17] Although he expressed concerns about trends in American churches, Kuyper, until his death, regarded the United States as the place where the Reformed faith was most healthy and where its prospects for the future were the best.

15.
A reformer in politics

Long before his trip to the United States, Abraham Kuyper had become leader of the Anti-Revolutionary Party in his homeland, where his newspaper *De Standaard* promoted Christian interests in national life. The party held eleven seats in parliament by 1880, and within its ranks was A. F. Savornin Lohman, who had a strong interest in obtaining justice for private schools. A central committee, of which Kuyper was chairman, directed the Anti-Revolutionary Party, and Savornin Lohman, a distinguished jurist, was one of its legal advisers. The party resolved to present an alternative to both liberalism and conservatism and to maintain a vigorous defence against socialism.

Kuyper's political stance

Abraham Kuyper, like John Calvin, favoured a republican political structure, but he supported the Dutch constitutional monarchy with its duly elected parliament. Perhaps that is why he called himself a democrat rather than a republican, even though he despised the doctrine of popular sovereignty, which is the theoretical basis for democracy. Kuyper's concept of sphere authority sometimes led him to protest against the growing power of the state over institutions that should be autonomous within their own spheres. He once asked his countrymen, 'What will remain of your personal freedom, when at length the caesarism which has sprung up out of the modern state and the modern imperialism, distributing its *panes et circenses* in its economic regulation of material advantages, permits everything to itself, because there is no man who withstands it for the very good reason that there is no man who can withstand it?'[1]

In order to discourage state authoritarianism, Kuyper favoured the division of political powers among national, provincial and local governments. He held that the king should rule only in time of war, and he argued that elementary education should be a local affair, while the provinces should control teachers' training colleges and *gymnasia* (academic high schools). The national government should have authority over higher education. He believed that the United States was a fine example of this arrangement, but he did not mention that there were no federal institutions of higher learning in America, and the accreditation of universities there was a state and regional matter.[2]

With regard to the foreign policy of his nation, Dr Kuyper supported a strong national defence, at least to the extent that this was practical for a small nation. He therefore promoted reforms to improve conditions of military service, and he called for strategic planning to prepare for the contingency of a major war in Europe. In colonial affairs Kuyper believed that Dutch officials at home should administer matters of defence and justice in the colonies, but internal matters should be left to the colonies themselves. He roundly condemned all exploitation of indigenous people subject to Dutch rule in the East and West Indies, and he contended that the Netherlands had a moral obligation to prepare the native inhabitants for economic progress and eventual self-rule. Kuyper called for Christian missions to the colonies, but he did not seek government support for any one church. He expected that the East Indian island of Java would progress to the point where it would one day have a free university. To encourage the development of native leadership, he said that nationals should staff the administration of the East Indies under the tutelage of European department heads.[3]

The development of the Anti-Revolutionary Party

Perhaps because the Anti-Revolutionary Party was so small, some of its members wanted to merge with Conservatives in order to win elections, but Groen and Kuyper rejected that proposal because it compromised the Christian principle of the antithesis. They agreed that Anti-Revolutionaries should co-operate with other parties in obtaining specific legislation for their common benefit, but they rejected humanism in all its forms. Groen and Kuyper wanted a political movement that operated on the basis of non-negotiable principles, not a pragmatic one that would compromise to win votes.

In order to advance the prospects for the Anti-Revolutionary Party, Kuyper promoted the development of a multi-party system. He contended that the two-party arrangement did not give voters genuine choices, because Liberals and Conservatives subscribed to the same humanistic principles that Christians rejected. A multi-party system did eventually become the pattern in Dutch politics, much to Kuyper's delight.

Because of his espousal of Christian beliefs and his service as a pastor, critics of his political movement sometimes called the Anti-Revolutionaries a clerical party. This was untrue, for it contradicted Kuyper's position. He participated in politics in his capacity as a citizen, not as a clergyman. In his scheme of sphere authority no church body has the right to operate a political party. He accused Dutch Liberals of intolerance because they would not acknowledge the right of Christians to offer an alternative world-view and to express it through political action.[4]

Conservatives, too, sometimes employed smear tactics to discredit the Anti-Revolutionary Party. One such irresponsible critic made the absurd charge that it was a Communist organization. Opponents from the right and left of the political spectrum feared the Anti-Revolutionary philosophy and correctly perceived that it threatened the practice of politics as usual.

On the pages of *De Standaard* Kuyper responded to attacks upon his party. He wrote, for example, to defend its position on Christian schools. He said, 'As long as there is injustice; as long as liberals, modernists, unbelievers, demand exclusively for themselves the right to educate children in public schools, so long shall every supporter of *recht* [law and justice], regardless of his point of view in the struggle of the Anti-Revolutionary Party, not be frightened by terms such as *Standaard man*, *Standaard Party* and *clerical*.'[5]

Abraham Kuyper was chairman of the Anti-Revolutionary Party for almost forty years, and during that time he watched it develop from a scorned and despised faction to a position of power in Dutch politics. The party enjoyed considerable growth in the 1880s, both in votes cast and in seats acquired in parliament. In the election of 1888 Anti-Revolutionaries and Roman Catholics supported each other's candidates and thereby won control of parliament, and Baron Aeneas Mackay became prime minister of a 'Christian coalition' government. Liberals denounced it as a 'monster alliance between Rome and Dort'. This was the government that initiated the reform of the school law that gave subsidies to private schools. It introduced legislation to protect women and children from exploitation in the workplace and to limit working hours for everyone.[6]

The problem of the East Indies

One matter of great concern for the Mackay government was the administration of the East Indies, which had long been an

enterprise of the Dutch East India Company. Along with its commercial privileges, the company received a mandate from the
States-General to promote Christianity in the islands. Due to
missionary efforts, the New Testament appeared in the Ma-
layan language in 1668 and the Old Testament in 1730, and by
the end of the eighteenth century seminaries were educating
native pastors.

The Netherlands Missionary Society came into being in 1797
as a means to spread Christianity among pagans in the Indies.
It was not a church agency, and some of its personnel came
from Protestant denominations which did not affirm the historic Reformed confessions.[7]

Slavery was a long-established practice of the Dutch rulers
in both the East and West Indies. Groen van Prinsterer opposed slavery and Jan Willem Gefken (1807-87), an Anti-Revolutionary colonial official in Surinam, West Indies, argued against
it on the basis that it ignores the personhood that the image of
God entails. Groen was among the first Dutchmen to criticize
the policies of the South African Boers towards Zulus and
Hottentots. The Netherlands abolished slavery in her East Indian colonies in 1857 and in the West Indies in 1863. Groen
and Gefken were leading figures in the Society for Abolition,
which promoted evangelism among colonial peoples as well as
emancipation from involuntary servitude.[8]

Reformed leaders eventually decided that the doctrinal character of the Netherlands Missionary Society was too broad to
merit their support, and they founded the Netherlands Missionary Union as a Reformed agency to spread the Christian faith
abroad. Like the Netherlands Bible Society, founded in 1814,
this Calvinist outreach was to exert considerable influence in
the East Indies. The missionaries won the largest number of
their converts from among animistic pagans.[9]

In spite of its claim that it was promoting the spread of Christianity among the natives of Indonesia, the Dutch East India
Company discouraged missionary work there, even to the point

of prohibiting distribution of the Scriptures in the Javanese language. In 1798 the Dutch government dissolved the company and soon assumed rule of the Indies for itself. This did not, however, quickly improve the prospects for missionary work, nor did it end exploitation of the indigenous people.

For a time during the era of wars against Napoleon (1796-1814), the French occupied the Netherlands, and the puppet government there promised to rule the East Indies for the benefit of the local inhabitants, but the rulers did very little to change things there. Forced labour, requisition of produce, monopolies and other abuses continued. The government still regarded the colonies as lands to be exploited for the advantage of the Netherlands. Since Great Britain was at war with Napoleon, British forces occupied the East Indies and subjected them to their rule until the defeat of Napoleon in 1814, when the United Kingdom returned the islands to Dutch rule. King William I assumed almost full control over Dutch colonial affairs, and his government adopted a 'Culture System' as its policy towards Indonesia. This required the local inhabitants to give the Dutch officials use of lands and control over native workers to produce crops for export. This was a great economic success, but it prevented the development of private enterprise and did not assign much importance to the well-being of indigenous peoples.[10]

Reforms in colonial policy came gradually, but the Netherlands did not abandon the Culture System until the 1870s, and the government did not inform the Dutch public fully about actual conditions in the East Indies. Because the king had full authority over colonies, he did not inform parliament. In 1848, however, a major revision of the constitution gave parliament authority over colonial policy, and soon a movement appeared to demand an end to exploitation. The East Indian Government Act in 1854 outlawed slavery and all forced labour, and it promised education for the local inhabitants. The abolition of slavery took effect in 1857. Enforcement of this law was not vigorous, but it did provide a basis for the development of an ethical school of thought regarding the treatment of subject peoples. Several Dutch cabinets and political parties contributed to the reforms, and when such measures did become effective, the cause was in part due to the demands of private investors for opportunities to trade in the East Indies. As the islands opened up to private development, the Dutch government became the protector of the indigenous peoples.[11]

Abraham Kuyper and the Anti-Revolutionary Party watched colonial affairs with intense interest. *Our Programme*, an Anti-Revolutionary statement of principles and policy published in 1889, declared that the Dutch kingdom had a moral responsibility towards the peoples it ruled in foreign lands. The statement asserted that exploitation was evil, whether due to private enterprise or to state policy, and it called for education of the native inhabitants to prepare them for self-rule. This Anti-Revolutionary appeal gradually won the endorsement of all political factions in the country, but full implementation of an ethical policy did not occur until after Abraham Kuyper became prime minister in 1901.[12]

In 1894, after seventeen years, Abraham Kuyper returned to parliament as a representative from the district of Sliedrecht. During the time of his absence problems in the East Indies had become critical.

The war with Acheh and its aftermath

Instability in the native Sultanate of Acheh, on the island of Sumatra, had not only threatened Dutch operations in Java and other islands, but appeared to be creating a serious international situation. The Dutch blamed the ruler of Acheh for piracy and general hostility towards areas which the Netherlands

ruled. Soon the colonial authorities learned that Acheh had
been seeking support from Turkey, the United States and perhaps other powers. There were rumours of American and Italian warships sailing for the East Indies. It is clear that Dutch
officials in the islands and others at home maintained an assertive posture towards Acheh and were eager to expand the In-
donesian territory subject to Dutch rule. As international interest in the region appeared to be increasing, the Netherlands
had declared war on Acheh in March 1873 (before Kuyper
entered parliament for the first time). The struggle was fierce,
protracted and costly for both countries.

Netherlanders in general supported the war at first, as did
both Roman Catholic and Anti-Revolutionary newspapers.
Abraham Kuyper held that it was a just conflict because American and/or Italian intervention appeared likely. When that did
not occur, and the war continued nevertheless, he became critical
of his government's policy. The war raged intermittently from
1873-80, and when it proved too costly to continue, the government ended it in 1881. Sporadic fighting continued for years
after that, however, and the Dutch navy blockaded some ports.
Humanitarians decried the loss of life on both sides, and prag-
matists lamented the financial expense. Most Christians came
to regard the war as an immoral effort to expand the Dutch
empire.

Kuyper's attitude towards the Dutch colonial holdings was
not one of opposition to colonialism as a principle. In 1879,
when it had appeared that British occupation of North Borneo
and New Guinea was imminent, he had urged his government
to annex those areas so as to preclude the British action. The
cabinet, however, had decided that Dutch resources were not
adequate to do so. Kuyper and Reformed Christians in general
realized that, as long as their nation held colonies, those terri-
tories presented great opportunities for missionary work. When
the Anti-Revolutionary Party increased its seats in parliament,

one of the uses to which it applied its new leverage was to demand the opening of the entire East Indies to Christian missions.

While the Anti-Revolutionary W. L. F. Keuchenius was Colonial Secretary (1889-90), he tried to improve the quality of Dutch officials serving in the East Indies, and he sought to combat Muslim influence there, but his critics controlled the First Chamber of parliament, which rejected the budget for colonies and compelled him to resign. He and Kuyper had called for an end to state-sponsored opium trade in the islands.[13]

The Ethical Policy

When Dr Kuyper returned to parliament in 1894, he promoted additional reforms in the colonies. He argued that the Netherlands should regard her posture towards the colonies as one of guardianship as a feature of an 'Ethical Policy' to improve life for the indigenous inhabitants by opening numerous schools under the direction of missionaries. When Kuyper became prime minister in 1901, this became state policy. Under the Ethical Policy the Dutch government assumed direct authority over areas of the East Indies where native rule was corrupt or oppressive, and the government took steps to alleviate the suffering caused by crop failures and diseases of cattle that had put the economy of the islands in decline by the opening of the twentieth century.[14] Also in line with the Ethical Policy, the Dutch took increasing numbers of nationals into the administration of the colony and, in 1918, they created a People's Council, which gradually became the major influence in the government of the East Indies.[15]

Implementing the Ethical Policy was difficult, and by 1900 only about 100,000 native children were in schools, while Java alone had a population of over twenty million. Very few of the indigenous people were receiving a higher education. The number of elementary school children did continue to rise, and by 1915 it had reached 300,000, by 1940 two million. Almost all instruction was in the native tongue.

The Ethical Policy, of which Kuyper had been the champion, raised the standard of living for most Indonesians, at least until World War I, and the Netherlands enjoyed greater profits from trade with the East Indies than ever before. From 1890-1910 the Dutch merchant fleet increased by 200%, and much of this growth was due to commerce with the islands.[16] Since Abraham Kuyper lived until 1920, he was able to watch with satisfaction the success of the reforms for which he had worked for many years.

Kuyper's rise to power

Since implementation of the Ethical Policy occurred after Kuyper became prime minister, it is appropriate at this point to explain how he attained to his country's highest office. Until 1892 he remained rector of the Free University of Amsterdam, and he taught and wrote about theology and applied the truths of the Reformed faith to a host of issues, at both personal and public levels. In 1894 he returned to parliament and in 1897 won re-election to the Second Chamber. He and the Anti-Revolutionary Party campaigned on their Christian principles, which included a rejection of both *laissez-faire* capitalism and statist socialism. The Anti-Revolutionaries called for support from those common people who had gained the franchise due to the Suffrage Reform Act (1896). By 1897 the Liberals had been in power for six years because the Anti-Revolutionary – Roman Catholic coalition had collapsed due to disagreement over matters pertaining to the armed forces. A Union of Socialists had formed in 1881 to promote improvements for the proletariat, but it suffered a schism in 1894, when Domela Nieuwenhuis, its leader, called for violence to accomplish its goals. The first split in socialist ranks produced the Social Democratic Workers' Party, and another led to the formation of the Social Democratic Party in 1902. The most radical socialists eventually became militant Marxists who affiliated with the Soviet *Comintern*, an agency of the Kremlin to promote worldwide revolution.[17]

The Suffrage Reform Act had increased the number of voters from 300,000 to 700,000, and the first election subsequent to the passage of that law occurred in June 1897. Kuyper won his seat, but the parties of the left-wing, Liberals, Socialists and Radicals, gained fifty-five seats in the Second Chamber to forty-five for their opponents, so a coalition of the left formed a cabinet. By this time Alexander de Savornin Lohman had broken with the Anti-Revolutionaries and had formed a faction known as the Free Anti-Revolutionaries, a rather aristocratic group that did not appreciate Kuyper's more democratic ideas.

In the election of 1897 the Anti-Revolutionary Party secured only seventeen seats. Kuyper was its leader in parliament, the chief spokesman for the opposition to the Liberal government. He quickly reaffirmed his party's rejection of popular sovereignty by asserting that the new monarch, Queen Wilhelmina (1898-1948), whose inauguration was pending, ruled by the grace of God, not merely by the will of the people. This, of course, angered humanists, both within the government and outside of it. The polarity of world-views in Dutch politics was obvious, and Kuyper strove to keep it in the public eye.

Although he led the major opposition party, Abraham Kuyper did not resist the government obstinately. On the contrary, he encouraged it to proceed with additional reforms, and he indicated a willingness to co-operate with it to the extent that the Christian principles of the Anti-Revolutionary Party would allow. One such reform was the Workers' Social Insurance Act, which became law in 1901. It provided financial compensation for employees injured while at work, the first measure of its kind in Dutch history, and Kuyper supported it vigorously.[18]

In 1899 tragedy struck the Kuyper family for the second time in that decade. Kuyper's nineteen-year-old son had died in 1892, and then his beloved wife, Johanna, passed away while they were on holiday in Switzerland. They had been married thirty-six years, and Abraham Kuyper did not remarry. He felt the loss keenly and, soon after his wife's death, he began publishing a series of articles that appeared later in his book *Asleep in Jesus*. That same year he, for the fourth time, was rector at the Free University of Amsterdam, and there he delivered an address entitled 'Evolution', which set forth clearly his opposition to the Darwinian world-view.[19] Before 1899 ended, the Anglo-Boer War erupted in South Africa, and Kuyper took a strong stand in favour of the Boers. He criticized the Dutch government for not inviting the Boer republics to send representatives to the Hague Peace Conference earlier that year.[20]

Although he never fully recovered from the loss of his wife, Kuyper did not allow personal grief to deter him from the performance of his duties. He continued to be the Anti-Revolutionary leader in parliament, where he made his influence felt in many debates. He supported the government where he could do so without compromise, but he always regarded it as a body of humanists who opposed God's rule over society. Kuyper was, therefore, eager to effect the defeat of the cabinet, and he looked forward to the election of 1901 as the next opportunity to do so.

The Anti-Revolutionary Party maintained voters' clubs across the nation, and those clubs chose delegates to their party's national convention. An executive committee led the party, and Kuyper's influence was paramount in the committee. The Anti-Revolutionary convention met in Utrecht in April 1901 and Kuyper delivered the keynote address as the kingdom prepared for elections in June. In his speech the Anti-Revolutionary leader did not assail personalities. He argued against the principles undergirding liberalism and socialism, principles he abhorred because they denied God's right to set the moral standards for public policy and national life. To Kuyper's delight, the parties on the right of the political spectrum won a majority of seats in the Second Chamber. The Anti-Revolutionaries took twenty-four seats, the Roman Catholics twenty-five, the Free Anti-Revolutionaries seven, and that combination gave them the basis on which to form a coalition government. Queen Wilhelmina then asked Dr Kuyper to organize a cabinet, and he became prime minister and Secretary for Internal Affairs. Three posts went to Roman Catholics, and the new government assumed authority on 1 August 1901.

Kuyper as prime minister

The demands of the premiership required Kuyper to suspend his activities at the Free University of Amsterdam, and he reduced his contributions to his newspapers. He then devoted himself to matters of state with characteristic energy. His objectives at the outset of his ministry were to achieve a final settlement of long-standing issues pertaining to private education, to provide adequate insurance for ill and elderly persons in a system of social security, and to continue efforts to protect and aid workers in danger of exploitation from employers.

His defeated opponents, of course, feared Kuyper, and he had given them reason to do so. In 1879 he had proclaimed the political objective of his movement when he wrote, 'We want both Liberals and Conservatives to be discredited.'[21] Such remarks were characteristic of his very assertive manner, a trait that sometimes hindered his work as an office holder. Kuyper sought to demolish idols in every sphere of life, not least of all in politics, and he could not do so gently. While he was prime minister, one critic accused him of trying to subvert the monarchy in order to establish a republic in the manner of Oliver Cromwell, the Puritan leader of England in the seventeenth century.[22]

Perhaps Liberals and Conservatives had underestimated Kuyper's ability as a political leader, but some foreign observers respected him highly. One American reporter met Kuyper in 1902 and published her impressions in the United States. Caroline Atwater Mason remarked: 'No pietist parson is more evangelical in his piety, more unrelenting in his orthodoxy, than this man who is capable of reversing the government of his nation and fusing elements the most diverse into an astounding political unity... We felt ourselves in the presence of a unique and powerful personality ... a man of genius, able to hold his own against the cleverest spirits in the Liberal camp.'[23]

The response of humanists in America was, of course, the opposite. Some of them scornfully referred to Kuyper's cabinet as a 'clerical government', and when his coalition fell from power in 1905, one American journal rejoiced about the end of 'clerical' rule in the Netherlands.[24] Kuyper's critics either failed to understand the difference between a confessional and a clerical party, or else they wilfully misrepresented him. The Anti-Revolutionary Party had no official connection with any church, and not all of its supporters adhered to the theology of the Reformed faith, but all accepted the political principles that developed from that persuasion. The Anti-Revolutionary – Roman Catholic coalition was a tactical alliance based upon mutual subscription to *some* principles. Neither party compromised anything, and Kuyper made it clear that Roman Catholicism as an interpretation of Christianity was not acceptable. In fact, Kuyper believed that the influence of the Roman Catholic Church was at least partly to blame for the French Revolution. He thought that the Roman Catholic Party was under the authority of its church, so conflict between it and the Anti-

Revolutionary Party was fundamental. In Kuyper's words, 'Rome says 1517 [the Protestant Reformation] led to 1789 [the French Revolution]. We say Roman Catholicism is responsible in church and state for 1789, as an illegitimate mother. Thus we cannot join Rome.'[25]

Dr Kuyper and his cabinet began their administration within the framework of sphere authority. Kuyper used the term 'society' to signify a structure much broader than the state. He worked on the premise that the state must respect the other spheres and protect society from both tyranny and anarchy. The state must prevent the spheres from infringing upon one another, and it may use compulsion when necessary to maintain order.[26] He feared the state, however, because, even if its officials are Christians, they are still sinners who might abuse their power. Kuyper's commitment to his biblical understanding of government is evident as he pursued his duties to follow divinely revealed moral precepts.

Along with his concern that government might exceed its God-given authority, Kuyper maintained that civil rule is a blessing of common grace and, in the hands of Christians, it could accomplish much good. Even though he had to share authority with the Roman Catholics, Kuyper, through the Anti-Revolutionary Party, was able to assert the rights of the Reformed minority in the Netherlands and to make faith once more a powerful influence in public life. Dutch liberals realized that the ideology of the Kuyper government was antithetical to their own, so they joined forces with the socialists to resist it.[27] The Liberal Party, nevertheless, went into recession from which it did not recover. The Liberal-Socialist alliance lasted only until 1908.[28]

Because he rejected the view of liberalism that autonomous human beings are at liberty to create their own social, political, educational and cultural forms without regard for God's ordinances, Abraham Kuyper made those very ordinances the basis for public policy.[29] He believed that, in politics, he was working in the domain of common grace, and he wrote extensively about that doctrine while he occupied the premiership of the kingdom. Common grace gave him a basis for trans-confessional co-operation to run the government.[30]

16.
Prime minister and
elder statesman

When Kuyper assumed office in August 1901, the eyes of the
world were fixed on South Africa, where the Anglo-Boer War
had been raging for two years. This is not the place to explain
that conflict in detail, but it is appropriate to relate Kuyper's
view of it and his efforts to bring it to a halt. Some description
of conditions in southern Africa is therefore necessary.

The background to the conflict

The Boers (Afrikaners) of the nineteenth century were descendants of Dutch settlers who had arrived at the Cape of Good
Hope in 1652 as agents of the Dutch East India Company.
Towards the end of the seventeenth century a few hundred
French Huguenots went to the Cape at the invitation of the
East India Company after King Louis XIV had revoked the Edict
of Nantes (1598) and thereby deprived Protestants in France of
their freedom of religion. The Europeans multiplied slowly and
began to cultivate farms and thus acquired the name *'Boers'*,
the Dutch word for farmers. The Boers imported slaves from
West Africa and Asia to work the soil, and they tried to avoid
contact with the primitive Bushmen and Hottentots, but the
need for meat required them to trade with the Hottentots for

cattle. In the process the Europeans expanded inland from the Cape.

In 1795, in the midst of their war against France, the British occupied the Cape, with the agreement of the exiled Prince of Orange, in order to prevent French seizure of this strategic post at the tip of Africa. By the Treaty of Paris (1814), which signalled Britain's victory over Napoleon, the United Kingdom took legal possession of the Cape and paid the Netherlands financial compensation for this imperial acquisition. Until 1825 a British governor ruled Cape Colony with no effective restraints upon his authority.

The establishment of British rule at the Cape brought missionaries and settlers from the United Kingdom, and conflicts between them and the older Boer population became frequent, especially as British political institutions and concepts of jurisprudence replaced the old Dutch system. In 1833 Britain abolished slavery throughout her empire, and the payments to compensate Boer slave-holders were, in their judgement, not adequate. Conflicts between Boers and interior tribes known as Bantus produced more trouble and worsened relations between Britons and Boers.

In 1835 about 10,000 Boers left the area of British jurisdiction to settle beyond the Vaal River, where they established the Transvaal Republic. Other Boers moved into Zululand and Natal, after tribal warfare had almost depopulated those regions. Those Boers established a Republic of Natal after defeating a powerful Zulu offensive. In 1842 the British imposed their rule upon Natal and gave protection to the tribes opposed to the Boers. Occasional fighting between Britons and Boers occurred as friction increased, and by 1857 the Boers had secured their hold on the Transvaal and the area known as the Orange River Colony, which they declared to be the Orange Free State, while the Transvaal announced it had become the South African Republic. The discovery of diamonds led to the development of a lucrative enterprise between the Vaal and Orange Rivers, and it excited the interest of European fortune-hunters. In 1871 the British government annexed the diamond-producing area, an action that infuriated the Boers. The goal of Britain was to bring all of southern Africa under British sovereignty.

By 1880 the Boers of the Transvaal could bear British interference no longer, and they resorted to armed revolt by which they regained independence for the South African Republic. The discovery of gold in that region in 1886 quickly focused world attention on South Africa once more, and soon British investors controlled most of the mining operations in the Boer-ruled state. In 1889 the Orange Free State and the South African Republic signed a treaty of mutual defence. After British financial magnate Cecil Rhodes became prime minister at the Cape in 1890, relations between his government and the Boer republics became critical. When he failed to convince the South African Republic to join a customs union, Rhodes began supporting a faction within the Transvaal that wanted to overthrow its government. Meanwhile, the British continued annexing lands, sometimes to frustrate Boer plans for expansion. Diplomatic efforts to resolve the problems failed, and the Anglo-Boer War erupted on 12 October 1899 and lasted until 31 May 1902.

Dutch support for the Boer cause

Long before the war Abraham Kuyper had corresponded with Paul Kruger (1825-1904), a Boer leader who became president of the South African Republic in 1888. Kruger, like Kuyper, was a zealous adherent to the Reformed faith who subscribed heartily to the *Canons of Dort*. He was a member of the Christian Reformed Church, which had been established in South Africa in 1859. It did not seek to become the state religion. Kruger expressed approval for Kuyper's concept of sphere authority as well as his theology in general.[1] Kuyper expressed a wish to visit South Africa, and he hoped that Christians there would establish a university comparable to the one he had founded in Amsterdam. Kruger endorsed the idea, but the people of the Transvaal showed little enthusiasm for the project.

As Kuyper watched the accumulating tensions in South Africa, he hailed the Boers for maintaining their cultural identity in the face of British intrusions, and he encouraged them to preserve their Calvinism and not to succumb to English materialism and the ritualism characteristic of the Anglican Church. Kuyper and the Dutch people in general were disgusted by British policy in South Africa, and the Anglo-Boer War intensified their resentment. On the pages of *De Standaard* Kuyper had protested against British annexations of territory at Boer expense, but he was at the same time critical of the Boers because of their treatment of the black tribes. Before Kuyper became prime minister, he wrote *La Crise Sud-Africaine*, and that essay soon appeared in English as *The South African Crisis*, which was published in at least fourteen editions. In 1899 Kuyper tried to enlist American president William McKinley to intercede on behalf of the Boers.[2]

After becoming prime minister he went to London to offer his help in achieving a negotiated settlement. Britain's Lord Lansdowne expressed gratitude for the Dutch effort, but he restated his government's policy of not allowing foreign intercession in disputes with the Boers. It was very unlikely that Kuyper could have succeeded, for the British knew he was not a disinterested party. In *The South African Crisis* he had written that the United Kingdom was waging 'a war of aggression which nothing can justify'.[3] He argued there that Britain's policy towards the Boers was a violation of her subscription to the Hague Peace Conference of 1899.

As Kuyper analysed the situation in South Africa, he extolled the Boers for their political and military ability and chose to credit them with founding a democratic society under the influence of their Calvinist faith. He said their morality was exemplary. The British, on the other hand, he accused of persistent injustice. Kuyper acknowledged that the early British efforts in South Africa were motivated by humane concern for the black peoples, but British imperialism was due to greed. Great Britain violated treaties with the Boer states because of her 'selfish and aggressive materialism' stimulated by diamonds and gold. British military intervention proceeded from the pretext that it was necessary to protect the tribes.[4] Kuyper took special pleasure in reminding his readers that many authorities on international law supported the Boers' argument against British claims.[5] When some British intellectuals claimed that the United Kingdom had a mission to civilize backward peoples, including the Boers, Kuyper indicted them for proposing to accomplish that 'mission' by war.[6]

Dr Kuyper blamed the capitalists for Britain's unjust war in South Africa, and he appealed to Britons to save their nation from its disgraceful policy of conquest. He warned, 'England must renounce … her dream of imperialism; otherwise imperialism will eventually destroy her, as it destroyed ancient Rome.'[7] Kuyper believed there was an evil principle at work in British policy, and that principle was social Darwinism, an application in this case of the 'survival of the fittest' to justify aggression against a weaker people. He criticized especially those British clergymen who supported the war on the grounds that it would extend the kingdom of God.[8]

The impassioned writing of Kuyper and his diplomacy as prime minister failed to convince the British government. At one point British authorities even denied a request from the Dutch Red Cross to send ambulances to aid wounded Boers.[9]

On another occasion they expelled 6,000 families from South Africa and forced them to go to the Netherlands, where they became impoverished refugees.[10] Perhaps in an effort to mitigate his lack of success in London, Prime Minister Kuyper asserted after the war that his approach to Lord Lansdowne had persuaded the latter to open peace negotiations with the Boers. If this is so, there is no documentary evidence to verify it.[11]

During the era of worsening tensions between Britons and Boers, many people in the Netherlands had tried to aid their counterparts in South Africa, and some spoke enthusiastically about developing a New Holland there. Liberals as well as Anti-Revolutionaries joined committees to aid the Boers by raising funds for them and sending petitions of protest against British policy to Queen Victoria. One Dutch Protestant labour organization had considered forming a volunteer army to go to South Africa to defend the Boers in their first war against Great Britain. In 1881 pro-Boers had formed the Dutch South African Association of which Kuyper was a member until disagreements with liberals in the organization led him to withdraw.

In 1884 Paul Kruger had led a delegation of Boers to the Netherlands to seek financing for a Boer national railway and national bank. These South Africans received a tumultuous welcome. The Dutch government at the time was, however, far less supportive towards the Boers than was the public at large. When war began in 1899, a specifically Christian National Boer Committee formed and soon had 5,500 members.[12]

When British forces finally conquered the Transvaal, President Kruger fled to the Netherlands aboard a Dutch warship. The Dutch government did not plan to make his arrival a state occasion, but public response was terrific, and Queen Wilhelmina and some political leaders greeted him warmly. When the British king Edward VII arrived in the Dutch city of Flushing, public reaction was hostile. A large crowd greeted him by singing the national anthem of the South African Republic. In the aftermath of the war Kuyper came to believe that the Boers could survive within the British Empire, and pro-Boer organizations continued to aid South Africans after the war, but dreams of a New Holland were gone.

Despite his sympathy for the Boers and his diplomatic efforts on their behalf, Abraham Kuyper's government remained officially neutral throughout the war. It could not have afforded to antagonize Great Britain, because to have done so might have provoked her to intervene in Indonesia. Kuyper denied that Dutch policy there was imperialistic, and he argued that the Netherlands had a moral obligation to rule the region well. In his view advanced races and nations must elevate the lower ones.[13] The British, of course, justified their position in South Africa in the same manner.

Trouble brewing at home

One of the important effects of Kuyper's efforts at peacemaking was that they distracted him from some pressing domestic concerns, and critics accused him of failing in his responsibilities to his own nation. Queen Wilhelmina fell seriously ill in early 1902, an event that cast a shadow of uncertainty over the cabinet as well as the kingdom. No bills could become law without her signature, so the government seemed to be at a standstill. She recovered by September and was then able to address parliament.

On 6 December 1902 the prime minister addressed the Second Chamber to specify the particular goals of his government. He began with a clear affirmation of pluralism, a promise that he sought equality, but not superiority, for the Christian portion of the population in the political life of the nation. He explained that it was time to end the public monopoly over education by granting equal status and support to private schools, and he called for laws to combat evils such as drunkenness, gambling and pornography. Finally, the prime minister asked parliament to enact measures to protect workers further from exploitation.[14]

By the time Kuyper's government came to power, socialism had acquired a diverse following in the Netherlands. Some socialists were Marxists in theory but had abandoned the pursuit of their goals through violent revolution. Others, however, were more radical than Marx in that they had no patience to await the necessary dialectical movement of history that he had predicted. They, on the contrary, were preparing for a revolutionary confrontation with the government at any time. These radicals were disciples of the Russian anarchist Mikhail Bakunin (1814-76). By the opening of 1903, they were ready to use violence in support of a labour strike to paralyse the nation in the hope of affecting the fall of the government.

In 1894 a Social Democratic Union had enlisted all Dutch socialists within its ranks, but the Social Democratic Labour Party, under the leadership of P. J. Troelstra, withdrew because it favoured parliamentary action rather than revolution. Most members of the union eventually supported the non-violent pursuit of their goals and thereby forsook Marxist methods, but labour agitation and occasional strikes had occurred, as socialists denounced the monarchs, industrialists and landowners. By 1903 a serious situation was emerging that had the potential to paralyse the country by disrupting the economy severely. The tactic of the Social Democratic Workers' Party was to agitate a general strike. A strike in 1900 had won higher wages and better working conditions for Amsterdam dock workers. This triumph for organized labour proved the effectiveness of a strike and consequently encouraged dissatisfied workers to employ it more often and more broadly. In 1902 the National Federation of Transport Workers decided to strike for better wages and improved working conditions.

The strike

When Kuyper learned that trouble was brewing in the port of Amsterdam, he promised that his government would be fair to both parties in the dispute. He did not, at that point, realize the gravity of the situation. The strike began on 10 January 1903, when workers refused to unload a ship and the owners of the affected company fired fifty-six of them and hired replacements. This led to more work stoppages and violence against company officials, and warehouse workers joined the strike. By the end of January gangs of angry unionists had begun assaulting replacement workers on the docks, even outside Amsterdam. Soon railway employees, too, refused to work. Kuyper hesitated to take forceful action because he did not want the government to take sides in the dispute, and he did not have enough troops at that time to enforce any decisions his cabinet might have made. Harassed employers made numerous concessions to the unions, so the strike had once again proved its value, and socialists and anarchists rejoiced over their victory.

The triumph of organized labour in January 1903 aroused workers who had not participated in the strikes to become more demanding and to threaten to use the same means to obtain satisfaction of their grievances. In February workers at the Amsterdam gas and water companies began to talk of striking, and municipal employees, even policemen and firemen, did the same. Dr Kuyper knew that government action was essential, so he presented bills to parliament that would enable the cabinet to deal with the crisis after the strike ended. His proposals called for creation of a railway brigade to keep essential trains running, the formation of a commission to consider workers' complaints and authority to deal with any criminal actions that might occur during a strike. Meanwhile, during the strike, Kuyper sent soldiers to protect railway facilities. When the prime minister asked parliament to outlaw strikes, the socialist-dominated movement answered with belligerence. His government incurred the charge that Christians did not care about the plight of deprived, abused workers, so the time for proletarian revolutionary action had arrived. By 29 January the long-dreaded strike had begun, with the initial disruption at the waterworks. It spread quickly to the railways, and soon 25,000 employees in Amsterdam refused to work and the strike spread to other cities. The socialists had issued their call for a general strike and the turmoil continued until May.

Throughout the crisis Abraham Kuyper remained determined to uphold the rule of law, but he sympathized with the grievances of the workers and wished to help them. The socialists, nevertheless, portrayed him as an enemy of labour and worked to defeat his government. They never forgave him for using force to suppress the strike, and they refused to believe that he sincerely cared about the workers.[15] They often referred caustically to Kuyper's cabinet as a 'clerical government', and they blamed him because Christian labour organizations had refrained from supporting the strike.

The clash of world-views demonstrated

The crisis of 1903 demonstrated clearly that a clash of world-views had occurred. Socialist materialism and commitment to the class struggle had collided with Christian ethics and a biblical view of civil government, and the sanctity of God's law as the basis for it. The antithesis between humanist relativism and Christian allegiance to the permanence of divine ordinances could not have been more evident.

It is interesting to note that, in spite of charges to the contrary, Kuyper was a friend of labour. That was one reason why he sought to enlarge the electorate, so that common people

A famous cartoon of Kuyper published during his time as prime minister

could have some influence over political decisions that affected their lives socially and economically. He often agreed with the socialists about the need for reforms, but he rejected their world-view and the confrontational, even violent, methods some of them employed. Long before he became prime minister, Kuyper had led the Anti-Revolutionary Party to adopt a programme of social reforms as a major feature of its aspirations. The *kleine luyden* were always a special concern for Kuyper, and he did not restrict that concern to Reformed Christians. The prime minister wanted voluntary co-operation between employers and workers to remove injustices, and he proposed laws to require such actions when voluntary co-operation did not take place. After 1910, when Kuyper was out of government, the Netherlands did require management and labour to conduct collective discussions in order to obtain contracts to regulate their relations. This changed the structure of industrial agreements, as Kuyper had desired.[16]

Recognition for Christian education

With the subsidence of labour violence behind him, the prime minister resumed his efforts to obtain justice for Christian education, particularly for his own Free University of Amsterdam, which had been operating since 1880 without public funding or state recognition of its degrees. In March 1903 Kuyper had proposed a Higher Education Bill to benefit private institutions, but serious consideration of this matter did not occur until February 1904.

In March 1904 the Second Chamber passed the Higher Education Bill, but the First Chamber rejected it. The prime minister then took the unusual step of asking the queen to dissolve parliament and to call new elections. Wilhelmina did so, and the result gave Kuyper the majority he needed. The bill became law on 22 May 1905. Christian higher education in this way gained the status of equality with that of humanist education in state universities. In the judgement of some historians, the Higher Education Law and the Ethical Policy in colonial rule are the most enduring achievements of Kuyper's government.[17]

Although the Free University of Amsterdam was the only immediate beneficiary of the new law, the provisions of that legislation applied to other institutions as well. It validated the diplomas of private *gymnasia* (schools preparing pupils for higher education) and it granted them increased public funding. The law authorized churches or private organizations to create special professorial chairs at the state universities. This could not, of course, make those institutions Christian, but it did allow for the presentation of Christian teaching to some extent in otherwise secular establishments.

The final provision of Kuyper's bill pertained to technological education. It elevated the Delft Polytechnic School to the level of a university, and it authorized the creation of an agricultural and a commercial institution of higher learning. Kuyper believed these measures would be a great stimulus to the nation's economic improvement. Much to his dismay, however, parliament approved only the elevation of the school at Delft. The opening of the agricultural and commercial universities came long after Kuyper had left office.[18]

Government as an agency of common grace

Although Abraham Kuyper never abandoned his view of the antithesis between Christian and non-Christian world-views, he invoked the doctrine of common grace as the basis for his government, because he regarded civil authority as an agency of common grace. While he was prime minister he wrote *De Gemeene Gratie* (Common Grace) in three large volumes, an amazing feat in the light of the enormous responsibilities of his office. He always considered politics a sacred calling for himself and for other Christians, for he believed that recipients of saving grace must minister to society and thereby assist the institutions of common grace for Christ the King *(Pro Rege)*. As believers apply their faith to all aspects of culture, they function as a leaven, an influential minority of people who promote the welfare of the whole.[19]

One way in which Kuyper believed Christians in government could help society was to deal with the growing consumption of alcoholic beverages, which was then becoming a major source of social problems. Since Dr Kuyper was not a total abstainer himself, he did not want to prohibit all use of alcoholic drinks. He realized, however, that intemperance was a great evil in itself and that it led to other serious problems. He believed that the incidence of drunkenness would decline appreciably if people drank in their homes, not in taverns. When the existing liquor control law expired in 1904, the prime minister saw another opportunity to introduce a reform. While he knew that government could not transform human nature, Kuyper believed it had a responsibility to restrain the evil tendencies of sinful humanity, including the abuse of alcohol. He wanted the state to provide services to alcoholics in the hope of emancipating them from their addiction. Parliament accepted Kuyper's proposal and established a procedure to license retail stores where people could buy liquor and take it home. The confessional government had gained another triumph.[20]

Electoral defeat

After four years in office the Anti-Revolutionary – Roman Catholic coalition had to face the voters again, and the opponents prepared for a militant campaign. Everyone expected a close contest, and the Anti-Revolutionary Party gave a ringing endorsement to Kuyper, his policies and the accomplishments of his government. Not everyone in the Christian camp, however, was pleased with Kuyper and his secular critics perceived that his base of support was weakening.

One of the criticisms of the government had to do with a continuing problem in the Dutch East Indies. A serious uprising in Acheh in 1902 required a costly intervention that brought the sultan into submission, but further disorders erupted in 1904. The deaths of Achin women and children provoked much disapproval in the Netherlands and worked against Kuyper's prospects for re-election.[21]

Another issue that perplexed Kuyper as the election of 1905 approached was the matter of suffrage. Broadening the electorate had led Savornin Lohman to withdraw from the Anti-Revolutionary Party in 1894, and the Christian Historical Union eventually developed from that schism as a rival for Kuyper's party. The exodus of the Historicals did not, at that time, hurt the Anti-Revolutionaries much, because it convinced many strict Calvinists to join Kuyper's movement, but the issue of suffrage remained unresolved. As a professing Christian Democrat, Kuyper made the family the basis for society and politics. He wanted the franchise for heads of families only. He feared that any greater democracy might encourage anarchy, and he argued that universal manhood suffrage had already damaged the United States, Germany and France. Socialists demanded suffrage for all adults, and they never ceased assailing him for suppressing the strike of 1903. Some people disliked him for limiting the sale of alcoholic drinks, and many secularists found his adherence to Calvinistic principles contemptible.[22] Then, too, there were Christians who did not join the Anti-Revolutionary Party, and they resented Kuyper for acting as though his party alone were truly Christian. Within his own government the prime minister's colleagues disliked the manner in which he lectured them as a father might chide naughty children.

The election brought defeat to the confessional coalition. The Roman Catholics retained their seats, but the Anti-Revolutionaries fell from twenty-four seats to fifteen. The Liberals and Socialists were able to win forty-five and seven seats respectively, enough to form a government, and Th. de Meester became prime minister. He remained in office only until 1907, when his government lost a vote of confidence over matters pertaining to national defence. When the defeat of

Kuyper became evident, the journal *De Gids* applauded it as the end of his career and exulted: 'The yoke of Kuyper has been shaken off... For a clerical government there is and can be no longer room in Holland.'[23]

The elder statesman

After vacating the premiership, Kuyper left for a nine-month tour around the Mediterranean Sea. Some of his followers resented his absence in the time of their defeat, and it appears that he lost some credibility as party leader because of it.[24] He remained in politics nevertheless, and in 1909, after the fall of the de Meester cabinet, it appeared that he might once again become prime minister. At that point P. Tideman, a lawyer from Bloemendaal, released some documents from Kuyper's premiership that made it appear that he had been unethical in obtaining funds for the Anti-Revolutionary Party. The former prime minister had broken no laws, but his actions seemed imprudent to some people and his image as a leader suffered accordingly.[25] Queen Wilhelmina then asked Theodorus Heemskerk to become leader of a cabinet composed of Anti-Revolutionaries, Roman Catholics and some non-partisan members.

In order to promote his own political recovery, Kuyper resumed editing *De Standaard.* He supported the Heemskerk government but sometimes criticized it in print. His articles continued to appear in *De Standaard* until the end of 1919 and in *De Heraut* into 1920. His last book was *Anti-Revolutionary Political Science*, which he produced in 1916. He resigned as leader of the Anti-Revolutionary Party in 1920, and gave up his seat in parliament the same year.

By the end of his political career, Kuyper had achieved his goal of 'an equitable public pluralism'. Membership of his party never exceeded twenty per cent of the population, but its

Abraham Kuyper at the age of eighty

coalition with the Catholic People's Party and some minor parties allowed it to exercise leadership in Dutch government long after Kuyper's demise.[26] The confessional coalition under Heemskerk remained in power until 1913, when a Liberal coalition won the election, and P. W. A. Cort van Linden became prime minister. It was fortunate for the kingdom that the new premier wanted to conciliate the Christian parties, and he did so by calling for a revision of the constitution that would allow for pluralism in education; that is, state funding for private as well as public schools, a cause dear to Kuyper's heart. The law to implement this came into effect in 1920, shortly before Kuyper died.

Although the Netherlands was too small a nation to play a major role in world affairs in the nineteenth and twentieth centuries, Kuyper's political philosophy would not allow him to ignore the international arena, as his efforts to end the war in South Africa demonstrate. He regarded Christ as King of the Universe, so he would not confine his political pronouncements to Dutch matters. Kuyper therefore often commented about the world situation, both through his journalism and while he was in public office. He warned, for example, that British, German and French imperialism in Africa and Asia could lead to war. During the Anglo-Boer War, Germany made intrusive diplomatic moves in southern Africa and expressed moral support for the Boers. Kuyper admired Germany at that point and regarded her as a means to create a new balance of power at Britain's expense. The Dutch people did not, however, favour closer association with Germany, and the queen rebuked him mildly by stating that her nation should remain neutral when disputes occurred among the major powers.

As Franco-German conflicts became intense early in the twentieth century, Kuyper wanted an active foreign policy of a pro-German character. Rumours circulated that he desired his country to adhere to the Triple Alliance, which Germany,

Austria-Hungary and Italy had concluded in 1882. There appears to have been no foundation for such rumours, but Kuyper's disapproval of British imperial policy made them credible at that time. He further demonstrated his dislike for Britain when he urged the Belgians, rulers of the Congo, to resist British expansion in central Africa.[27]

Despite his well-known disdain for British imperialism, some Britons admired Kuyper and valued his opinions, even about their own nation. The Parliament Bill of 1911 was a measure on the part of the Liberal government of Herbert Asquith to eliminate the House of Lords as an effective wing of the legislature. In London the *Daily Telegraph* published a series of articles about the controversy and invited Dr Kuyper to participate in the debate. The same newspaper had earlier praised his efforts to end the war in South Africa, and it cited him as being an authoritative political thinker.

In the requested article Kuyper expressed his preference for a two-house legislature as a safeguard against tyranny, but he held that the whole parliament should represent the entire nation. Neither house should promote the interests of factions only. He disliked the House of Lords because he thought it acted for the aristocrats and the clergy and opposed the interests of common people. Kuyper seemed to think there was a class conflict in British politics, even though the major social reforms of the previous century had been accomplished with the leadership of several distinguished noblemen and wealthy members of the House of Commons.

Kuyper argued that the time when the monarch should select the members of the Upper House had passed. The king should not ally with any political faction, but should be impartial in partisan affairs. The Dutch statesman suggested that the United Kingdom abolish hereditary membership in the House of Lords and require the peers to stand for election by constituencies they would represent, as did members of the Commons.[28]

Britain did not accept this advice. Instead, when the Parliament Bill became law, it deprived the Lords of almost all authority, while leaving it a body composed chiefly of aristocrats, many of whom held their seats by inheritance from their titled parents. The effect of this change was to produce more democracy than even Kuyper desired. After 1912 any bills dealing with finance would become law even without the consent of the Lords. For non-financial bills the Upper House could delay enactment, but three successive votes of the Commons would override even that. As a consequence Great Britain was left with no effective checks and balances in government, since the Commons controls both legislative and executive functions. There could be no preventing the movement towards socialist democracy, which the United Kingdom became by the mid-twentieth century. Kuyper did not live to see this development, but had he done so, he might have regretted the advice he gave to Britain.

In World War I Kuyper expressed support for Germany, as did the faculties at the Universities of Delft and Utrecht, perhaps because memories of the Anglo-Boer War made many Dutchmen anti-British. When the former Boer generals Jan Christian Smuts and Louis Botha supported Britain, Kuyper and many of his countrymen were dismayed.[29]

In 1918 a confessional coalition gained a slim majority over parties of the left, and the Anti-Revolutionaries filled three cabinet positions, but Kuyper expressed concern because Prime Minister C. J. M. Ruys de Beerenbrouck was a Roman Catholic. Kuyper's public remarks weakened the coalition, but the socialist leader Troelstra unintentionally strengthened it. He became excited by socialist victories in Germany and began talking about a Dutch republic with himself as president. This caused all non-socialist parties to support the government. Troelstra boasted that the army and the police were with him, perhaps to frighten the government into submission, but he failed. The cabinet responded to the threat by calling the militia to active duty, and pro-government citizens rallied to support the queen. All non-socialists in the Second Chamber denounced Troelstra. Even within the Social Democratic Workers' Party, Troelstra enjoyed little support. Discredited by his own ambitions, he retreated from his militancy. Christian troops loyal to the government volunteered to suppress disturbances and, when the threat of revolution had subsided, soldiers appeared at the home of Dr Kuyper, where they joined him in a spontaneous service of thanksgiving.

One incident connected with the fear of revolution that caused particular concern occurred in the Dutch Reformed Church. A pastor in Nieuweniedorp, north of Amsterdam, espoused Communism and preached it from his pulpit. This was a strange aberration, but it shows the sad condition of the former National Church at the time. After Dutch socialists renounced revolution, they made large gains among the electorate.[30]

Until his death on 8 November 1920, Abraham Kuyper remained mentally lucid and so maintained a keen interest in the life of the Dutch nation. He was amazingly productive as a writer in his later years, and the Anti-Revolutionary Party promoted his causes long after his demise. His three-volume work *Pro Rege*, originally a series of articles in *De Heraut*, appeared in 1911-12, a tribute to his ceaseless efforts to extol the lordship of Christ over all of life, private and public.[31] In this book, as throughout his career, Dr Kuyper set forth the antithesis between Christianity and humanism and called his readers to submit to Christ's authority. It is fitting that a recent author has referred to Kuyper as the 'Incarnation of the Antithesis'.[32]

17.
A far-reaching legacy

Towards the end of 1919 Abraham Kuyper seemed to realize that his life on earth would soon be over. At the age of eighty-two he became seriously ill but made a remarkable recovery. He continued to work to the best of his ability, and he read to keep informed about developments at home and abroad. Another spell of sickness befell him late in the winter of 1920, but once again he recovered and continued writing articles for *De Heraut*. He could not attend the national convention of the Anti-Revolutionary Party that year, but he was satisfied to learn that the body elected Hendrik Colijn as party chairman. Colijn was a fervent Reformed Christian committed to Anti-Revolutionary principles. When Kuyper was dying Colijn wrote to assure him that the party would maintain his principles. The new chairman said, 'I shall devote all my energies to holding our people to the paths in which you have led us.'[1] Content that his work was finished and that his successors would be faithful in implementing and expanding it, Kuyper passed into eternity. As his will directed, he lies beneath a headstone with this inscription:

DR. A. KUYPER
BORN OCTOBER 29, 1837

AND FALLEN ASLEEP IN
HIS SAVIOUR
NOVEMBER 8, 1920.

Since Kuyper's public career spanned fifty-seven years
(1863-1920), it should surprise no one that his legacy has been
far-reaching to the point where many Christians today are
pleased to identify themselves as Kuyperians. His influence remains strong within Reformed circles, even more so in the United
States, Canada and South Africa than in his native country.
Several of his expositions of Reformed theology are available
in English, as are his Stone Lectures, some of his devotional
writings and occasional essays about specific issues of peren-
nial concern to Christians. Even without a knowledge of the
Dutch language, one may obtain an appreciation of the contributions of God's Renaissance Man.

His influence in the field of apologetics

Kuyper has exerted an especially significant influence upon the
discipline of apologetics — the philosophic defence of the faith
— and in this regard he helped to promote a major departure
from traditional methods. When Kuyper went to Princeton Theological Seminary in 1898, the great Dutch theologian-statesman
was in the company of America's most distinguished advocate
of rationalist-evidentialist apologetics. The renowned Benjamin
B. Warfield (1851-1921) was a vigorous proponent of the belief that the proper way to defend the claims of Christianity is to
demonstrate their reasonableness, and in the process to supply
evidences to validate specific portions of the Bible assailed by
the critics. Warfield wanted to prove the validity of Christianity
before exegesis and systematic theology expounded it. Kuyper,

on the contrary, held that believers do not need proof, and they should proceed with the study of theology as preparation for their contests with the enemies of the faith. In expressing his view of the matter, Dr Kuyper admonished his readers: 'To oppose rationalism by mere counter-argumentation is voluntarily to deprive yourself of the mighty powers the Lord puts into your hands for the purpose of touching the conscience of your antagonists and rousing the enthusiasm of the people in your church.'[2]

Kuyper believed that faith is a prerequisite for all learning. Non-Christians lack *saving* faith, but not faith *per se*. Faith makes scholarship possible because belief about things always precedes examination of the evidence. Scientists, for example, examine only a tiny part of the available data but from such examinations conclude that the laws of science are universally true. This is a demonstration of their faith, without which their enquiries would not be possible. All scholars proceed with their arguments on the basis of axioms which are expressions of their faith. They assume these axioms are valid. Faith makes learning possible, and reason progresses from it to more learning.

As a Reformed theologian, Dr Kuyper realized that sin has had debilitating effects upon the human mind. These noetic effects of sin prejudice people against the claims of God's Word and lead them to assume a posture of autonomy as they stand before it. Unbelievers are therefore unaware of their own spiritual depravity, so they do not appreciate their lack of competence to judge God's claims upon them. Even when Christian and non-Christian thinkers agree about particular phenomena in creation, they disagree about principles, such as the doctrine of creation itself, because they approach the study of the world with mutually opposing assumptions. The special revelation of God in Scripture is essential for the correct understanding of all created things, and regeneration by the power of the Holy Spirit is necessary before anyone can accept the authority of that revelation. Because humans are sinners, they cannot test divine revelation. Revelation is, nevertheless, ultimate because it comes from God and so is not subject to human judgement.[3]

Warfield thought that apologetics would be a major influence in the Christian conquest of the world as preparation for the post-millennial return of Christ. He believed Christianity would '*reason* its way to dominion ... and it is solely by reasoning that it will put all its enemies under its feet'.[4] Kuyper did not share that belief about eschatology. He expected the antithesis between the City of God and the City of This World to continue until Christ returns and defeats all enemies by his personal intervention, so the realm of scholarship would remain a battleground until then. Kuyper crisply summarized his position about apologetics when he exclaimed, 'Do not exhaust your strength in attacking the enemy on his own ground [reason]; this is doomed to failure!'[5] Such declarations and the foundational principles from which they proceeded excited the interest of Cornelius Van Til (1895-1987), a Dutch-born American theologian educated at Princeton Theological Seminary, who became one of the founders of Westminster Theological Seminary in Philadelphia. Van Til, a Ph.D. from Princeton University, became an appreciative but not uncritical disciple of Kuyper, one who analysed, expanded and applied Kuyper's arguments. Van Til thereby became the most distinguished advocate of what is known as presuppositional apologetics, for which his seminary is duly famous.[6]

This is not the place to analyse Van Til's system, but it is appropriate to mention Kuyper's influence upon him, because the presuppositional approach to apologetics has become a potent school of thought, the teachings of which now extend well beyond traditional circles of Reformed belief. Proponents of the traditional rationalist-evidentialist apologetics find the presuppositional approach disturbing, especially because its influence appears to be spreading.[7]

To cite Abraham Kuyper as the foundational figure in the development of presuppositional apologetics is accurate but might be misleading nevertheless. Van Til and his followers have gratefully accepted Kuyper's contributions, but they have found significant flaws in his defence of the faith. They concur enthusiastically that Scripture enables believers to understand general revelation, and that it is the first principle of theology. All other conclusions must be derived from it, and Scripture is self-attesting. Humans are not entitled to pass judgement upon it. Presuppositionalists do not, however, follow Kuyper in practically dismissing the value of apologetics, at least for reasoning with unbelievers.

Warfield feared that Kuyper's attitude towards reason might lead to an irrational subjectivism. Warfield argued that Christian faith has specific content — Christians do not believe irrationally. He contended forcefully for the rational character of Christian belief and showed from Scripture that sinful minds suppress the truth of God's being, which confronts them through general revelation. The Princeton scholar's error, which Kuyper corrected, was his assumption that human reason, in spite of the noetic effects of sin, is competent to understand general revelation without preceding regeneration by the Holy Spirit. Warfield, in the judgement of presuppositionalists, failed to assign sufficient weight to humanity's ethical alienation from God. Kuyper, on the other hand, assigned too much weight to human depravity in that he saw little value in the intellectual defence of the Christian faith.[8]

Kuyper appeared at times to be ambivalent about the noetic effects of sin. Although he postulated a radical antithesis between regenerate and unregenerate scholarship and stressed the influence of their contradictory world-views, he thought that unregenerate scholars could apply their minds to external or exact sciences without experiencing the noetic effects of sin. Van Til and his school of apologists vigorously deny this.[9] They agree heartily with Kuyper that evidences which support the claims of Christianity will not, by themselves, convince unbelievers. Unregenerate minds reject the principles that constitute the basis of the faith, so they reject the evidences as well. Apologetics is, then, a contest between principles, not only an argument about evidences.[10]

His dislike for arguing with unbelievers notwithstanding, Abraham Kuyper was a fervent apologist for biblical Christianity, as his entire career demonstrates clearly. He was at times intemperate, even acidic, in asserting his position, but he conveyed some advice that was better than some of his actions. In his judgement, when fundamental principles are at stake, Christians must defend them, but 'Bitterness, ill-will, malice, and love of dispute should never characterize a Christian in his defence of the truth... When peace is injurious to the truth, peace must give way. Peace with God is of greater value than peace with men.'[11]

In all dealings with unbelievers Kuyper advised Christians to display concern for the eternal well-being of those with whom they are in disagreement. He said, 'Enter into their condition; show them not your wisdom but your heart[s]. Always show them that you care about their eternal salvation.'[12]

His contribution to thinking about education and culture

In addition to his important influence upon the principles and practices of apologetics, Dr Kuyper made a monumental contribution to Christian thinking about culture. As this study has already shown, his doctrine of common grace leads to a profound appreciation for the creation, and it calls believers to implement the requirements of the cultural mandate (Genesis 1:28). Kuyper's Stone Lectures of 1898 expound this concept in a systematic, substantial manner. On the basis of his understanding of the cultural mandate, Kuyper decried the tendency to retreat from the world into enclaves of believers in order to find protection from evil, as many Anabaptists of the Reformation era had done, and as some of their spiritual descendants continue to do. Kuyper maintained that Christians must strive 'to push the development of this world to an even higher stage, and to do this in constant accordance with God's ordinance, for the sake of God, upholding in the midst of so much painful corruption everything that is honourable, lovely, and of good report among men'.[13]

One way in which Christians can promote the healthful development of culture is to work in the arts and sciences for God's glory and in so doing to confer benefits upon humanity. Kuyper believed that Calvinists are in the best position to lead such efforts because of their complete confidence in God's sovereignty over all he has made. Kuyper remarked, 'The Calvinistic dogma of predestination [is] the strongest motive ... for the cultivation of science.' This dogma affirms one universal principle that governs everything, and thereby it 'forces upon us the confession that there must be stability and regularity ruling over everything'. Without predestination an orderly universe would be impossible. Calvinists maintain that God's decrees form 'one organic programme of the entire creation and the entire history'.[14]

Dr Kuyper's commitment to divine sovereignty, and to human responsibility to implement the cultural mandate, led him to establish the Free University of Amsterdam. It was not just a school of theology and obviously not an institute of technology. Since, in Kuyper's view, all of life is religion, human beings must pursue truth in all disciplines, and Kuyperians have concurred with this dictum of their mentor by establishing Christian schools on all levels of instruction to explore the wonders of creation for the honour of the Creator. Calvin College in Michigan, Dordt College in Iowa, and Trinity Christian College in

Illinois all embraced Kuyper's holistic concept of culture, and some colleges outside the Reformed tradition have also realized the necessity of teaching all subjects from the perspective of Scripture. Then, too, Kuyperians began an Association for Reformed Scientific Studies in 1956, and in 1967 an Institute for Christian Studies opened in Toronto. This organization has not maintained strict adherence to the Reformed faith, but the inspiration which led to its foundation came from Kuyper's legacy.

Although Christian colleges that adhere to the Reformed faith perpetuate in some measure the legacy of Abraham Kuyper, no institution comparable to the Free University of Amsterdam exists in the United States. In South Africa, however, Kuyperians did establish Potchefstroom University for Christian Higher Education, modelled on the Free University, and it became the nucleus for the creation of Christian schools at all levels.

It is ironic that Kuyper's university, which he hoped would inspire the founding of comparable institutions in other lands, has for the most part abandoned his theology and his world-view. By the end of the Second World War the drift away from its foundations was becoming evident. There was no chair of philosophy at the Free University until 1926, when Herman Dooyeweerd and D. H. T. Vollenhoven joined the faculty. These scholars, at least to some extent, attempted to apply Kuyper's concepts in their construction of a Calvinistic philosophy, but theologians at the university resisted such endeavours.[15] Later Johan H. Bavinck and G. C. Berkouwer came to dominate the faculty of theology, and they gained the respect of an increasingly secular department of philosophy by accepting its critique of theology. Even before that occurred, Leendert Bouman, professor of psychology, had been lecturing approvingly about the theories of Sigmund Freud. By 1960, when it was receiving state funding, a large number of the 12,000 students at the Free University expressed no allegiance to the Christian faith.

In 1971 the institution discarded its commitment to Calvinism but declared it would keep the gospel of Christ as the basis for its teaching. The university Kuyper had founded to combat secular humanism had become humanistic itself within ninety years of its opening. In the realm of higher education Kuyper's influence is stronger in North America and in South Africa than in his homeland.[16]

The decline of his university notwithstanding, Kuyper's call for the subjection of all thinking to the authority of God's Word continues to command an international following. The concepts of the antithesis and common grace are flourishing in the works of scholars who appreciate his legacy. Louis Berkhof (1873-1957), once President of Calvin Theological Seminary, tried to implement Kuyper's idea for separate Christian organizations in education, trade unions, social agencies, etc. Although his work enjoyed but little success, it demonstrates the deep impression that Kuyper had made in the United States. Berkhof was a prolific writer of Reformed theology, and his works reflect the influence of Kuyper.[17]

The current popularity of Christian schools in America would have pleased Dr Kuyper, even though many of the people who operate them are not aware of his pioneering efforts in that realm. The persistence of Reformed believers in maintaining parent-controlled Christian schools shows the ongoing significance of Kuyper's teaching about sphere authority. By denying the state the opportunity to dictate what their children will learn, Christian parents are asserting their own authority over the sphere of education.[18]

In the area of Christian scholarship the influence of Abraham Kuyper remains strong, as his recent disciples have interpreted the creation in the light of divine revelation. This is evident, for example, in the writings and films of Francis A. Schaeffer (1912-84), who, like Kuyper, had the ability to communicate with common people as well as with other scholars. Schaeffer's book *How Should we then Live?* and the film series of the same title call Christians to obey the cultural mandate on the basis of common grace while maintaining a systematic antithesis in opposing anti-Christian world-views.[19]

In 1887 Abraham Kuyper produced an improved edition of John Calvin's *Institutes of the Christian Religion* and included Theodore Beza's life of Calvin with it. His intention was to promote a return to the Reformed faith at a time when most clergymen had imbibed anti-biblical philosophies. In 1960, when American Calvin scholars John T. McNeill and Ford Lewis Battles rendered the *Institutes* into a new English version, they used an 1891 reprint of Kuyper's Latin edition as their text. As a consequence, those who study Calvin's masterpiece in this edition owe a debt to Kuyper, although they might not be aware of it.[20]

Under the influence of Kuyper's concept of social justice, Reformed believers in the United States established Christian mental hospitals in Michigan and New Jersey and one for tuberculosis patients in Colorado. They opened homes for the care of elderly people as well.

A legacy lost

Although Kuyper spent many years in politics, he always loved his church and remained a champion of her interests. The secession of 1886 and the union of 1892 produced the Reformed Churches in the Netherlands, and credit for the success of those movements belongs largely to Kuyper for his dynamic leadership. Developments within that body since his demise have not, however, preserved his legacy. The same critical attitude towards Scripture that earlier infected the Dutch Reformed Church appeared in the Netherlands Reformed Churches as well. Parallel with the defection from Kuyper's teachings at the Free University of Amsterdam there occurred corresponding changes in the church he loved and served so well. His church eventually adopted a synodal government comparable to that of the former National Church which its founders had renounced. Spiritual and doctrinal declension became evident after World War II, and the Netherlands Reformed Churches now have fraternal relations with the Dutch Reformed Church, and eventual reunion appears to be likely. To genuine Kuyperians this amounts to a repudiation of their mentor and of his Saviour, a defection that gives reason for another *Doleantie*.

Confusion within the Reformed churches during the German occupation (1940-45) led to very detrimental consequences. A Dutch Nazi Party had formed before the war, and about 8,000 members of the Netherlands Reformed Churches affiliated with it, even though the synod of that body denounced the Nazi movement in 1936. During the war Kuyper's grandson Willem joined the German SS and died while fighting on the eastern front. Willem's father, Dr H. H. Kuyper, discouraged the Netherlands Reformed Churches from taking disciplinary action against church members who supported the Nazis.[21]

Another casualty among Kuyper's causes was his newspaper *De Standaard*. This was due to its failure to resist the Nazi occupation regime during the Second World War. Because *De Standaard* cited the German rulers as constituting a lawful government, the paper lost credibility and impaired the work of the anti-German underground movement. After the war the Dutch government forbade publication of *De Standaard*.[22] *Trouw (Fidelity)* was its would-be successor, but it assumed an ecumenical rather than a Reformed posture, and its political pronouncements were often favourable to socialism.

The movement towards the left in Dutch education, religion and journalism occurred in politics, too, and had very damaging consequences for the Anti-Revolutionary Party. When the party obtained public funds for private schools, it agreed to accept universal suffrage, a democratic goal of the socialists, so the most determined enemies of Kuyper gained in the long run because of a concession from the Anti-Revolutionaries that encouraged popular sovereignty. Some Christians complained that the Anti-Revolutionary Party had discarded the antithesis in order to gain political influence. Whatever immediate gain public funding of private schools had produced, one eventual effect was to strengthen the socialists.

Eventually some intellectuals within the Anti-Revolutionary Party argued that Kuyper's concept of the antithesis was no longer applicable, and they advocated accommodations to modern culture as the basis for their programmes. The same attitude encouraged co-operation between the Dutch Reformed and the Netherlands Reformed churches. Within the Christian Historical Union, too, younger leaders denied the antithesis and called for broad collaboration with Social Democrats, liberal Catholics and secular humanists. Dr Kuyper had been able to maintain his doctrine of common grace without sacrificing the antithesis, but some of his heirs abandoned the antithesis and appealed to common grace as justification for doing so.[23] Some people who claimed to be disciples of Kuyper ignored his emphasis upon personal piety and made their Christianity largely a matter of seeking political and social goals by whatever means were at hand, without regard for biblical principles.[24]

The schisms that occurred within the Anti-Revolutionary Party saddened Kuyper, and they continued after his death. In 1961 his party issued a statement of principles which affirmed divine sovereignty in the manner that Kuyper had taught. By 1975, however, the party Groen and Kuyper had founded showed little attachment to their principles. Winning elections had become its priority, and in 1980 it merged with the Catholic People's Party to form the Christian Democratic Appeal. To Kuyper's heirs the antithesis no longer mattered. In the troubled period after World War II a Dutch National Movement had called for an end to confessional politics and Christian social and labour organizations because such movements were deemed divisive. Many Christians responded positively, perhaps because they thought that would hasten recovery from the damage of the war. Synthesis replaced antithesis in their thinking, and the result was the end of the road for some of Kuyper's most cherished projects.

Although most of the organized expressions of Abraham Kuyper's Neo-Calvinism have not endured, his influence remains powerful among Reformed Christians in various countries, for there are still thousands of believers who stand ready at all times to declare with their mentor: 'God's majesty and sovereignty require that we believe God's Word, not because of what it says, but because *it is his Word*, not because we think it beautiful and true, but because *he has spoken it*.'[25]

18
Conclusion and critiqu e

Abraham Kuyper was, is, and will remain, a controversial figure. His deep convictions, amazing energy and assertive manner impressed people powerfully, whether they regarded him as a champion of their faith or as a dangerous threat to their entire view of life. No one in the public life of the Netherlands could afford to ignore Dr Kuyper. People were for him or against him, but they were not apathetic towards him. Although some of his cherished projects have not endured, as an exponent and defender of orthodox Christianity he stands among the giants of the faith. Even though secular humanism appears to be in the ascendant at the start of the twenty-first century, Neo-Calvinists continue to assert Kuyper's principles and to call all Christians to apply their faith to the whole of life, to proclaim the kingship of Christ over all creation.

Kuyper's teaching distorted to justify apartheid

Efforts to apply Kuyper's Calvinistic principles have continued to provoke debates about the wisdom and appropriateness of his concepts. This became especially evident in South Africa, where advocates of apartheid, separate development of the races, sometimes invoked the idea of sphere authority in support of their ideology. Some Afrikaners regarded themselves as the only true Calvinists, while they distorted Kuyper's teaching to promote a civil religion of Afrikaner nationalism. Within the South African National Party some leaders aspired to make it a movement like the Anti-Revolutionary Party of the Netherlands, but loyalty to nationalism was the priority for the party membership in general.

Neo-Calvinism became prominent within South Africa during the 1930s because many Afrikaner theologians and pastors studied at the Free University of Amsterdam. Some of them found the concept of sphere authority an ideal instrument with which to sanctify Afrikaner nationalism in opposition to British domination and the rising potential for black political power. Kuyper never designated a particular ethnic group *(volk)* as a sphere, but some South African theologians did so, nevertheless.

Part of the difficulty in appraising the influence of Kuyper upon South African nationalists is due to ambiguity in his pronouncements about South Africa. In his Stone Lectures Kuyper hailed the United States as a melting-pot of ethnic groups, and he cited the 'commingling of blood' as a healthful development, one of which Calvinism approves.[1] In *The South African Crisis*, however, he extolled the Boers for their defence of Dutch ethnicity as well as the Reformed faith, and he charged the blacks with a racism of their own, a 'racial passion' that American Negroes continued to express. He knew that the Boers regarded blacks as inferior peoples whom they did not think it possible to elevate to equality with whites. Kuyper did not believe that black people are inherently inferior, but he observed that their culture in Africa was inferior to that of Europe and America, where the influence of Christianity has been strong for centuries. Although he disliked the Boer attitude towards the blacks, Kuyper argued that Boer influence was having a civilizing effect upon the tribes of South Africa.[2]

The lack of clarity in Kuyper's statements about South Africa's racial situation led to conflicting applications of his theology. A. P. Treurnicht, an Afrikaner zealot, cited Kuyper in support of his contention that a special *Afrikaner Volksgees* (national spirit) made the Boers a separate people.[3] This kind of argument became especially pronounced after the Anglo-Boer War, when Afrikaners came to believe that the preservation of their identity required separation from other ethnic groups. When Britain tried to impose the English language upon the schools, the Boers concluded that their fears were appropriate. Their churches in general rallied to the support of Afrikaner identity. The National Party and the Reformed churches became custodians of a culture threatened by Britons and Bantus. It became common then to employ Kuyper's teaching to validate separate political and social development as essential for Afrikaner survival.[4] A thorough study of Kuyper's writings in the context of those times shows, however, that he desired South African Christians to evangelize the Bantus and to promote their cultural development so that they would eventually attain to equality with the whites.[5] Kuyper had always contended for equality before the law, a point of view that negates racism and the injustice that it produces.

Afrikaners did not follow Kuyper in forming a Christian political party. Instead they adapted his teachings to support their civil religion through the National Party. Reformed Christians, with some exceptions, did not protest against apartheid because they thought that policies pertaining to race belonged to the sphere of the state, so churches should not become involved. Unlike Kuyper, those who thought in that way refrained from assuming a prophetic posture towards injustice.[6] Many Afrikaner nationalists, in their desire to preserve apartheid, assigned far more authority to the state than Kuyper would have deemed legitimate. In that way they violated his doctrine of sphere authority.[7]

Questions raised concerning his theology

While some interpreters of Abraham Kuyper dispute the significance of his teachings for South Africa, others point to flaws in
his theology. Although Kuyper was a fearless champion of historic orthodoxy, he maintained some points of doctrine that do
not accord with the Reformed tradition and, as a consequence,
there have been critics of Kuyper who contend that he was not
truly Reformed. The areas of dispute are: supralapsarianism,
justification from eternity, and regeneration and Baptism.
Although I have found no one who has raised the issue about
Kuyper's concept of *Sola Scriptura*, I would add it to the list of
controversial beliefs.

Supralapsarianism

Supralapsarianism is a particular interpretation of the doctrine
of predestination that does not find expression in the Three
Forms of Unity, that is, the *Belgic Confession*, the *Heidelberg
Catechism* and the *Canons of Dort*, or in any other Reformed
confessions of faith, although some noteworthy Reformed theologians have espoused it. Kuyper knew the history of doctrine
well, so he realized he was not alone in his understanding of
this rather obscure question.

In the late sixteenth and early seventeenth centuries, when
the Dutch Reformed Church experienced much agitation due
to the Arminian Remonstrance, Franz Gomarus (1563-1641)
had defended Calvinism against the Arminians. In doing so he
set forth the supralapsarian view of predestination as it pertains
to divine decrees. The debate with the Arminians was only the
beginning of the controversy, for disagreement remains within
Reformed circles even today.

Supralapsarians believe that, when God decreed to create
humanity, he ordered a sequence of events that would have to
come to pass. According to this view, that sequence is as follows: God decided (1) to elect some people whom he would
create for everlasting life and to reject others; (2) to create humanity; (3) to allow the fall into sin; (4) to provide a Saviour for
his chosen ones; (5) to send his Holy Spirit to apply redemption to his elect.

Although Gomarus' defence against the Arminians succeeded
in repelling their challenge to the Dutch Reformed Church, the
canons of the Synod of Dort did not affirm his supralapsarianism.
A different view of the sequence of events that accomplish the
divine decree became dominant in Reformed theology, a position known as infralapsarianism. In this understanding of predestination the sequence is as follows: God decided (1) to create the human race; (2) to allow the Fall; (3) to choose some
people from among the fallen race for salvation and to leave
the others to perish in their sins; (4) to send a Redeemer for his
elect; (5) to send his Holy Spirit to apply redemption to the
elect.[8]

A prominent objection to the supralapsarian view is that it
appears to make God the author of sin, although adherents to
that position have always denied that implication of their belief. Kuyper, of course, never suggested that God is responsible
for sin but, by embracing the supralapsarian doctrine, he incurred that criticism.

It is ironic that the champion of Neo-Calvinism did not concur with his own mentor in this regard. John Calvin taught
infralapsarianism. He held that God loves the entire human
race, and common grace is an expression of his love, even to
the non-elect.[9] Because Calvin and historic Reformed theology
have upheld the infralapsarian position, Kuyper's view of this
matter seemed odd in his day, and it somewhat diminished his

credibility among strict Calvinists. The Christian Reformed Church in America debated this issue vigorously at times but did not accept Kuyper's teaching.[10]

Not only did Dr Kuyper maintain a non-traditional view of predestination, he espoused it tenaciously and contended that the other view denigrates God and had led to heretical beliefs. This attitude was sometimes pronounced in Kuyper's relations with other Reformed thinkers who did not share his perspective on particular points of doctrine. Kuyper, in this matter, imposed a logical construction on a mysterious subject that Scripture leaves unexplained. The Bible does not reveal God's precise relationship to sin, but supralapsarians purport to explain it anyway.[11]

Justification

The second interpretation that has placed Kuyper at odds with his colleagues in the Reformed tradition is his understanding of justification through faith alone, the doctrine on which Martin Luther said the church would stand or fall. While Kuyper concurred with Luther's contention, he maintained a belief about justification that has never received endorsement in any major Protestant confession of faith. Kuyper's peculiar view appears in his great book *The Work of the Holy Spirit*, in a chapter entitled 'Justification from Eternity'.[12]

In his zeal to affirm God's sovereignty over salvation, Kuyper emphasized that justification, God's judicial declaration that he has accepted elect sinners as righteous, proceeds from his own will without regard to human merit, actual or foreseen. With this conviction all Reformed Christians agree, but Kuyper deduced from this belief the conclusion that the justification of the elect took place in eternity before God created his chosen people. Just as God imputed the guilt of Adam to Adam's unborn posterity, so the Creator has imputed the righteousness of Christ to his elect, even before he created them. In Kuyper's words, 'The Sacred Scripture reveals justification as an *eternal* act of God, i. e., an act which is not limited by any moment in the human existence.'[13] In other words, justification occurred in eternity, even though the elect would not become aware of their righteous standing before God until, through faith, they embrace Christ. Conversion then marks the point at which believing sinners experience a consciousness of their justification. Kuyper made his view of this explicit when he wrote, 'It is ... evident that the sinner's justification need not wait until he is converted, nor until he has become conscious, nor even until he is born.'[14]

Despite Kuyper's claim that justification from eternity is the teaching of Scripture he did not, in his book about the Holy Spirit, cite any biblical texts to support his interpretation. Most Reformed Bible scholars contend that there is no biblical warrant for this doctrine. Reformed theologians hold that, while election occurred in eternity, other aspects of the *ordo salutis* (the sequence of events in salvation) take place in time as parts of an individual's spiritual experience. Regeneration, justification and sanctification, for example, flow from eternal election, but they occur in this temporal sequence. Dr Kuyper's understanding of this matter appears to have been due to his unwitting attachment to deductive logic in the manner of medieval Scholastic philosophers, scholars he often criticized for indulging in speculation.

Baptism and regeneration

While Kuyper's teaching about supralapsarianism and justification from eternity have aroused criticism from within the Reformed community, his peculiar position on regeneration and baptism has been even more controversial. In the tradition of the Protestant Reformation, Kuyper believed that infant baptism is a sign and seal that the one baptized is a member of the community of God's covenant people. Baptism is the New Testament successor to Old Testament circumcision. Reformed theologians have not, however, assumed that those the church baptizes as infants have been regenerated by the Holy Spirit. Just as circumcision did not guarantee salvation for people in Old Testament times, so baptism is no assurance of a preceding regeneration. Kuyper, nevertheless, advanced a doctrine of *presumed* regeneration as the basis for baptism.

In contrast with Roman Catholicism, which teaches that baptism itself produces regeneration, the Reformed faith does not attribute such power to that sacrament. Regeneration is, in Reformed belief, a sovereign operation of the Holy Spirit by which he applies the grace of the new life to his elect. With this Kuyper heartily agreed, as when he wrote, 'He who is not born again cannot have a substantial knowledge of sin, and he who is not converted cannot possess certainty of faith; he who lacks the *testimonium Spiritus Sancti* [witness of the Holy Spirit] cannot believe in the Holy Scriptures.'[15]

Together with Reformed theologians across the centuries, Abraham Kuyper maintained that baptism *per se* does not regenerate, but he taught that it is a sign and seal of a regeneration that has already taken place by a work of the Holy Spirit.[16] To support this interpretation Kuyper cited the case of John the Baptist. The Gospel of Luke states that Mary, the mother of Jesus, while still pregnant with the Christ child, visited her cousin Elizabeth, who was expecting the birth of John, and when Mary met Elizabeth, her cousin reported that her unborn child 'leaped in my [Elizabeth's] womb for joy' (Luke 1:39-45). Kuyper took this to mean that John had been regenerated while yet in his mother's womb, so the Holy Spirit may, at his pleasure, perform the work of the new birth for his chosen people even before they are born physically. It is therefore appropriate to baptize children of Christian parents on the presumption that they have been born again.[17]

One difficulty with Kuyper's doctrine which other Reformed scholars have perceived is that it seems to diminish, or even to eliminate, the role of God's Word as an instrument of the Holy Spirit to effect regeneration. If spiritual birth occurs before an infant's baptism, then that child is regenerated by a direct act of the Holy Spirit, and the Word of God is not involved. Kuyper may have failed to see this implication of his belief, because he did at times connect the Word with regeneration.[18] His critics have often pointed to the doctrine of presumed regeneration as a serious flaw in Kuyper's theology, one which may reflect another evidence of his reliance upon Scholastic deductive reasoning in a case where Scripture offers no explicit support for his position. The logic of Kuyper's argument could lead to the conclusion that people who were 'baptized' as infants but later deny Christ were not truly baptized at all, because there is no evidence of regeneration. Kuyper must have realized that this description applies to large numbers of people within Christian churches.[19]

Even though Dr Kuyper's understanding of regeneration and baptism is highly speculative, it quickly gained acceptance in the Reformed Churches in the Netherlands, perhaps because of his stature as its most eminent scholar. In 1905 the synod of that church body issued a proclamation to clarify its position about this matter. Article 158 of the *Acts* of that synod declares: 'According to the confession of our churches, the seed of the covenant, by virtue of the promise of God, is to be considered regenerated and sanctified in Christ, until the contrary should become evident from their doctrine and conduct, as they grow up.'[20]

Abraham Kuyper did make the necessary distinction between regeneration as a work of the Holy Spirit in which the recipients are passive, and conversion, a conscious experience of grace in which they respond with faith and repentance. He therefore called on pastors to summon all baptized persons to repentance. This is a message pastors must address to their whole congregations, and they must realize that the non-elect within them will not respond.[21] It appears, therefore, that Kuyper thought his presumption about the regenerate state of baptized infants would, at least in some cases, be mistaken.

The doctrines of supralapsarianism, justification from eternity and presumed regeneration put Dr Kuyper at odds with historic Reformed teachings, and despite his great stature as a defender of the faith, many scholars and pastors in various Reformed church bodies have rejected his peculiar views about these matters. Kuyper's willingness to separate the grace of regeneration from the Word of God was, and is, especially objectionable to most orthodox Reformed believers, many of whom think it was his most serious error.

A tendency towards mysticism

When an author decides to write about the life and work of some great person, admiration for that person is often the motive, as is true of the author of this volume. Admiration is appropriate, but uncritical approbation is not. Kuyper made no pretence about being above error, and it should surprise no one that his mistakes were damaging to the cause he loved and served so well. In the interest of objectivity, it is therefore proper to expose his flaws and to examine one that seems to have escaped the notice of even his most outspoken critics. The error in question pertains to Kuyper's inconsistency with regard to *Sola Scriptura*, the sole authority of Scripture, which is the bedrock principle of the Reformed faith.

Abraham Kuyper's confidence in the entire trustworthiness of the Bible is obvious throughout his writings. It was because of attacks upon the Bible that he assumed leadership of the Reformed movement and invested his whole career in defending it. Kuyper loved Scripture and never, after his conversion, doubted that its message is the very Word of God. In theology, education, journalism, social theory, government and public policy, he strove to implement biblical principles, so he deserves recognition as one of the greatest exponents and defenders of Christianity. There was, nevertheless, in his thinking an evident proclivity towards mysticism which sometimes led him to make decisions and to issue pronouncements incompatible with his fervent espousal of *Sola Scriptura*. Although this profound Christian thinker disavowed any claim to extra-biblical revelation, his writings contain statements that appear to be just that.

Mystics purport to enjoy direct communication with God apart from, or in addition to, the ordinary means of general and special revelation. Kuyper sometimes warned believers about the dangers inherent in mystical practices, but an inclination towards such practices is apparent in his own life. This is especially so in his book *Near unto God*, a warm-hearted expression of his deep love for his Lord that Kuyper published in 1918. There he asserted a strong belief that individual Christians may receive messages directly from God, who 'from the throne of his glory can look down upon us and can whisper to us in the soul'.[22] He held that Christians acquire a knowledge of God by 'the understanding, feeling and imagination'.[23] Moreover, Kuyper seems to have suggested that believers today may hear the voice of God in the way that Jacob did when he wrestled with a heavenly messenger and concluded that he had seen the face of God (Genesis 32:22-31).[24]

It seems strange that, in the same book which contains the expressions quoted above about subjective guidance, Kuyper

denied that such direction was any longer available. He argued
that God did not ordain continuing revelation in the manner by
which he spoke to the biblical prophets and apostles: 'This does
not mean ... that now God cannot give anyone personal leading and direction. But nothing more is added to revelation. To
the truth as it has been revealed there is no augmentation, and
sickly mysticism that imagines this is still possible has not been
able these nineteen centuries to add a line to the Scriptures.'[25]

Were statements about receiving personal messages from
God confined to only one of Kuyper's books, it might be proper
to conclude that they appeared in a time of personal crisis and
that they do not reflect his overall understanding about, and
application of, *Sola Scriptura*. A careful review of his writings
across the span of his career will, however, show that he maintained a mystical posture towards divine revelation. For
example, in 1874, when he was uncertain about becoming
a member of parliament, Kuyper wrote to Groen van Prinsterer,
'I have never taken weighty decisions of this kind without receiving a sign from the Lord. That is what has always made my
tone so sure and my step so steady. I would usually receive
such a sign only at the acme of my spiritual strain. You understand that waiting of the soul, do you not? That fear to act
against his [God's] will, to depart from his way and be going
away from him.'[26]

It appears that Dr Kuyper regarded a strong conviction, or a
sense of impulsion, as a revelatory sign from God to direct his
course of action. His own description of this belief indicates
that he resorted to this method of discerning God's will, and it
is clear that he thought other believers had the same access to
divine direction. In his great treatise *The Work of the Holy Spirit*
Kuyper, while extolling Martin Luther and other heroes of Christian history, declared, 'Only he that has ears [spiritual receptiv-
ity] can hear what the Spirit has spoken secretly to these children of God.'[27]

Statements such as those just quoted leave little room for doubt that Kuyper believed in extra-biblical means for ascertaining God's will. He did not, however, identify such divine disclosures as revelation *per se*, nor did he elevate them to a status of equality with Scripture. He called such mystical experiences 'illuminations', not 'inspirations' from God. Inspiration he attributed only to the writers of Scripture as the Holy Spirit imparted truth to them, and 'Inspiration ... is ... an abnormal, temporal, organic process, the fruit of which lies before us in the Holy Scriptures.'[28]

Kuyper often asserted that special revelation is now complete in the Bible,[29] and he did not see any tension between his vigorous affirmation of *Sola Scriptura* and his occasional claims to direct divine guidance. This is difficult to understand, because he had an extensive knowledge of church history, which shows clearly that numerous heresies and pseudo-Christian cults arose because charismatic leaders claimed to know God's will by means of their subjective experiences.[30] Kuyper was neither a heretic nor a cult leader, however.

The continuance of miracles

In addition to his belief about personal illumination, with its implications for the sole authority of Scripture, Kuyper deviated from traditional Reformed belief about the continuance of miracles since New Testament times. Orthodox Christians have always accepted the historicity of all miracles recorded in the Bible, and Kuyper, of course, concurred. Reformed theologians have, however, regarded miracles as temporary phenomena which God performed to support the claims of the apostles until the completion of the New Testament. Miracles occurred only during the era of special revelation, and that era ended with the conclusion of the New Testament.[31]

Kuyper disagreed with conventional Reformed thinking about miracles by asserting that God continues to bestow the supernatural gift of healing, at least to allow Christians to cure 'the sick suffering from nervous and psychological diseases'.[32] Perhaps his own nervous collapse made him think about this matter and led him to attribute his recovery to a miraculous intervention in his life.

Physical healing, too, continues to occur miraculously, Kuyper contended. He taught that when Jesus gave his disciples the gift of healing, he thereby restored the natural human ability Adam and Eve possessed before the Fall.[33] Since there was no sickness before the Fall, Kuyper should have explained this idea more clearly, but he did not. Instead he said, 'This power to heal through prayer is available to us even today. It has not been abrogated.'[34] This is so even though the special purpose of miracles to accredit divine revelation ended with the closure of the apostolic age.[35] It would be interesting to know how he would have assessed the claims of the numerous faith-healers and television evangelists who now profess to exercise miraculous powers.

Implications for the authority of Scripture

Kuyper's affirmation of extra-biblical guidance and his belief that the channels of special revelation remain intact put him at odds with the *Westminster Confession of Faith,* a statement he revered profoundly, one which he appealed to American Presbyterians not to modify. Article I of that confession proclaims *Sola Scriptura* in unequivocal terms by stating that, since Scripture is complete, and 'those former ways of God's revealing his will unto his people being now ceased', therefore, 'The whole counsel of God, concerning all things necessary for his own glory, man's salvation, faith and life, is either expressly set down in Scripture, or by good and necessary consequence may be deduced from Scripture; unto which nothing at any time is to be added, whether by new revelations of the Spirit or traditions of men.'

A major difficulty confronting anyone who believes in extra-biblical guidance and/or post-biblical miracles is the absence of any objective standard by which to judge whether such phe-nomena have occurred. Even Kuyper admitted that satanic in-fluence can lead people astray in this regard, but he could cite no adequate means of verification to apply in situations which he thought warranted divine disclosures, or when extraordi-nary events seemed to be miraculous in character. In this mat-ter Kuyper's practice appears to have conflicted with his own firmly declared principle. He wrote, 'Nothing is further from our minds than to exercise ourselves in things too high for us, or to penetrate into mysteries hid from our view. Where Scrip-ture stops, we shall stop; to the difficulties left unexplained, we shall not add what must be only the result of human folly.'[36]

Relationships with others

Although Abraham Kuyper was a Christian thinker of excep-tional intelligence and faith, he was, of course, a fallible sinner, as he often lamented. It is not realistic to expect perfect consist-ency from him or from any other mortal of Adam's race. When Oliver Cromwell was Lord Protector of England (1653-58), he sat for an official portrait executed by an artist who had earlier painted members of the royal family. Cromwell knew that the artist had flattered his patrons, but the Protector insisted that he appear on canvas as he actually was. He said, 'Omit neither scar nor blemish.' Because of his clear understanding of his own sinfulness, Kuyper would not have wanted anyone to de-pict him otherwise, either in portraits or in print. It is appropriate therefore to conclude these studies of God's Renaissance Man with some observations about his relations with friends and foes.

Dr Kuyper once described the human being, because of the Fall, as 'born without ... original righteousness ... with an impaired body ... with a soul out of harmony with itself ... with a personal ego which is turned away from God'.[37] Saving grace alters the human condition fundamentally, but the effects of sin linger, and the sanctification of believers is only partial so long as they remain in this corrupted world. As a consequence of this condition, even the finest Christians often fail in their personal relationships, and Kuyper was no exception. The strength of his convictions sometimes expressed itself in opinionated, stridently assertive ways that offended even his friends and supporters.

Modesty and mild manners were not characteristics of Kuyper's personality. He saw himself as a warrior in battle against forces of evil, so the antithesis about which he spoke and wrote prolifically was not only a clash of world-views; it was that of soldiers defending all that was dear to them. In the conflict Kuyper was sometimes impatient with those who did not employ his confrontational methods, and offended co-workers were known to forsake the Anti-Revolutionary movement because they found his style of leadership intolerable. His fellow theologian Herman Bavinck resigned from the executive committee of the Anti-Revolutionary Party in 1909 for that reason.

Kuyper understood the imitation of Christ to entail battle for Christ's kingship in all areas of life, and he held that no one could pursue that goal in a passive manner. His associates agreed, but they sometimes found it necessary to rebuke their leader for failing to follow Christ's example of humility and gentleness.[38] There might have been even more such protests, but Kuyper's great popularity in Reformed circles intimidated people who might otherwise have criticized him. When he was old and becoming enfeebled, Kuyper refused to relinquish leadership of the Anti-Revolutionary Party until his physical condition forced him to do so.

An impossible goal?

Dr Kuyper did not claim to be the oracle of the Reformed faith, and he did encourage his students at the Free University to engage in independent study and to develop their own understanding of the faith. His great prestige as a scholar, however, led some of them to regard his teaching as the final word, which negated the need for fresh investigations. This was an unfortunate effect of Kuyper's commanding presence, but one for which he was not responsible. After Kuyper passed from the scene, this tendency declined, and later professors began rejecting some of his concepts, especially his doctrine of the antithesis. As a consequence, the socialism he despised gained the support of many faculty members at his university. Perhaps Kuyper himself unwittingly prepared the way for this development by his frequent calls for state intervention to rectify injustices in society. He assailed the French Revolution for justifying state intrusion into the lives of citizens and for demanding that individuals surrender to the interests of the group. He, however, promoted policies that affirmed society's claims against individual rights. His belief that the state should use taxation to deprive some people so it could endow others is the fundamental premise of socialism. Kuyper's complaints about the ruthless individualism of the capitalists were often appropriate, but he did not find a means to combat it without encouraging an ever-increasing amount of state intervention, with its consequent diminution of personal freedom. Perhaps there is no way to achieve the balance Kuyper desired. Did he pursue an impossible goal?[39]

Restoring a God-centred view

To identify a great leader's faults is not to depreciate his contributions, which, in the case of Abraham Kuyper, were colossal. In the providence of God he was the recipient of exceptional talents, which he employed gratefully for the glory of his Redeemer. In the Italian Renaissance humanists became fascinated with their own abilities, especially in the arts and scholarship. They sought and obtained recognition and material reward for their achievements. With the ancient Greek Protagoras they believed, 'Man is the measure of all things.' Their man-centred world-view reflected their admiration for pagan antiquity, the 'good old days' before Christianity asserted the rights of the triune God to rule his own creatures. Christianity, by contesting ancient humanism, had set forth the antithesis between opposing world-views. By the nineteenth century it appeared that humanism had overcome the influence of the Protestant Reformation and was poised to grasp the victory, but Guillaume Groen van Prinsterer, Abraham Kuyper and the Neo-Calvinists rose to block its path. Biblical Christianity was still alive and vigorous, ready to assert Christ's claim to every inch of his creation.

Renaissance humanists exulted in their man-centredness, but for the most part that meant promoting the pleasures of an artistic and intellectual élite. Abraham Kuyper, God's Renaissance Man, on the contrary, sought to bring all of life into subjection to Christ, and in so doing he sought the well-being of the *kleine luyden*, the little people, whom humanists of the Renaissance often viewed with contempt. In the nineteenth and twentieth centuries humanists eventually came to embrace the common people, and they promoted socialism as the means to satisfy their needs. Kuyper and the Anti-Revolutionaries also sought to meet such needs, but material progress alone was not their goal. As Christians, they sought to prepare people for eternity by encouraging them to turn to Christ and to acknowledge his lordship over their lives and over the entire universe. This means that Christians must never confine their faith within church walls. All of life is religion, so there is no dichotomy between faith and public practices. As Dr Kuyper stated this truth, 'In his Word God absolutely forbids every inclination and every effort to break up your life into two parts, one part for yourself and the other part for him.'[40]

Notes

Preface
1. Frank Vanden Berg, *Abraham Kuyper* (Grand Rapids: William B. Eerdmans Publishing Co., 1960); Louis Praamsma, *Let Christ be King* (Jordan Station, Ontario: Paideia Press, 1985).

Introduction
1. An appropriate critique of Kuyper's doctrine of common grace appears in Cornelis Pronk, 'Neo-Calvinism,' *Reformed Theological Journal,* 11 (1995), pp.42-56. Pronk is more critical than the present writer, but he has raised questions which students of Kuyper should not ignore.

Chapter 1 — Home and heritage
1. A contemporary of Abraham Kuyper referred to his father as 'a man of liberal tendencies'. See Henry Beets, 'Dr. Abraham Kuyper,' *Banner of Truth,* 39 (1904), p.65.
2. Catherine M. E. Kuyper, 'Abraham Kuyper, His Early Life and Conversion,' *International Reformed Bulletin,* 5 (1960), p.21. This is the work of Kuyper's daughter.
3. Abraham Kuyper, *Confidentie: Schrijven aan den Weled. Heer J. Abraham. Van der Linden* (Amsterdam: Höveker & Zoon, 1873), p.35. Translations from *Confidentie* are the work of McKendree R. Langley.
4. Catherine Kuyper, 'Abraham Kuyper,' p.22.
5. Quoted by Kuyper's comrade Witsius Abraham De Savornin Lohman, 'Dr. Abraham Kuyper,' *The Presbyterian & Reformed Review,* IX (1878), p.564.
6. Charlotte M. Yonge, *The Heir of Redcliffe,* 2 vols (New York: Garland Publishing Co., 1975 reprint of 1853 edition).
7. Quoted by De Savornin Lohman, 'Dr. Kuyper,' p.565. The full account of Kuyper's conversion, told by himself, appears in his *Confidentie,* pp.48-53.

Chapter 2 — The fall of a great church
1. A succinct account of these developments appears in Walter Lagerway, 'The History of Calvinism in the Netherlands,' in *The Rise and Development of Calvinism,* ed. John Abraham Bratt (Grand Rapids: William B. Eerdmans Publishing Co., 1959), pp.63-102. For additional coverage see Pieter Geyl, *The Netherlands in the Seventeenth Century,* I (London: Ernest Been, Ltd, 1961).

2. Bernard H. M. Vlekke, *Evolution of the Dutch Nation* (New York: Roy Publishers, 1945), pp.279-38.

3. Kenneth Scott Latourette, *Christianity in a Revolutionary Age,* II (Grand Rapids: Zondervan Publishing House, 1969 reprint of 1959 edition), pp.207-38.

4. D. H. Kromminga, *The Christian Reformed Tradition* (Grand Rapids: William B. Eerdmans Publishing Co., 1943), pp.80-82.

5. The secession that began with de Cock was not actually the first withdrawal from the Dutch Reformed Church. In 1822 a small secession led to the formation of the Restored Church of Christ, which affirmed the Three Forms of Unity. See John H. Kromminga, *'De Afscheiding:* Review and Evaluation,' *Calvin Theological Journal,* 20 (1985), pp.43-57.

6. *Ibid.,* p.45. Extensive coverage of the *Afscheiding* appears in Gerrit J. ten Zythoff, *Sources of Secession* (Grand Rapids: William B. Eerdmans Publishing Co., 1987).

7. Johan G. Westra, 'Abraham Kuyper on Church and State,' *Reformed Review,* 38 (1985), pp.122-3.

8. Jantje Lublegiena van Essen, 'Guillaume Groen van Prinsterer and his Conception of History,' trans. Herbert Donald Morton, *Westminster Theological Journal,* 44 (1982), pp.205-49; Bernard Zylstra, *Who was Groen?* (Grand Rapids: The Groen van Prinsterer Society, 1956). These are concise, insightful studies of this remarkable man.

9. Gerrit Hendrik Hospers, 'Groen van Prinsterer and his Book,' *Evangelical Quarterly,* 7 (1935), p.269.

Chapter 3 — The decline of a great theology

1. Helpful summaries of these schools of thought appear in Louis Praamsma, *Let Christ be King* (Jordan Station, Ontario: Paideia Press, 1985), pp.31-8.

2. Eldred Vanderlaan, *Protestant Modernism in Holland* (London: Oxford University Press, 1924), pp.12-16.

3 James Hutton Mackay, *Religious Thought in Holland during the Nineteenth Century* (London: Hodder & Stoughton, 1911), p.30.

4. *Ibid.,* p.69.

5. Daniel Chantepie de la Saussaye, *La Crise Religieuse en Hollande* (Leiden: De Breuk & Smits, 1860).

6. Praamsma, *Let Christ be King,* pp.34-5. It is interesting that the Ethicals tolerated a broad diversity of beliefs because they held dogma to be of little importance. However, they became highly intolerant of Kuyper when he rose to defend the historic Christian faith.

7. Chantepie, *La Crise,* pp.82ff.; Mackay, *Religious Thought,* pp.112-15.

8. *Ibid.,* pp.128-9.

9. Hendrikus Berkhof, *Two Hundred Years of Theology: Report of a Personal Journey,* trans. John Vriend (Grand Rapids: William B. Eerdmans Publishing Co., 1989), pp.106-7.

10. *Ibid.,* pp.98-9.

11. Vanderlaan, *Protestant Modernism,* pp.45-9; Gustave Thils, 'Abraham Kuyper (1837-1901) Ethicals et la Théologie Protestante aux Pays-Bas,' *Ephemeides Theologicae Louvanienses,* 25 (1949), pp.92-6.

12. Although the writings of most Dutch liberals remain untranslated, some of Kuenen's works are available in English. See his *The Religion of Israel to the Fall of the Jewish State,* trans. Alfred Heath May (London: Williams and Norgate, 1875) and *The Prophets and Prophecy in Israel,* trans. Adam Milroy (London: Longmans, Green, & Co., 1877).

13. Jean Reville, *Liberal Christianity: Its Origin, Nature, and Mission,* trans. Victor Leuiette (New York: G. P. Putnam's Sons, 1903), pp.82-3.

14. *Ibid.,* p.175 (emphasis mine).

Chapter 4 — The rise of a great defence

1. Savornin Lohman, 'Dr. Abraham Kuyper,' p.565.
2. Quoted in Catherine Kuyper, 'Abraham Kuyper,' p.24.
3. Kuyper, *Confidentie*, p.45.
4. *Ibid.*, p.48.
5. Catherine Kuyper, 'Abraham Kuyper,' p.24.
6. McKendree R. Langley, 'A Sketch of Abraham Kuyper's Life,' *Reformed Ecumenical Synod Theological Forum*, XVI (1988), pp.4-8.
7. Some church leaders who heard Kuyper's inaugural sermon at the *Domkerk* thought they discerned traces of his liberal background within it. Even if this were so, he was in the process of discarding them as he grew in his understanding of the Reformed faith and learned to avoid the language he had acquired when a student at Leiden. See Frank Vanden Berg, *Abraham Kuyper* (Grand Rapids: William B. Eerdmans Publishing Co., 1960), pp.46-7.
8. Praamsma, *Let Christ be King*, p.51.
9. Kuyper, *Confidentie*, p.72.
10. Savornin Lohman, 'Dr. Abraham Kuyper,' pp.567-8.
11. Quoted by G. C. Berkouwer, *A Half-Century of Theology*, trans. & ed. Lewis B. Smedes (Grand Rapids: William B. Eerdmans Publishing Co., 1977), p.12.
12. Savornin Lohman, 'Dr Abraham Kuyper,' p.585.
13. *Ibid.*, p.581.
14. McKendree R. Langley, The Legacy of Groen van Prinsterer,' *Reformed Perspective*, 4 (1985), pp.25-8. This is an excellent introduction to Groen's principles.
15. Vlekke, *Evolution of the Dutch Nation*, p.317.
16. The text of this sermon appears in Abraham Kuyper, *Predicatien Door Dr. A. Kuyper* (Kampen, Netherlands: J. H. Kok, 1913), pp.327ff., a book that contains selected messages delivered at Beesd, Utrecht and Amsterdam between 1867-73.
17. Helpful accounts of Kuyper's experiences while a pastor in Amsterdam appear in Praamsma, *Let Christ be King*, pp.56ff, and in Vanden Berg, *Abraham Kuyper*, pp.56-68.
18. Kuyper, *Confidentie*, p.85.
19. *Ibid.*, p.104.
20. *Ibid.*, p.106.
21. *Ibid.*, p.81.

Chapter 5 — Reformation through journalism, education and social action

1. Kuyper, *Confidentie*, p.7.
2. This lecture appears as a chapter in Gerrit Hendrik Hospers, *The Reformed Principle of Authority* (Grand Rapids: The Reformed Press, 1921), pp.15-35.
3. *Ibid.*, p.17.
4. *Ibid.*, p.20. Kuyper's imagery here is a reference to a phenomenon in nature that sometimes occurs on the coast of Sicily, when atmospheric conditions create an illusion of palaces and grazing animals.
5. *Ibid.*
6. *Ibid.*, p.25.
7. *Ibid.*, p.29 (emphasis Kuyper's).
8. *Ibid.*, pp.32-3.
9. McKendree R. Langley, 'The Political Spirituality of Abraham Kuyper,' *International Reformed Bulletin*, 76 (1979), pp.4-9.
10. Groen van Prinsterer, *Unbelief and Revolution*, trans. & eds Henry van Dyke and Donald Morton (Amsterdam: The Groen van Prinsterer Fund, 1953).
11. Interesting coverage of this and related matters appears in Justus M. van der Kroef,

'Abraham Kuyper and the Rise of Neo-Calvinism in the Netherlands,' *Church History,* 17 (1948), pp.316-34.

12. Groen van Prinsterer, *Unbelief and Revolution,* pp.31-4.

13. See J. William. Deenick, 'Christocracy in Kuyper and Schilder,' *The Reformed Theological Review,* 43 (1984), pp.42-50; Jantje Lubbegiena van Essen, 'Guillaume Groen van Prinsterer and his Conception of History,' *Westminster Theological Journal,* 44 (1982), pp.205-49.

14. McKendree R. Langley, 'Groen van Prinsterer: What Does it Mean to be a Christian in the World?' *The Presbyterian Guardian,* 46 (1976), pp.8-9, 12-13.

15. Bernard Zylstra, *Who was Groen?* (Grand Rapids: the Groen van Prinsterer Society, 1956), pp.9-12.

16. For a splendid narrative and analysis of Groen, Kuyper and the Anti-Revolutionary Party, see McKendree R. Langley, *The Practice of Political Spirituality* (Jordan Station, Ontario: Paideia Press, 1984).

17. Vlekke, *Evolution of the Dutch Nation,* pp.316-21.

18. E. H. Kossmann, *The Low Countries, 1780-1940* (Oxford: the University Press, 1978), p.302; Praamsma, *Let Christ be King,* p.74.

19. Kossmann, *Low Countries,* pp.303-5.

20. *Ibid.,* pp.352-5.

21. Succinct coverage of these developments appears in George Edmundson, 'Holland,' in *Cambridge Modern History,* XII, ed. A. W. Ward, *et al.* (Cambridge: The University Press, 1910), pp.243-50.

22. Vlekke, *Evolution of the Dutch Nation,* p.323.

23. Abraham Kuyper, 'Het Penningske der Weduwe,' *De Standaard,* 14 August 1879. A helpful analysis of Kuyper's philosophy of education is Anthony H. Nichols, 'The Educational Doctrines of Abraham Kuyper: an Evaluation,' *Journal of Christian Education Papers,* 52 (1975), pp.26-38.

24. Gordon J. Spykman, 'Pluralism: Our Last, Best Hope?' *Christian School Review,* 10 (1981), pp.99-115.

25. Savornin Lohman, 'Dr. Abraham Kuyper,' pp.572-6; Wilhelm Kolfhaus, *Dr. Abraham Kuyper, 1837-1920: Ein Lebensbericht,* 2nd ed. (Elberfeld, Germany: Buchhandlung des Erziehungs-Vereins, 1925), pp.163-4; W. F. A. Winkel, *Leven en Arbeid van Dr. A. Kuyper* (Amsterdam: W. Ten Have, 1919), pp.68-75; Vanden Berg, *Abraham Kuyper,* pp.101-14; James A. De Jong, 'Hendricus Beuker and De Vrije Kerk on Abraham Kuyper and the Free University,' in *Building the House: Essays on Christian Education,* eds James A. De Jong & Louis Y. van Dyke (Sioux Center, IA: Dordt College Press, 1981), pp.27-46.

26. This is the interesting observation of James D. Bratt, 'Big Ideas, Little People: Theological Education in the Dutch Neo-Calvinist Tradition,' an unpublished lecture delivered at Westminster Theological Seminary in March 1994.

27. Jonathan Z. Smith, *Imagining Religion: From Babylon to Jonestown* (Chicago: the University Press, 1982), pp.102-3.

28. Kolfhaus, *Abraham Kuyper,* pp.167ff.

29. Anthony H. Nichols, 'Abraham Kuyper — a Summons to Christian Vision in Education,' *Journal of Christian Education,* 16 (1973), p.90.

30. Langley, *Political Spirituality,* pp.105-9.

31 For interesting coverage of this matter, see Hendrik van Riessen, *The University and its Basis: Christian Perspectives,* 1963 (St Catherine's, Ontario: Association for Reformed Scientific Studies, 1963), pp.41-51.

32. A tribute to Kuyper's philosophy of education appears in Bernard L. Ramm, *The Christian College in the Twentieth Century* (Grand Rapids: William B. Eerdmans Publishing Co., 1963), pp.73-95.

Chapter 6 — The authority of the spheres
1. Abraham Kuyper, *Sovereiniteit in Eigen Kring* (Amsterdam: J. H. Kruyt, 1880), p.35. An English translation of this speech in unpublished form appears in Wayne A. Kobes, 'Sphere Sovereignty and the University: Theological Foundations of Abraham Kuyper's View of the University and its Role in Society,' Ph. D. dissertation at Florida State University, 1993, pp.281-302. Another translation is on file in typescript at Calvin College without the translator's name being indicated. Quotations from this speech in the present work are taken from both of the above sources, with some slight modifications.
2. *Ibid.*
3. *Ibid.,* pp.9-12.
4 John Locke, *Two Treatises of Government,* ed. Thomas I. Cook (New York: Hafner Publishing Co., 1966); Jean-Jacques Rousseau, *The Social Contract,* trans. Charles Frankel (New York: Hafner Publishing Co., 1947).
5. Abraham Kuyper, 'False Theories of Sovereignty,' *The Independent,* 50 (1898), p.1920. In this article Kuyper succinctly explained his entire philosophy of politics and government.
6. *Ibid.,* pp.1920-21.
7. Edmund Burke, *Reflection on the Revolution in France,* ed. Russel Kirk (New Rochelle, New York: Arlington House). In this exceptionally penetrating analysis Burke predicted that the revolution would produce civil strife and bloodshed within France and imperialistic war against France's neighbours, and that it would lead to military despotism at home. He was right on all points.
8. Kuyper, 'Calvinism: Origin and Safeguard of our Constitutional Liberties,' *Bibliotheca Sacra,* 52 (1895), pp.385-410, 646-75.
9. Van Essen, 'Groen and his Conception of History,' p.241. Cf. James Edward McGoldrick, 'Edmund Burke: Christian Activist,' *Modern Age,* 17 (1973), pp.275-86 for an analysis of Burke's political philosophy and its Christian basis. A helpful comparison of Burke and Groen appears in E. L. Hebden Taylor, *The Christian Philosophy of Law, Politics, and the State* (Nutley, NJ: Craig Press, 1966), pp.222-47.
10. Van Essen, 'Groen and his Conception of History,' p.228.
11. Dirk Jellema, 'Groen van Prinsterer,' *Calvin Forum,* 19 (1954), pp.114-16.
12. Van Dyke, *Groen's Lectures,* p.51. This is an especially valuable work for the way it traces the sources of some of Groen's most significant ideas.
13. *Ibid.,* p.224.
14. Guillaume Groen van Prinsterer, *The Anti-Revolutionary Principle,* trans. J. Faber (Amsterdam: Groen van Prinsterer Society, 1956), pp.33-4.
15. For a keen analysis of this matter see Edward J. Ericson, 'Abraham Kuyper: Cultural Critic,' *Calvin Theological Journal,* 22 (1987), pp.210-27.
16. Kuyper, 'Calvinism: Origin and Safeguard of Liberties,' p.395.
17. Kuyper, 'Christian-Liberal or Christian and Liberal?' *De Standaard,* 13 October 1879.
18. Kuyper, 'The Defeat of England's Conservatives,' *De Standaard,* 7 April 1880; but cf. D. W. Bebbington, *William Ewart Gladstone* (William B. Eerdmans Publishing Co., 1993).
19. Kuyper, 'Calvinism: Origin and Safeguard of Liberties,' pp.396-7.
20. *Ibid.,* pp.388-92.
21. *Ibid.,* p.663.
22. *Ibid.*
23 *Ibid.,* p.656. It appears that Kuyper was not aware that Luther preceded Calvin in so explaining the role of inferior magistrates. See James Edward McGoldrick, *Luther's English Connection* (Milwaukee: Northwestern Publishing House, 1979), pp.182 ff.
24. Kuyper, 'Calvinism: Origin and Safeguard of Liberties,' p.662.
25. *Ibid.,* p.666.

26. *Ibid.*, p.674.

27. Westra, 'Kuyper on Church and State,' p.124. This otherwise fine article asserts the strange conclusion that Kuyper sought a theocracy, while all the evidence points to his acceptance of pluralism.

28. See Henry H. Meeter, *The Basic Ideas of Calvinism,* 5th ed. (Grand Rapids: Baker Book House, 1956), pp.93ff.; for Kuyper's understanding of the Sabbath and the state's responsibility to maintain it, see his *The Lord's Day Observance* (s' Gravenhage, the Netherlands: J. Bootsma, Electrische Boeken Kunstdrukkerij, 1915). *Tractaat van den Sabbath* (Amsterdam: J. A. Wormser, 1890) is a fine specimen of Kuyper's exegetical skill as a practitioner of biblical theology.

29. For an unusual critique of Kuyper on this matter see Raymond O. Zorn, *Church and Kingdom* (Philadelphia: Presbyterian & Reformed Publishing Co., 1962), pp.188-90.

Chapter 7 — Christians as social reformers

1. F. A. Hayek, ed., *Capitalism and the Historians* (Chicago: The University Press, 1954) is an important reply to the argument that industrial capitalism was inherently exploitative.

2. See Henry Ryskamp, 'Calvinistic Action and Modern Economic Problems,' in *God-Centered Living or Calvinism in Action,* Clarence Bouma, *et al.* (Grand Rapids: Baker Book House, 1951), pp.177-97.

3. Dirk Jellema has produced brief but insightful studies of Kuyper's thinking about political economy. See: 'Abraham Kuyper: Forgotten Radical?' *Calvin Forum,* 15 (1950), pp.211-13, 241-2; 'Abraham Kuyper's Attack on Liberalism,' *Review of Politics,* 19 (1957), pp.472-85; 'Abraham Kuyper's Answer to Liberalism,' *Reformed Journal,* 15 (1965), pp.10-14. Cf. Bob Goudzwaard, 'Christian Social thought in the Dutch Neo-Calvinist Tradition,' in *Religion, Economics, and Social Thought,* eds Walter Block and Irving Hexham (Vancouver, BECAUSE: the Fraser Institute, 1986), pp.251-79.

4. 'Domela Nieuwenhuis, a Great Dutch Socialist,' *American Monthly Illustrated Review of Reviews,* XXIX (1904), pp.746-7.

5. H. Daalder, 'Parties and Politics in the Netherlands,' *Political Studies,* 3 (1955), pp.1-16.

6. Abraham Kuyper, 'The Anti-Revolutionary Programme,' trans. & eds Harry der Nederlanden and Gordon Spykman in *Political Order and the Plural Structure of Society* (Atlanta: the Scholars Press for Emory University, 1991), p.255. This is a selection from articles in *De Standaard.*

7. For a worthwhile treatment of such matters, see Steven E. Meyer, 'Calvinism and the Rise of the Protestant Political Movement in the Netherlands,' unpublished Ph.D. dissertation at Georgetown University, 1976.

8. Kuyper, 'Anti-Revolutionary Programme,' p.237.

9. Praamsma, *Let Christ be King,* p.27.

10. Langley, *Political Spirituality,* p.61; cf. Ronald H. Nash, *Social Justice and the Christian Church* (Milford, MI: Mott Media, 1983).

11. Langley, *Political Spirituality,* pp.26-8.

12. Jellema, 'Abraham Kuyper: Forgotten Radical?' p.241.

13. Two English translations of this long address are available: *Christianity and the Class Struggle,* trans. Dirk Jellema (Grand Rapids: Piet Hein Publishers, 1950) and *The Problem of Poverty,* ed. James W. Skillen (Grand Rapids: Baker Book House, 1991). Citations in the present work are from the more recent version, except where otherwise indicated.

14. Leo XIII, 'On the Condition of Labor,' in *Five Great Encyclicals,* ed. Gerald C. Treacy, S. J. (New York: Paulist Press, 1939), pp.1-30.

15. Kuyper, *Problem of Poverty,* pp.24-6.

16. *Ibid.,* pp.29-30.
17. *Ibid.,* p.32.
18. *Ibid.,* p.34.
19. *Ibid.,* pp.37-8.
20. *Ibid.,* pp.40-41.
21. Kuyper, *Christianity and the Class Struggle,* p.30, n.14.
22. Kuyper, *Problem of Poverty,* p.42.
23. *Ibid.,* p.45.
24. *Ibid.,* pp.47-8.
25. *Ibid.,* p.52 (emphasis Kuyper's). Kuyper cited 1 Corinthians 12:12ff. in support of this concept, even though the passage refers to the church, not to a nation.
26. *Ibid.,* p.61; Kuyper, *Christianity and the Class Struggle,* p.48, n. 34.
27. Kuyper, *Problem of Poverty,* pp.70-71; see Deuteronomy 24:5; 24:14; Leviticus 19:13; Malachi 2:10; cf. Luke 10:7; James 5:4.
28. *Ibid.,* p.72.
29. *Ibid.,* p.78.
30. Langley, *Political Spirituality,* pp.39-41.

Chapter 8 — *Doleantie:* A sorrowful separation

1. Mackay, *Religious Thought in Holland,* pp.47ff.
2. *Ibid.,* pp.141-5.
3. *Ibid.,* pp.145-6.
4. A helpful analysis of Kuyper's view of modernism appears in Gary Scott Smith, *The Seeds of Secularization: Calvinism, Culture, and Pluralism in America, 1870-1915*(Grand Rapids: Christian University Press, 1985), pp.43ff. Cf. Kuyper's 'Modernism a Fata Morgana'.
5. *Ibid.,* p.34.
6. Kuyper, *Confidentie,* p.63.
7. *Ibid.,* p.69.
8. G. Groningen, 'The Effects of the *Doleantie* on the Christian Reformed Church,' *Calvin Forum,* 19 (1954), pp.227-32; 20 (1955), pp.33-40.
9. Abraham Kuyper, *A Pamphlet on the Reformation of the Church,* trans. Herman Hanko, collated from *The Standard Bearer,* pp.54-63 (1977-86), by Randall K. Klynsma, section 51.
10. *Ibid.,* section 49.
11. *Ibid.,* section 58.
12. *Ibid.,* section 59.
13. *Ibid.,* section 63.
14. See James Edward McGoldrick, 'Every Inch for Christ,' *Reformation & Revival,* 3 (1994), pp.91-9.
15. John Cairns, 'The Present Struggle in the National Church of Holland,' *The Presbyterian Review,* 9 (1887), pp.87-108.
16. Helpful coverage of this and of Kuyper's ecclesiology in general appear in Henry Zwaanstra, 'Abraham Kuyper's Conception of the Church,' *Calvin Theological Journal,* 9 (1974), pp.149-81.
17. Vanden Berg, *Abraham Kuyper,* pp.128-61 offers detailed coverage of these trying times.
18. Kuyper, *Pamphlet on Reformation,* section 49.

Chapter 9 — Abraham Kuyper's theology : The triune God

1. Abraham Kuyper, *The Antithesis between Symbolism and Revelation* (Edinburgh: T. & T. Clark, 1899), p.19.
2. *Ibid.,* p.11.
3. *Ibid.,* pp.16-17.
4. *Ibid.,* p.20 (emphasis Kuyper's).
5. Abraham Kuyper, 'The Biblical Criticism of the Present Day,' *Bibliotheca Sacra,* 61 (1904), pp.409-42, 666-88.
6. *Ibid.,* pp.417-18.
7. *Ibid.,* p.685.
8. *Ibid.,* p.422.
9. Abraham Kuyper, *Principles of Sacred Theology,* trans. J. H. De Vries (Grand Rapids: Baker Book House, 1980 reprint of 1898 edition), p.450 (emphasis Kuyper's).
10. Quoted in Richard Gaffin, Jr, 'Old Amsterdam and Inerrancy,' *Westminster Theological Journal,* 44 (1982), p.268. This is a very important article for understanding Kuyper's view of Scripture.
11. *Ibid.,* pp.271-5.
12. Hospers, *The Reformed Principle of Authority,* p.98.
13. Kuyper, 'Biblical Criticism,' p.430.
14. *Ibid.,* p.668.
15. *Ibid.,* p.670.
16. *Ibid.,* p.682. Cf. Kuyper, *Principles of Sacred Theology,* p.366.
17. *Ibid.,* pp.351, 452.
18. Abraham Kuyper, 'Calvinism and Confessional Revision,' *Presbyterian and Reformed Review,* 2 (1891), pp.378-9.
19. Kuyper, *Principles of Sacred Theology,* pp.213-14.
20. Abraham Kuyper, *To be Near unto God,* trans. J. H. De Vries (Grand Rapids: William B. Eerdmans Publishing Co., 1925), p.674.
21. Kuyper's collaborator, Herman Bavinck, produced a helpful account of the state of religion in the Netherlands. See his 'Recent Dogmatic Thought in the Netherlands,' *Presbyterian And Reformed Review,* 3 (1892), pp.209-28.
22. Abraham Kuyper, 'Pantheism's Destruction of Boundaries,' trans. J. H. De Vries, *Methodist Review,* 75 (1893), p.527.
23. *Ibid.,* p.529.
24. *Ibid.,* p.530.
25. Abraham Kuyper, *Evolutie,* unpublished translation by George Kamps (Amsterdam: Hovekker & Wormser, 1899), p.3.
26. *Ibid.*
27. *Ibid.* (emphasis Kuyper's).
28. Kuyper, 'Pantheism's Destruction of Boundaries,' p.765.
29. Kuyper, *Evolutie,* p.18.
30. Kuyper, 'Pantheism's Destruction of Boundaries,' pp.533-4.
31. *Ibid.,* pp.769-70.
32. *Ibid.,* p.531; for a keen analysis of the issues raised in connection with evolution, see Ilsen Bulhof, 'The Netherlands' in *The Comparative Reception of Darwinism,* ed. Thomas F. Glick (Austin, TX: University of Texas Press, 1972), pp.269-306.
33. Abraham Kuyper, *You Can do Greater Things than Christ,* trans. Jan H. Boer (Jos, Nigeria: Institute of Church and Society, 1991), p.80; cf. Kuyper, *Principles of Sacred Theology,* pp.215, 425.

34. Abraham Kuyper, *Asleep in Jesus,* trans. J. H. De Vries (Grand Rapids: William B. Eerdmans Publishing Co., 1929), p.14.

35. Jan Karel Van Baalen, *The Heritage of the Fathers* (Grand Rapids: William B. Eerdmans Publishing Co., 1948), p.186.

36. Abraham Kuyper, *Keep thy Solemn Feasts,* trans. J. H. De Vries (Grand Rapids: William B. Eerdmans Publishing Co., 1928), p.26.

37. Kuyper, *To be Near unto God,* p.45.

38. Abraham Kuyper, *The Work of the Holy Spirit,* trans. J. H. De Vries (Grand Rapids: William B. Eerdmans Publishing Co., 1979 reprint of 1900 edition), pp.56, 60.

39. *Ibid.,* p.76.

40. *Ibid.,* p.73.

41. Kuyper, *Principles of Sacred Theology,* pp.360-61.

42. Kuyper, *Work of the Holy Spirit,* p.175.

43. *Ibid.,* p.193.

44. *Ibid.,* pp.176-7.

45. *Ibid.,* p.211.

Chapter 10 — Abraham Kuyper's theology: Sin and salvation

1. Kuyper, Abraham, *When thou Sittest in thine House,* trans. J. H. De Vries (Grand Rapids: William B. Eerdmans Publishing Co., 1929 reprint of 1899 edition), pp.137-8.

2. Abraham Kuyper, *The Death and Resurrection of Christ,* trans. Henry Zylstra (Grand Rapids: Zondervan Publishing House, 1960), p.17.

3. Kuyper, *Keep thy Solemn Feasts,* p.23.

4. Abraham Kuyper, 'The Dominion of Christ's Kingship,' *Christian Renewal,* 1 (1982), p.20.

5. Abraham Kuyper, *His Decease at Jerusalem,* abridged & ed. Stuart P. Garver (Grand Rapids: William B. Eerdmans Publishing Co., 1946), p.30.

6. *Ibid.,* pp.31-2.

7. Kuyper, 'Election and Selection,' *The Independent,* 51 (1899), pp.1693-4.

8. Kuyper, 'Calvinism and Confessional Revision,' pp.381-2.

9. Abraham Kuyper, *Women of the New Testament,* trans. Henry Zylstra (Grand Rapids: Zondervan Publishing House, 1962 reprint of 1934 edition), p.13.

10. Abraham Kuyper, *Women of the Old Testament,* trans. Henry Zylstra (Grand Rapids: Zondervan Publishing House, 1961 reprint of 1933 edition), pp. 69-70.

11. *Ibid.,* p.96.

12. Kuyper, *Women of the New Testament,* pp.88, 98.

13. Kuyper, *The Work of the Holy Spirit,* p.295.

14. Abraham Kuyper, *The Biblical Doctrine of Election,* trans. G. M. Van Pernis (Grand Rapids: Zondervan Publishing House, 1934), p.308.

15. *Ibid.,* p.5.

16. *Ibid.,* p.9.

17. *Ibid.,* pp.12-13.

18. *Ibid.,* p.20.

19. Kuyper, *Keep thy Solemn Feasts,* p.98.

20. Kuyper, *The Work of the Holy Spirit,* p.338.

21. *Ibid.,* p.420.

22. *Ibid.,* pp.587-8.

23. *Ibid.,* p.81.

24. *Ibid.,* p.253.

25. Kuyper, *Principles of Sacred Theology,* pp.106-9.

26. *Ibid.,* p.112.
27. *Ibid.,* p.113.
28. *Ibid.,* p.114.
29. *Ibid.,* pp.210-12.
30. *Ibid.,* pp.223-5.
31. *Ibid.,* pp.248-54.
32. Kuyper, *The Death and Resurrection of Christ,* p.82.
33. Kuyper, 'Calvinism and Confessional Revision,' p.388.
34. Kuyper, *The Work of the Holy Spirit,* p.421.
35. Kuyper, *Keep thy Solemn Feasts,* p.28 (emphasis Kuyper's).
36. Kuyper, *The Work of the Holy Spirit,* p.435.
37. *Ibid.,* pp.454-5.
38. *Ibid.,* pp.463, 467.
39. *Ibid.,* p.455 (emphasis Kuyper's).
40. Abraham Kuyper, 'The Work of God in our Work,' *Homiletic Review, LV* (1908), p.273a.
41. Kuyper, *The Work of the Holy Spirit,* pp.486-8.
42. Abraham Kuyper, *The Practice of Godliness,* trans. Marian M. Schooland (Grand Rapids: Baker Books, 1977 reprint of 1948 edition), p.22.
43. *Ibid.,* p.28.
44. *Ibid.,* pp.30-31.
45. *Ibid.,* p.56.
46. Kuyper, *Keep thy Solemn Feasts,* p.297.
47. *Ibid.,* p.181.
48. Abraham Kuyper, *The Revelation of St. John,* trans. J. H. De Vries (Grand Rapids: William B. Eerdmans Publishing Co., 1963 reprint of 1935 edition), p.39.
49. *Ibid.,* p.145.

Chapter 11 — Abraham Kuyper's theology: The church

1. Kuyper, *Asleep in Jesus,* pp.150-51.
2. Henry Zwaanstra, 'Abraham Kuyper's Conception of the Church,' *Calvin Theological Journal,* 9 (1974), pp.149-50. This concise treatment of the subject is very helpful.
3. *Ibid.,* pp.161-4, 169-70.
4. Kuyper, *Women of the New Testament,* p.88.
5. Kuyper, *Lectures on Calvinism,* pp.64-5; *Pamphlet on the Reformation of the Church,* section 15.
6. *Ibid.,* section 13.
7. *Ibid.,* section 19.
8. *Ibid.,* section 18.
9. *Ibid.,* section 19.
10. *Ibid.,* section 22.
11. *Ibid.,* section 25.
12. *Ibid.,* section 26.
13. Abraham Kuyper, 'Alexander Comrie: His Life and Work in Holland,' *The Catholic Presbyterian, VII* (1882), p.280.
14. *Ibid.,* p.198.
15. Kuyper, *Pamphlet on the Reformation of the Church,* section 38.
16. *Ibid.,* section 39.
17. *Ibid.,* section 44.
18. Kuyper, *Principles of Theology,* pp.325-6.

19. Kuyper, *Practice of Godliness,* p.61.

20. All citations from the Three Forms of Unity come from *The Creeds of Christendom,* 3, ed. Philip Schaff and rev. David Schaff (Grand Rapids: Baker Book House, 1983 reprint of 1931 edition).

21. Louis Berkhof, *Systematic Theology,* 4th ed. (Grand Rapids: William B. Eerdmans Publishing Co., 1941), p.608.

22. Kuyper, *Holy Spirit,* pp.299-300.

23. *Ibid.,* pp.318, 336.

24. Kuyper, 'Calvinism and confessional Revision,' p.388.

25. Abraham Kuyper, *The Implications of Public Confession,* 5th ed., trans. Henry Zylstra (Grand Rapids: Zondervan Publishing House, 1941), p.608.

26. *Ibid.,* p.47.

27. *Ibid.,* p.26.

28. Kuyper, 'Calvinism and Confessional Revision,' p.387; cf. *Canons of Dort,* chapter I, article XVII.

29. Kuyper, *Holy Spirit,* pp.342, 353.

30. Kuyper, *Implications of Public Confession,* p.24.

31. Cf. Kuyper, 'Calvinism and Confessional Revision,' p.387 and *Implications of Public Confession,* p.17.

32. See Archibald Alexander, *Thoughts on Religious Experience* (Philadelphia: Presbyterian Board of Publication, 1841), pp.26f., which espouses a position opposite to that of Kuyper.

33. Quoted from Carl A. Schouls, '1892-1992: Lessons for Today?' unpublished essay written in Vineland, Ontario, in September 1992.

34. *Ibid.,* pp.10-14; cf. William Young, 'Historic Calvinism and Neo-Calvinism,' *Westminster Theological Journal,* 22 (1973), pp.48-64, 156-73.

35. Peter De Jong, 'Where are we Going with the Kingdom?' *The Outlook,* 24 (1974), pp.2-6.

36. Young, 'Historic Calvinism and Neo-Calvinism,' p.64.

37. J. Douma, *Infant Baptism and Conversion* (Winnipeg, Manitoba: Premier Publishing, 1979), pp.28-9.

38. Kuyper, *Implications of Public Confession,* p.13.

39. For a concise explanation of Luther's doctrine, see James Edward McGoldrick, *Luther's English Connection* (Milwaukee: Northwestern Publishing House, 1979), pp.154-61.

40. Kuyper, *Implications of Public Confession,* pp.13-14.

41. *Ibid.,* p.22.

42. *Ibid.,* p.28.

43. *Ibid.,* p.85; cf. *Belgic Confession,* article XXVIII.

44. Kuyper, *Holy Spirit,* p.544.

45. Kuyper, *To be Near unto God,* p.227.

Chapter 12 — Antithesis and common grace

1. R. B. Kuiper, *To Be or Not to Be Reformed* (Grand Rapids: Zondervan Publishing House, 1959), pp.117-18.

2. For a concise treatment of this matter, see Henry Stob, 'Observations on the Concept of the Antithesis,' in *Perspectives on the Christian Reformed Church,* eds Peter De Klerk & Richard R. De Ridder (Grand Rapids: Baker Book House, 1983), pp.241-58.

3. Abraham Kuyper, 'Concerning the Antithesis,' trans. Henry Van Til, *Torch and Trumpet,* 4 (1955), p.31.

4. Trans. McKendree R. Langley in foreword to Abraham Kuyper's, *Christianity as a Life-System* (Memphis, TN: Christian Studies Center, 1980), p.viii (emphasis Kuyper's).

5. *Ibid.,* p.ix (translation slightly altered).

6. Kuyper, *Lectures on Calvinism,* p.12; Jacob Klapwijk, 'Dooyeweerd's Christian Philosophy: Antithesis and Critique,' *Reformed Journal,* 30 (1980), p.21.

7. Abraham Kuyper, 'Common Grace in Science and Art,' in *De Gemeene Gratie,* 3, unpublished translation by Wayne Bornholdt and Has van de Hel (Amsterdam: Hoeveker & Wormser, 1904), p.7.

8. An excellent analysis of this subject appears in Del Ratzsch, 'Abraham Kuyper's Philosophy of Science,' *Calvin Theological Journal,* 27 (1992), pp.277-303.

9. Kuyper, *Lectures on Calvinism,* pp.131-4.

10. Ratzsch, 'Abraham Kuyper's Philosophy of Science,' pp.298-9.

11. Kuyper, *Lectures on Calvinism,* p.147.

12. Calvin, quoted *Ibid.,* p.153.

13. *Ibid.,* pp.155-7.

14. Kuyper, 'Common Grace in Science and Art,' p.33.

15. *Ibid.,* p.39 (translation slightly altered).

16. Kuyper, *When thou Sittest in thine House,* p.279.

17. Kuyper, 'Common Grace in Science and Art,' p.44.

18. *Ibid.*

19. *Ibid.,* p.7.

20. *Ibid.,* p.20.

21. Kuyper, *You Can do Greater Things than Christ,* p.34.

22. *Ibid.,* p.38.

23. Kuyper, *Lectures on Calvinism,* p.17; see James W. Skillen, 'Kuyper was on Time and ahead of his Time,' *Reformed Ecumenical Synod Theological Forum, XIV* (1988), pp.15-19.

24. See the very helpful analysis of S. U. Zuidema, *Communication and Confrontation,* trans. Harry Van Dyke (Assen/Kampen: Royal Van Gorcum, Ltd & J. H. Kok, Ltd, 1972), pp.52-101.

25. Henry R. Van Til, *The Calvinistic Concept of Culture* (Philadelphia: Presbyterian & Reformed Publishing Co., 1972), p.120; see Kuyper, *De Gemeene Gratie,* I, pp.252-3, 200-201.

26. Zuidema, *Communication and Confrontation,* pp.72-89.

27. *Ibid.,* pp.52-4.

28. Kuyper, *Lectures on Calvinism,* p.120.

29. *Ibid.,* p.125 (emphasis Kuyper's).

30. *Ibid.,* pp.127-40.

31 *Ibid.,* p.171.

32. *Ibid.,* pp.190-97.

33. *Ibid.,* p.69.

34. John Calvin, *Institutes of the Christian Religion,* III, XIX.

35. For a concise, perceptive analysis of this matter, see Henry J. Van Andel, 'The Christian and Culture,' *The Presbyterian Guardian,* 13 (1944), pp.17-18, 28-30.

36. Jacob Klapwijk, 'Antithesis and Common Grace,' in *Bringing into Captivity every Thought,* eds Jacob Klapwijk, Sander Griffioe and Gerben Groenewoud (Lanham, MD: University Press of America, 1991), pp.169-90, is an incisive study of these ideas.

37. Kuyper, 'Concerning the Antithesis,' pp.32ff; cf. Klapwijk, 'Rationality in the Neo-Calvinian Tradition,' in *Rationality in the Neo-Calvinian Tradition,* eds H. Hart, *et al.* (Lanham, MD: University Press of America, 1983), pp.93-111.

38. Praamsma, *Let Christ be King,* pp.81-3.

39. For important critiques of Kuyper, see: Cornelis Pronk, 'F. M. Ten Hoor: Defender of Secessionist Principles against Abraham Kuyper's *Doleantie* Views,' unpublished Th.M.

thesis at Calvin Theological Seminary, 1987; Klaas Schilder, *Christ and Culture,* trans. G. Van Ronger & W. Helder (Winnipeg, Manitoba: Premier Printing, 1977); Rudolf Van Reest, *Schilder's Struggle for the Unity of the Church,* trans. Theodore Plantinga (Neerlandia, Alberta: Inheritance Publications, 1990); Herman Hoeksema, *Reformed Dogmatics* (Grand Rapids: Reformed Free Publishing Association, 1966).
40. See, for example, Kuyper, *The Practice of Godliness.*
41. Van Reest, *Schilder's Struggle for the Unity of the Church,* contains harsh criticism of Kuyper on these points.

Chapter 13 — Church and state
1. Kuyper, *Near unto God,* p.7.
2. *Ibid.,* p.599.
3. For a helpful study of this matter, see James W. Skillen, 'God's Ordinances: Calvinism in Revival,' *Pro Rege,* VIII (1980), pp.24-33.
4. Sometimes when Kuyper referred to the church as an 'organism', he meant the whole body of believers working outside of, as well as within, the visible ecclesiastical institution. See Arnold De Graaf, *The Educational Ministry of the Church* (Phillipsburg, NJ: Craig Press, 1968), pp.68-70.
5. Kuyper, *Lectures on Calvinism,* p.79 (emphasis Kuyper's).
6. *Ibid.,* p.85.
7. Kuyper, *Pamphlet on Reformation,* section 62; cf. Helmut Thielicke, *Theological Ethics,* II, ed. William H. Lazareth (Philadelphia: Fortress Press, 1969), pp.599-603.
8. Kuyper, *Keep thy Solemn Feasts,* pp.78-9; *Lectures on Calvinism,* pp.99-100.
9. Kuyper, 'Calvinism and Confessional Revision,' p.376.
10. Skillen, 'God's Ordinances,' p.30.
11. Kuyper, *Lectures on Calvinism,* pp.65-6, 99.
12. *Ibid.,* pp.101-3.
13. *Ibid.,* pp.106-8.
14. *Ibid.,* pp.31, 103.
15. James W. Skillen, 'Societal Pluralism: Blessing or Curse for the Public Good?' in *The Ethical Dimension of Political Life,* ed. Francis Canavan (Durham, NC: Duke University Press, 1983), p.169.
16. Abraham Kuyper, *Souvereiniteit in Eigen Kring* (Amsterdam: J. H. Kruyt, 1880), p.16. A fine English translation of this address appears as an appendix in Wayne A. Kobes, 'Sphere Sovereignty and the University: Theological Foundations of Abraham Kuyper's View of the University and its Role in Society' (unpublished Ph.D. dissertation at Florida State University, 1993), pp.281-302.
17. Kuyper, *Souvereiniteit in Eigen Kring,* p.19.
18. A helpful examination of these issues appears in H. Van Riessen, *The Society of the Future,* trans. & ed. David Hugh Freeman (Philadelphia: Presbyterian and Reformed Publishing Co., pp.69-84.
19. Kuyper, *Souvereiniteit in Eigen Kring,* p.35.

Chapter 14 — Kuyper and America
1. Kuyper, *Lectures on Calvinism,* p.87.
2. Quoted, *Ibid.,* p.78.
3. Witsius De Savornin Lohman, 'Dr. Abraham Kuyper,' *The Presbyterian and Reformed Review,* IX (1898), p.565.
4. Herb Brinks, 'Abraham Kuyper: It might have been,' *The Kuyper Newsletter,* I (1980), pp.4-5.

5. Herb Brinks, 'Kuyper in Michigan,' *The Kuyper Newsletter,* II (1981-82), pp.2-3.

6. *The Princeton Press,* 1 October 1898.

7. 'Dr. Kuyper,' *The Presbyterian,* LXVIII (1898), p.7.

8. Dirk Jellema, 'Kuyper's Visit to America in 1898,' *Michigan History,* 42 (1958), pp.227-9.

9. *Ibid.,* p.230.

10. *Ibid.,* pp.234-6.

11. Henry Zwaanstra, *Reformed Thought and Experience in a New World* (Kampen, Netherlands: J. H. Kok, 1973), pp.3-27.

12. *Ibid.,* pp.75-83.

13. Henry Lucas, *Netherlanders in America* (Grand Rapids: William B. Eerdmans Publishing Co., 1989), p.572. This is useful for a study of the European background of the Dutch immigrants, and it relates Kuyper's influence upon Reformed Christians in America.

14. Edwin H. Rian, *The Presbyterian Conflict* (Grand Rapids: William B. Eerdmans Publishing Co., 1940), pp.18-23.

15. Abraham Kuyper, 'Calvinism and Confessional Revision,' *Presbyterian and Reformed Review,* 2 (1891), pp.369-99.

16. Abraham Kuyper, 'The True Genius of Presbyterianism,' *The Presbyterian,* 76 (1906), pp.12-14.

17. For a view of the American Revolution contrary to that of Kuyper, see James Edward McGoldrick, '1776: A Christian Loyalist View,' *Fides et Historia,* XI (1977), pp.26-40. A helpful survey of Kuyper's tour of America appears in Praamsma, *Let Christ be King,* pp.123-34.

Chapter 15 — A reformer in politics

1. Quoted by Savornin Lohman, 'Dr. Kuyper,' pp.588-9.

2. *Ibid.,* p.598.

3. *Ibid.,* pp.606-7.

4. Succinct coverage of these matters appears in McKendree R. Langley, 'Pioneers of Christian Politics,' *Vanguard,* II (1971), pp.7-10, 22.

5. Abraham Kuyper, 'Standaard Mannen,' *De Standaard,* 20 June 1879, trans. McKendree R. Langley.

6. Westra, 'Kuyper on Church and State,' p.128.

7. Kromminga, *The Christian Reformed Tradition,* pp.38-9, 73.

8. Dirk Th. Kuiper, 'Theory and Practice in Dutch Calvinism on the Racial Issue in the Nineteenth Century,' *Calvin Theological Journal,* 21 (1986), pp.55-9.

9. Kenneth Scott Latourette, *A History of the Expansion of Christianity,* V (New York: Harper & Brothers, 1943), pp.284-6.

10. Amry J. Vandenbosch has produced two fine studies of these matters in *The Dutch East Indies: Its Government, Problems, and Politics* (Berkeley, CA: University of California Press, 1944) and 'The Dutch in the Far East,' in *The Netherlands,* ed. Bartholomew Landheer (Berkeley, CA: University of California Press, 1944), pp.233-45.

11. *Ibid.,* pp.337-8.

12. J. S. Furnivall, *Netherlands India: A Study of Plural Economy* (Cambridge: The University Press, 1967 reprint of 1939 edition), p.229.

13. Maarten Kuitenbrouwer, *The Netherlands and the Rise of Modern Imperialism: Colonial and Foreign Policy,* 1870-1902, trans. Hugh Beyer (New York: Berg Publications, 1991), pp.88-123, 160-63.

14. Furnivall, *Netherlands India,* p.233.

15. Vandenbosch, 'Dutch in the Far East,' p.339; E. H. Kossman, *The Low Countries,* 1780-1940 (Oxford: Clarendon Press, 1978), pp.389-405.

16. *Ibid.*, pp.412-15.
17. E. S. De Klerck, *A History of the Netherlands East Indies*, II (Rotterdam: W. L. & J. Brusse, 1938), p.81.
18. Langley, *Political Spirituality*, pp.54-66.
19. This address has recently become available in a fine English translation. See 'Evolution,' trans. Clarence Menninga, *et al., Calvin Theological Journal*, 31 (1996), pp.11-50.
20. Kuyper analysed the situation in South Africa in his essay *The South African Crisis*, 14th ed., trans. A. E. Fletcher (London: Clock House for the Stop the War Committee, 1900).
21. Abraham Kuyper, 'The Coming Downfall of Liberalism,' I, *De Standaard*, 1 August 1879, trans. McKendree R. Langley.
22. See the interesting article by Rex Ambler, 'The Christian Mind of Abraham Kuyper,' in *Profitable for Doctrine and Reproof*, excerpted from the *Evangelical Magazine* (London: Puritan and Reformed Studies Conference, 1967), pp.5-14.
23. Caroline Atwater Mason, 'The New Premier of Holland,' *The Outlook*, 70 (1902), pp.333-7.
24. 'The Fall of the Kuyper Ministry in Holland,' *American Monthly Illustrated Review of Reviews*, XXXII (1905), pp.356-7.
25. Abraham Kuyper, 'The Coming Downfall of Liberalism' II, *De Standaard*, 4 August 1879, trans. McKendree R. Langley.
26. An appreciative yet critical analysis of Kuyper's thinking about these matters appears in Irving Hexham, 'Christian Politics According to Abraham Kuyper,' *Crux*, 19 (1983), pp.2-7.
27. For a fine introduction to Kuyper's political ideas, see Edward J. Tanis, 'Abraham Kuyper, Christian Statesman,' *Calvin Forum*, 3 (1937), pp.53-6.
28. Dirk Jellema, 'Abraham Kuyper's Attack on Liberalism,' *Review of Politics*, 19 (1957), pp.472-85, covers this subject well.
29 Kuyper, *Lectures on Calvinism*, pp.70-71.
30. James D. Bratt, 'Abraham Kuyper's Public Career,' *Reformed Journal*, 37 (1987), pp.9-12.

Chapter 16 — Prime minister and elder statesman

1. *The Memoirs of Paul Kruger*, trans. A. Teixeira de Mattos (London: T. Fisher Unwin, 1902), pp.84-8, 415-17.
2. Kuyper, *South African Crisis;* cf. P. Kasteel, *Abraham Kuyper* (Kampen, The Netherlands: J. H. Kok, 1938), pp.274-5.
3. Kuyper, *South African Crisis*, p.1.
4. *Ibid.*, pp.10-12,20-29.
5. *Ibid.*, p.51.
6. *Ibid.*, p.54.
7. *Ibid.*, p.67.
8. *Ibid.*, pp.70-72.
9. *The Times* (London), 13 May 1902.
10. *The Times*, 3 April 1902; for British reaction to the Dutch offer, see *The Annual Register, A Review of Public Events at Home and Abroad* (London: Longmans, Green & Co., 1902), pp.50 ff.
11. Kasteel, *Abraham Kuyper*, p.276.
12. Kuitenbrouwer, *The Netherlands and the Rise of Modern Imperialism*, pp.192-224.
13. *Ibid.*, pp.305-19.
14. Langley, *Practice of Political Spirituality*, p.86.

15. Extensive coverage of these matters has not yet appeared in English. The major Dutch-language treatment is by Adolf J. C. Rüter, *Spoorweg-Stakingen van 1903: Een Spiegel der Arbeidersbeweging in Nederland* (Leiden: E. J. Brill, 1935). McKendree R. Langley has supplied me with a summary in English. Cf. Langley, *Practice of Political Spirituality,* pp.91-101; Erik Hansen & Peter A. Prosper, Jr, 'Religion and the Development of the Dutch Trade Union Movement, 1872-1914,' *Historie Sociale-Social History,* 9 (1956), pp.357-83.

16. Bob Goudzwaard, *A Christian Political Option,* trans. Herman Praamsma (Toronto: Wedge Publishing Foundation, 1972), pp.48-9.

17. Chessman, *The Low Countries,* p.495.

18. More extensive coverage of the Higher Education Act may be found in Langley, *Practice of Political Spirituality,* pp.103-13; Vanden Berg, *Abraham Kuyper,* pp.221-42.

19. John H. Kromminga, 'Abraham Kuyper (1837-1920),' in *A History of Religious Educators,* ed. Elmer L. Towns (Grand Rapids: Baker Book House, 1975), pp.288-96.

20. Langley, *Practice of Political Spirituality,* pp.115-20.

21. Edmundsen, 'Holland,' p.248.

22. Van der Kroef, 'Rise of Neo-Calvinism,' pp.237-38, 333.

23. Quoted by *American Monthly Illustrated, Review of Reviews,* XXXII (1905), p.357.

24. This is the judgement of Bratt, 'Raging Tumults of the Soul,' p.12.

25. A. J. Barnouw, *Holland under Queen Wilhelmina,* foreword by E. W. Bok (New York: Charles Scribner's Sons, 1923), p.72; cf. Langley, *Practice of Political Spirituality,* pp.135-6.

26. James W. Skillen, 'From Covenant of Grace to Equitable Public Pluralism,' *Calvin Theological Journal,* 31 (1996), p.88; Langley, *Practice of Political Spirituality,* pp.154-5.

27. Chessman, *The Low Countries,* pp.429-33.

28. Abraham Kuyper, 'Parliament Bill: As others see us: Foreign Statesmen on the Constitutional Crisis. Dr. Kuyper,' *The Daily Telegraph* (London), 22 August 1911.

29. Barnouw, *Holland under Wilhelmina,* pp.169-70.

30. *Ibid.,* pp.190-94, 300-301.

31. There is a fine analysis of *Pro Rege* in Praamsma, *Let Christ Be King,* pp.145-55.

32. R. E. L. Rodgers, *The Incarnation of the Antithesis: An Introduction to the Educational Thought and Practice of Abraham Kuyper* (Durham, England: Pentland Press, 1992).

Chapter 17 — A far-reaching legacy

1. Quoted by Edward J. Tanis, 'Abraham Kuyper, Christian Statesman,' *Calvin Forum,* 3 (1937), p.56.

2. Kuyper, 'Alexander Comrie,' p.282.

3. A helpful analysis of Kuyper's position appears in Bernard L. Ramm, *Varieties of Christian Apologetics* (Grand Rapids: Baker Book House, 1961), pp.181ff. Cf. Gerritt H. Hospers, *Apologetics: A Study and a Critique* (Ontario, NY: published by the author, 1924). This remarkably concise, lucid pamphlet contains a brief essay by Kuyper at the end.

4. Warfield, quoted by Hospers in *Apologetics,* p.24. The emphasis is Warfield's own. For an appreciative but critical study of this matter see Stephen R. Spencer, 'A Comparison and Evaluation of the Old Princeton and Amsterdam Apologetic,' unpublished Th.M. thesis at Grand Rapids Baptist Theological Seminary, 1980; Cornelius Van Til, *A Christian Theory of Knowledge* (Philadelphia: Presbyterian & Reformed Publishing Co., 1969).

5. Kuyper, 'Editorial on Apologetics,' in Hospers, *Apologetics,* p.31.

6. William White, Jr, *Van Til, Defender of the Faith* (Nashville: Thomas Nelson Publishers, 1979), is an authorized biography by a zealous disciple. A more thorough and balanced

treatment is that by John M. Frame, *Cornelius Van Til: An Analysis of his Thought* (Phillipsburg, NJ: Presbyterian & Reformed Publishing Co., 1995).

7. See Frame, *Cornelius Van Til.* An entire school of vigorous presuppositionalists is now active in defending the faith on the foundation of Kuyper's arguments as developed and applied by Van Til. See, for example, William Edgar, 'Without Apology: Why I am a Presuppositionalist,' *Westminster Theological Journal,* 58 (1996), pp.17-27; Richard Pratt, *Every Thought Captive* (Phillipsburg, NJ: Presbyterian & Reformed Publishing Co., 1979); and Van Til's *Defense of the Faith,* 2nd ed., revised and abridged (Philadelphia: Presbyterian & Reformed Publishing Co., 1963).

8. Van Til, *Christian Theory of Knowledge,* pp.232-46.

9. Van Til, *Defense of the Faith,* pp.192-3. For a brief critique of Kuyper's antithetical view of scholarship, see Thedford Dirkse, the Extent of the Antithesis,' *Calvin Forum,* 19 (1954), pp.147-9.

10. Ramm, *Varieties of Apologetics,* pp.192-3.

11. Kuyper, *Practice of Godliness,* pp.51-2.

12. Kuyper, *Near unto God,* p.651 (emphasis Kuyper's).

13. Kuyper, *Lectures on Calvinism,* p.73.

14. *Ibid.,* pp.112-15.

15. Fred H. Klooster, 'The Kingdom of God in the History of the Christian Reformed Church,' in *Perspectives on the Christian Reformed Church: Studies in its History, Theology, and Ecumenicity,* eds Peter De Klerck & Richard R. De Ridder (Grand Rapids: Baker Book House, 1983), p.209.

16. This appraisal of developments at the Free University of Amsterdam comes from an unpublished lecture by James D. Bratt entitled 'Big Ideas, Little People: Theological Education in the Neo-Calvinist tradition' delivered at Westminster Theological Seminary, Philadelphia in March 1994. A detailed history of the Free University is now available in Dutch. It is the work of J. Stellingwerff, *Dr. Abraham Kuyper en de Vrije Universiteit* (Kampen, the Netherlands: J. H. Kok, 1987). This is the work of a librarian at the university who took pleasure in exposing its eventual rejection of Kuyper's world-view. A critical review of this book may be found in *Westminster Theological Journal,* 51 (1989), pp.403-6. M. R. Langley, the reviewer, was once a graduate student at the Free University.

17. Louis Berkhof, 'Dr. Abraham Kuyper and the Revival of Calvinistic Doctrine,' *Calvin Forum,* 3 (1937-38), pp.104-6.

18. Anthony H. Nichols, 'The Educational Doctrines of Abraham Kuyper: an Evaluation,' *Journal of Christian Education Papers,* 52 (1975), pp.26-38; Donald Oppewal, *The Roots of the Calvinistic Day School Movement* (Grand Rapids: Calvin College Monograph Series, 1963).

19. Francis A. Schaeffer, *How Should we then Live?* (Old Tappan, NJ: Fleming H. Revell Co., 1976).

20. James A. De Jong, 'Abraham Kuyper's Edition of the *Institutes,*' *Calvin Theological Journal,* 21 (1986), p.231.

21. W. H. Velema, 'Abraham Kuyper — Born 150 Years Ago: A Study in Strengths and Pitfalls,' *Reformed Ecumenical Synod Theological Forum,* XVI (1988), pp.9-14, is a helpful look at the eventual failure of Kuyper's most cherished projects. Cf. Van Reest, *Schilder's Struggle,* pp.231ff.

22. Frederick Nymeyer, 'What Happened to the Daily Newspaper Abraham Kuyper Founded?' *Progressive Calvinism,* 1 (1955), pp.324-8.

23. D. Th. Kuiper, 'Historical and Sociological Development of ARP and CDA,' in *Christian Political Options,* ed., C. Den Hollander, *et al.,* trans. A. J. Van Dijk & G. Groenewoud (The Hague: AR-Partijstiching, 1980), pp.22-5.

24. Joel R. Beeke, 'The Second Dutch Reformation,' *Calvin Theological Journal,* 28 (1993), p.321.

25. Kuyper, *Practice of Godliness,* p.99 (emphasis Kuyper's).

Chapter 18 — Conclusion and critique

1. Kuyper, *Lectures on Calvinism,* pp.37 ff.

2. Kuyper, *The South African Crisis,* pp.25-7; cf. Kobus Smit, 'Kuyper and Afrikaner Theology,' *Reformed Ecumenical Synod Theological Forum,* XVI (1988), pp.20-28.

3. D. E. M. Strauss, 'An Analysis of S. A. Calvinist Theology,' *Journal of Theology for Southern Africa,* 19 (1977), pp.29-34; Alan Davis, *Infected Christianity: A Study of Modern Racism* (Montreal: McGill-Queens University Press, 1988), pp.94-5.

4. A very insightful analysis of this matter appears in David J. Bosch, 'Afrikaner Civil Religion and the Current South African Crisis,' *Princeton Seminary Bulletin,* 7 (1986), pp.1-14.

5. P. J. Strauss, 'Abraham Kuyper, Apartheid, and the Reformed Churches in South Africa in their Support of Apartheid,' *Reformed Ecumenical Synod Theological Forum,* XXIII (1995), pp.4-27. This is a persuasive article, one free from excessive desire to detach Kuyper's influence from the development of apartheid.

6. Jaap Durand, 'Church and State in South Africa: Karl Barth vs. Abraham Kuyper,' in *On Reading Karl Barth in South Africa,* ed. Charles Villa-Vicencio (Grand Rapids: William B. Eerdmans Publishing Co., 1988), p.133. Although this author is an enthusiast for Barth, he does not blame Kuyper for apartheid.

7. Kuiper, 'Theory and Practice in Dutch Calvinism,' p.77; for the perspective of a South African Jew, see Charles Bloomberg, *Christian Nationalism and the Rise of the Afrikaner Broederband, 1918-48,* ed. Saul Dubow (Bloomington, IN: Indiana University Press); a concise account of the history of Calvinism in South Africa appears in D. J. Bosch, 'The Roots and Fruits of Afrikaner Civil Religion,' in *New Faces of Africa,* eds J. W. Hofmeyer & W. S. Vorster (Pretoria: University of South Africa, 1984), pp.14-35.

8. For a succinct explanation of predestination, see Loraine Boettner, 'Predestination,' in *Baker's Dictionary of Theology.* A more thorough coverage appears in the same author's *Reformed Doctrine of Predestination* (Grand Rapids: William B. Eerdmans Publishing Co., 1932).

9. Calvin, *Institutes of the Christian Religion,* I, II, xvi.

10. John Kromminga, *The Christian Reformed Church: A Study in Orthodoxy* (Grand Rapids: Baker Book House, 1949), pp.52-6.

11. A valid criticism of Kuyper on this and on some other doctrines appears in Cornelis Pronk, 'F. M. Ten Hoor: Defender of Secessionist Principles against Abraham Kuyper's *Doleantie* Views,' unpublished Th.M. thesis at Calvin Theological Seminary, 1987.

12. Kuyper, *Work of the Holy Spirit,* pp.367-71.

13. *Ibid.,* p.369 (emphasis Kuyper's).

14. *Ibid.*

15. Kuyper, *Lectures on Calvinism,* p.137; Kuyper, *Principles of Sacred Theology,* pp.338-9.

16. Kuyper, *Work of the Holy Spirit,* p.299.

17. *Ibid.,* p.295.

18. Kuyper, *Principles of Sacred Theology,* pp.554-5.

19. One such criticism appears in Van Reest, *Schilder's Struggle for Unity,* p.47.

20. Quoted in *Ibid.,* p.11.

21. Kuyper, *Work of the Holy Spirit,* p.340.

22. Kuyper, *Near unto God,* p.51.

23. *Ibid.,* p.192.

24. *Ibid.,* p.127.

25. *Ibid.,* pp.409-10 (emphasis mine).

26. Quoted in Louis Praamsma, 'The Reformed First Principles,' *Christian Renewal,* 5 (1986), pp.10-11.

27. Kuyper, *Work of the Holy Spirit,* p.4.

28. Kuyper, *Principles of Sacred Theology,* p.354.

29. *Ibid.,* p.401; Kuyper, *Work of the Holy Spirit,* p.73.

30. For an examination of many such charismatic leaders and their movements, see James Edward McGoldrick, *Baptist Successionism: A Crucial Question in Baptist History* (Metuchen, NJ: Scarecrow Press, 1994).

31. Kuyper's friend Benjamin B. Warfield was especially adamant about this. See his *Counterfeit Miracles* (Edinburgh: Banner of Truth Trust, 1976 reprint of 1918 edition).

32. Kuyper, *Work of the Holy Spirit,* p.189.

33. Kuyper, *You Can do Greater Things than Christ,* pp.22-3.

34. *Ibid.,* p.25.

35. *Ibid.,* p.28.

36. Kuyper, *Work of the Holy Spirit,* pp.206-7.

37. *Ibid.,* p.91.

38. John Bolt, *Christian and Reformed Today* (Jordan Station, Ontario: Paideia Press, 1984), p.146.

39. Frederick Nymeyer, 'The Anti-Revolutionary Party: The Founder was Confusilated from the Beginning,' *Progressive Calvinism,* I (1955), pp.195-200. This is a highly critical appraisal of Kuyper's thinking.

40. Kuyper, *Near unto God,* p.595.

Annotated bibliography of materials in English

Works by Kuyper

Abraham Kuyper: A Centennial Reader, ed. James D. Bratt. Grand Rapids; William B.
Eerdmans Publishing Co.
> An excellent selection of Kuyper's writings about a variety of important subjects.
> Several of the items have not been available in English until now.

Abraham Kuyper on Evolution, ed. & trans. Steve van der Weele. Grand Rapids: Youth
and Calvinism Group, 1950.
> Translation of summaries of Kuyper's address in 1899 by J. C. Rullman and W.
> F. A. Winckel; shows Kuyper's strong hostility to Darwin and his disciples.

'Alexander Comrie: His Life and Work in Holland,' *Catholic Presbyterian,* VII (1882),
pp.20-29, 192-201, 278-84.
> Kuyper's tribute to an eighteenth-century Scotsman who served the Dutch church
> and defended orthodoxy against rationalism. Valuable for insight into Kuyper's own
> theology and his view of apologetics.

'The Anti-Revolutionary Program,' trans. & eds. Harry der Nederlander & Gordon
Spykman, in *Political Order and the Plural Structure of Society,* eds James W. Skillen
& Rockne McCarthy. Atlanta: Scholars Press for Emory University, 1991.
> Excerpts from *De Standaard, Ons Program* and *Souvereiniteit in Eigen Kring.*

The Antithesis between Symbolism and Revelation. Edinburgh: T. & T. Clark, 1899.
> A lecture to Philadelphia's Presbyterian Historical Society; assails the rise of
> modernism and its symbolic rather than biblical conception of religion; sees symbol-
> ism as leading to pantheism and subversion of revealed truth, as in Freemasonry and
> the decadent Church of England.

Asleep in Jesus, trans. J. H. De Vries. Grand Rapids: William B. Eerdmans Publishing
Co., 1929.
> Often repetitive and somewhat speculative meditations about life after death to
> console believers who face death themselves or the loss of loved ones; awkward
> translation.

'The Biblical Criticism of the Present Day,' trans. John Hendrik De Vries, *Bibliotheca Sacra,* 61 (1904), pp.409-42, 666-88.

Kuyper's inaugural address as rector at the Free University of Amsterdam; attacks modernists and Ethicals for denying the supreme authority of the Bible and assuming the right to judge it; shows Kuyper's indignation at those who claim to revere the Bible while rejecting its infallibility.

The Biblical Doctrine of Election, trans. G. M. Van Pernis. Grand Rapids: Zondervan Publishing House, 1934.

A translation of a small portion of *De Voto* that shows Kuyper's rigorous supralapsarian Calvinism.

'Blessed are the Pure in Heart,' trans. J. H. De Vries, *Christianity Today,* VII (8 December 1936), pp.183-4.

A devotional meditation.

'But Some Doubted,' trans. J. H. De Vries, *Christianity Today,* VII (5 September 1936), pp.111-12.

Devotional meditation on Matthew 28:17.

'By the Resurrection of the Dead,' trans. J. H. De Vries, *Christianity Today,* VII (6 October 1936), pp.137-9.

Devotional meditation on Romans 1:4.

'Calvinism and Art,' *Christian Thought: Lectures and Papers in Philosophy, Christian Evidence, Biblical Elucidation,* IX (1891-92), pp.259-82, 447-59.

Kuyper's argument to show that Calvinism is not antithetical to the arts, but rather provides the biblical basis for appreciation and development of art.

'Calvinism and Confessional Revision,' trans. Geerhardus Vos. *The Presbyterian and Reformed Review,* 2 (1891), pp.369-99.

An exceptionally important article that expresses Kuyper's views on the most significant features and procedures of the Reformed faith.

'Calvinism: The Origin and Safeguard of our Constitutional Liberties,' trans. J. H. De Vries, *Bibliotheca Sacra,* 52 (1895), pp.385-410, 646-75.

An undocumented and somewhat uncritical affirmation of Calvinism as the basis for enduring liberty in England, the Netherlands, Switzerland and the United States; some questionable judgements.

Chiliasm, or the Doctrine of Premillennialism, trans. & ed. G. M. Van Pernis. Grand Rapids: Zondervan Publishing House, 1934.

A vigorous rejection of chiliasm as incompatible with Scripture and Reformed confessions. Kuyper seems to have attacked Dispensationalism without realizing that historic premillennialism does not espouse the re-creation of a Jewish state and resumption of religious practices.

Christianity and its Class Struggle, trans. Dirk Jellema. Grand Rapids: Piet Hein Publishers, 1950.

Original English translation of Kuyper's 1891 address to the First Christian Social Congress.

Christianity as a Life-System: The Witness of a World-View, foreword by McKendree R. Langley. Memphis: Christian Studies Center, 1980.
> An abridgement of the Stone Lectures with a valuable foreword.

'Church and State,' in *De Gemeene Gratie,* v. 3, unpublished translation by Wayne Bornholdt & Hans van de Hel. Amsterdam: Hoeveker & Wormser, 1904.
> A very awkward translation of an important treatise that shows Kuyper was not a theocrat but an advocate of the separation of church and state and a champion of freedom for all religions.

'Common Grace in Science and Art,' in *De Gemeene Gratie,* v. 3, unpublished translation by Wayne Bornholdt & Hans van de Hel. Amsterdam: Hoeveker & Wormster, 1904.
> This is a substantial portion of important writing that shows Kuyper's perspective on culture; awkward translation has caused obscurity as to his meaning at some points.

'Concerning the Antithesis,' trans. Henry R. Van Til, *Torch and Trumpet,* 4 (1955), pp.31-2.
> A clear statement of the antithesis in world-views between Christians and secularists, especially since the French Revolution.

Confidentie, unpublished translation by McKendree R. Langley. Amsterdam: Höveker & Zoon, 1873.
> Two open letters in which Kuyper expressed his longing for the restoration of orthodoxy in the Dutch Reformed Church. Vital for understanding his thinking about ecclesiology.

'The Courses of the Age are His,' trans. J. H. De Vries, *Christianity Today,* VI (8 January 1936), pp.183-4.
> A devotional meditation.

The Death and Resurrection of Christ, trans. Henry Zylstra. Grand Rapids: Zondervan Publishing House, 1960 (1888).
> Moving devotional expositions of Christ's passion and resurrection which reflect Kuyper's Reformed persuasion. Numerous insights into the meaning of soteriology and the proper response to Christ's suffering and triumph. Unclear about the extent of atonement. Readable.

'The Dogma of Evolution,' *Christian Renewal,* 3 (1985), p.2.
> A brief excerpt from Kuyper's 1899 attack upon evolution in a speech to the Free University of Amsterdam.

'The Dominion of Christ's Kingship,' *Christian Renewal,* 1 (1982), pp.1-2, 20-21.
> A ringing affirmation of Christ as King and a call to churches to proclaim the royalty and sovereignty of Christ as Lord.

'An Editorial on Apologetics,' in *Apologetics: A Study and a Critique,* by Gerrit H. Hospers. Ontario, NY: published by the author, 1924, pp. 30-32.
> An affirmation of presuppositional apologetics in connection with Hospers' rebuttal of Warfield's evidentialism.

'Election and Selection,' *The Independent,* 51 (1899), pp.1693-4.
> A concise argument in favour of predestination and election, in opposition to the fatalistic natural selection of the Darwinians.

'Every one which seeth the Son,' trans. J. H. De Vries, *Christianity Today,* VI (9 February 1936) pp. 203-4.
> A devotional meditation.

Evolutie, unpublished translation by George Kamps. Amsterdam: Hovekker & Wormser, 1899.
> Kuyper's attack on the theory of evolution; shows his remarkable scientific learning as well as his philosophic grasp of its consequences. Poor translation.

'Evolution,' trans. Clarence Menninga, *et al. Calvin Theological Journal,* 31 (1996), pp.11-50.
> The first adequate translation of this 1899 address; shows the amazing breadth of Kuyper's learning and stipulates his objections to the evolutionary world-view.

The Evolution of the Use of the Bible in Europe. New York: American Bible Society, 1916.
> A lecture delivered to the World's Bible Congress in 1915; extols the influence of Bible in Protestant lands and holds that it has promoted healthful social and political, as well as religious, developments.

'False Theories of Sovereignty,' *The Independent,* 50 (1898), 1918-21.
> A lucid and concise critique of popular sovereignty, as held by French Revolutionaries, and the state sovereignty of the German pantheists; presents the Calvinist concept of divine sovereignty as the defence of true freedom.

'The Firstborn from the Dead,' trans. J. H. De Vries, *Christianity Today,* VI (11 April 1936), pp.250-52.
> A devotional meditation on Colossians 1:18.

'Glory to God in the Highest!' *Christian Renewal,* 1 (1982), pp.5-6. A Christmas devotion.

His Decease at Jerusalem, abridged & ed. Stuart P. Garver. Grand Rapids: William B. Eerdmans Publishing Co., 1946.
> An insightful and moving devotional treatise on the meaning of the atonement.

'Immanuel,' trans. J. H. De Vries, *Christianity Today,* VI (7 December 1935), pp.155-6.
> A devotional meditation.

The Implications of Public Confession, 5th ed., trans. Henry Zylstra. Grand Rapids: Zondervan Publishing House, 1934.
> Valuable for an understanding of Kuyper's ecclesiology and its numerous implications for the Christian life; unclear about baptism and regeneration.

'In the Beauties of Holiness,' *The Christian Intelligencer,* 69 (1900), pp.50-51.
> A devotional article relating to sanctification.

In the Shadow of Death, trans. John Hendrik De Vries. Grand Rapids: William B. Eerdmans Publishing Co., 1929.
>   Meditations to console the sick and dying and those who care for them; confidence in divine sovereignty underlies all admonitions. Clumsy translation.

Keep thy Solemn Feasts, trans. John Hendrik de Vries. Grand Rapids: William B. Eerdmans Publishing Co., 1928.
>   Devotional meditations about traditional Christian holidays such as Christmas, Easter, Pentecost, etc.

Lectures on Calvinism. Grand Rapids: William B. Eerdmans Publishing Co., 1931.
>   The celebrated Stone Lectures of 1898 that present Calvinism as the basis for an integrated biblical world-view.

'The Lord Reigns,' *Christian Renewal*, 1 (1982), pp.1-2, 14-15.
>   A New Year's Eve devotion to arouse concern to love God and to serve his cause in the brevity of life.

The Lord's Day Observance. s'Gravenhage, Netherlands: Js Bootsma, Electrische Boeken Kunstdrukkerij, 1915.
>   An address to promote the Lord's Day as the Christian Sabbath which individuals, churches and civil governments are obliged to maintain.

'A Meditation on the Resurrection — "Highly Exalted",' trans. J. H. De Vries, *Christianity Today*, VI (10 March 1936), pp.227-9.
>   Devotional meditation on Philippians 2:9.

'Modernism, A Fata Morgana in the Christian World', in Gerrit Hendrik Hospers, *The Reformed Principle of Authority.* Grand Rapids: The Reformed Press, 1924, pp.15-35.
>   An important polemic against modernism and its seductive appeals.

'On Political Cartooning,' trans. Gordon Spykman, *Reformed Journal*, 26 (1972), pp.18-21.
>   Kuyper's response to a publisher who proposed to issue a collection of cartoons about him; offers an excellent insight into his sometimes magnanimous attitude towards his critics.

A Pamphlet on the Reformation of the Church, trans. Herman Hanko, *The Standard Bearer*, v. 54-63 (1977-86).
>   A series of articles, each of which contains a portion of Kuyper's pleas for reformation.

'Pantheism's Destruction of Boundaries,' trans. J. Hendrik de Vries. *Methodist Review*, 75 (1893), pp.520-37, 762-78.
>   A penetrating critique of pantheism and evolution as they affect the Christian faith.

'Parliament Bill: As Others See Us. Foreign Statesmen on the Constitution Crisis. Dr. Kuyper,' *The Daily Telegraph* (London), 22 August 1911, pp.4-5.
>   Kuyper's suggestions to reform the House of Lords so as to make it representative of the whole nation rather than just of the aristocracy and clergy.

The Practice of Godliness, trans. Marian M. Schoolland. Grand Rapids: Baker Book
House, 1977 (1948).
> A very insightful Reformed view of sanctification in a devotional format.

Principles of Sacred Theology, trans. J. Hendrik De Vries, intro. Benjamin B. Warfield.
Grand Rapids: Baker Book House, 1980 reprint of 1898 ed.
> An erudite but verbose examination, or 'theological encyclopaedia'. Extensive
definitions of terms and examinations of methodology; important for an understanding of the subject's doctrine and manner of expounding and defending it.

The Problem of Poverty, ed. James W. Skillen. Grand Rapids: Baker Book House, 1991
edition of 1950 publication.
> An improved translation of *Christianity and the Class Struggle.* Helpful bibliog-
raphy. Appeals for a Christian alternative to both socialism and capitalism.

'The Resurrection of our Lord Jesus Christ,' trans. J. H. De Vries, *Christianity Today,* VII,
3 July 1936, pp. 53-5.
> Devotional meditation on Revelation 1:18.

The Revelation of St. John, trans. John Hendrik de Vries. Grand Rapids: William B.
Eerdmans Publishing Co., 1963 (1935).
> A futurist and amillennarian interpretation; this originated as a series of articles
late in Kuyper's life.

'The Sign of Jonas,' trans. J. H. De Vries, *Christianity Today,* VII 7 (November 1936), pp.
160-62.
> Devotional meditation on Matthew 12:39.

'The Signs of the Times,' trans. J. H. De Vries, *Christianity Today,* VII (9 January 1937),
pp. 206-7.
> A devotional meditation.

The South-African Crisis, trans. & preface by A. E. Fletcher, 14th ed. London: Clock
House, for the Stop the War Committee, 1900.
> Kuyper blamed capitalism, social Darwinism and imperialism for the British role
in the Boer War; he expressed great affection for the Boers, whom he regarded as
fellow Calvinists waging a just defence.

'Swallowed up in victory,' trans. J. H. De Vries, *Christianity Today,* VII (1 May 1936), pp.
10-13.
> Devotional meditation on 1 Corinthians 15:54.

'Thou hast Shown me the Path of Life', trans. J. H. De Vries, *Christianity Today,* VII (4
August 1936), pp. 90-91.
> Devotional meditation on Psalm 16:11.

To be Near unto God, trans. John Hendrik De Vries. Grand Rapids: William B. Eerdmans
Publishing Co., 1925.
> A fine example of Kuyper's intense personal piety and his pastoral admonitions
to others; emotionally charged language and the author's undefined mysticism leave
his meaning obscure at points.

'The True Genius of Presbyterianism,' *The Presbyterian,* 76 (1906), pp.12-14.
> Kuyper's fraternal greetings to American Presbyterians, in which he emphasized the distinctives of Calvinism and the healthful development of those principles in America.

'Use and Abuse of Apologetics,' *Bibliotheca Sacra,* 65 (1908), pp.374-9.
> A vigorous call for Christians to go beyond defensive measures to confront critics of their faith.

'Whatsoever ye Do, Do it Heartily, as to the Lord', trans. J. H. De Vries, *Christianity Today,* VI (6 November 1935), pp. 130-31.
> Devotional meditation on Colossians 3:23.

When thou Sittest in thine House, trans. J. H. De Vries. Grand Rapids: William B. Eerdmans Publishing Co., 1929 (1899).
> Somewhat ambiguous meditations about family life; reflects the author's disdain for capitalism. Clumsy translation.

'Whereupon are the Foundations thereof Fastened?' *The Christian Intelligencer,* 70 (1899), pp.2-3.
> A devotional article that stresses God's omnipotence and providence as the foundation for all of life.

'Who Quickeneth the Dead,' trans. J. H. De Vries, *Christianity Today,* VII (2 June 1936), pp. 33-5.
> Devotional meditation on Romans 4:17.

The Woman's Position of Honour, unpublished trans., Irene Brouwer Konyndyk. Kampen, Netherlands: J. H. Kok, 1932.
> An anti-feminist tract that argues against giving women the right to vote except when, as widows, they are heads of households.

Women of the New Testament, trans. Henry Zylstra. Grand Rapids: Zondervan Publishing House, 1962.
> Thirty vignettes, some of minor characters about whom the New Testament contains little information; very readable devotional material; some insights into Kuyper's doctrine and hermeneutics.

Women of the Old Testament, trans. Henry Zylstra. Grand Rapids: Zondervan Publishing House, 1961.
> Fifty devotional vignettes in readable form; reflects Kuyper's strict adherence to male authority and female submission.

'The Work of God in our Work,' *Homiletic Review,* LV (1908), insert between pp.273-4.
> A devotional article about good works as the instrumental means of sanctification while God's grace is the effectual means.

The Work of the Holy Spirit, trans. Henri De Vries, with introduction by Benjamin B. Warfield. Grand Rapids: William B. Eerdmans Publishing Co., 1979 reprint of 1900 edition.

A thorough exposition of practically every aspect of the subject; many illustrations of Kuyper's great devotion; somewhat verbose, but well worth reading.

You Can do Greater Things than Christ, trans. Jan H. Boer. Jos, Nigeria: Institute of Church and Society, 1991.
An excerpt from *Pro Rege* that emphasizes supernaturalism and belief in miracles as the foundation for a correct world-view.

Works about Kuyper or which provide additional information on topics covered in this book

Alvarado, Ruben C. 'Calvinism, Arminianism, and Theocracy: Hoedemaker's Critique of Kuyper'. Nioeville, FL: Biblical Horizons, 1992 (audio-tape).
A lecture that maintains theocracy is the truly Reformed view of church and state and therefore criticizes Kuyper's pluralism.

Ambler, Rex. 'The Christian Mind of Abraham Kuyper,' in *Profitable for Doctrine and Reproof,* excerpted from the *Evangelical Magazine.* London: Puritan and Reformed Studies Conference, 1967, pp.5-14.
A readable sketch divided into topics that cover most of Kuyper's contributions; a fine introduction to Kuyper's thinking.

Anderson, Norman. *Christianity and World Religions.* Downers Grove, IL: Inter-Varsity Press, 1984.
A vigorous defence of the uniqueness and superiority of biblical Christianity as compared with its competitors. Cites Kuyper as an example of orthodox scholarship.

The Annual Register, A Review of Public Events at Home and Abroad. London: Longmans, Green & Co., 1902.
Reports Kuyper's efforts to mediate an end to the Anglo-Boer War and the British refusal to accept Dutch good offices.

Barnouw, A. J. *Holland under Queen Wilhelmina,* foreword by E. W. Bok. New York: Charles Scribner's Sons, 1923.
An interesting topical history of the quarter century when Kuyper's career was at its apex. The author's perspective is that of a liberal who was rather critical of the Anti-Revolutionaries.

Bavinck, Herman. 'The Future of Calvinism,' *The Presbyterian and Reformed Review,* 17 (1894), pp.1-24.
An enthusiastic survey and appraisal of Calvinism's accomplishments and a wishful proposal for its future influence. Does not mention Kuyper by name but extols the Neo-Calvinist movement.

The Philosophy of Revelation, trans. Geerhardus Vos, Nicholas M. Steffans & Henry E. Dosker. Grand Rapids: Baker Book House, 1979 reprint of 1909 edition.
Most of these essays were Stone Lectures in 1908-9; the material corresponds closely with Kuyper's views.

'Recent Dogmatic Thought in the Netherlands,' trans. Geerhardus Vos, *The Presbyterian and Reformed Review,* 3 (1892), pp.209-28.
> An important survey of theological trends of the nineteenth century and Kuyper's reaction to them.

Beattie, Francis P. *Calvinism and Modern Thought.* Philadelphia: Westminster Press, 1902.
> Affirms the compatibility of the Reformed faith with wholesome advances in history, philosophy, science, sociology, etc; comparable to Kuyper's world-view.

Bebbington, David W. *William Ewart Gladstone.* Grand Rapids: William B. Eerdmans Publishing Co., 1993.
> An important analysis of Gladstone's beliefs about Christianity and politics; shows that he was an Anglo-Catholic with a liberal attitude towards evolution and Higher Criticism. Kuyper misunderstood Gladstone.

Beeke, Joel R. 'Cornelius Van Til and Apologetics,' *The Banner of Truth,* 342 (1992), pp.17-22.
> A clear exposition of presuppositionalism as an expansion of Kuyper and Bavinck.

'The Second Dutch Reformation,' *Calvin Theological Journal,* 28 (1993), pp.298-327.
> An interesting survey of Dutch church history in the seventeenth and eighteenth centuries with helpful historiographical comments; cites Kuyper as a critic of pietism despite the piety evident in his own writings.

Beekenkamp, C. 'The Dr. Kuyper Institute,' *Calvin Forum,* 3 (1937), pp.107-9.
> Shows how Calvinists have tried to preserve the Anti-Revolutionary heritage of Kuyper while promoting his influence in public life.

Beets, Henry. 'The Calvinism of Abraham Kuyper,' *The Banner,* 56 (1921), p.69.
> A strong defence of Kuyper's historic Calvinism and a tribute to his elaboration of the Reformed faith into a consistent world-view.

The Christian Reformed Church: Its Roots, History, Schools, and Mission Work. Grand Rapids: Baker Book House, 1946.
> A useful account of the European background and development in America; shows some of Kuyper's influence upon the Christian Reformed Church in America.

'Dr. Abraham Kuyper,' *Banner of Truth,* 39 (1904), pp.65-8.
> A laudatory sketch; a useful introduction to Kuyper's work.

'Dr. Abraham Kuyper,' *The Banner,* 42 (1907), pp.520-21.
> A readable biographical sketch on the occasion of Kuyper's seventieth birthday.

'Dr. Abraham Kuyper,' *The Banner,* 55 (1920), pp.730-31.
> An obituary tribute that reviews Kuyper's life and extols him as an example of faithfulness to Christ and orthodoxy.

'Dr. Abraham Kuyper, His Life and Principles,' *Banner of Truth*, 36 (1902), pp.70-74, 186-8; 37 (July 1902), pp.10-13.
>A helpful biographical sketch and a summary and analysis of the Stone Lectures.

'Publishing the Works of Dr. A. Kuyper,' *The Banner,* 56 (1921), pp.164-5.
>A proposal to render Kuyper's writings into English and other languages.

'Publishing the Works of Dr. A. Kuyper,' *The Banner,* 56 (14 April 1921), p.229.
>An editorial about a proposal to render Kuyper's writings into English and other languages; this project has not been completed.

'Two Publications of Loving Tribute to Dr. A. Kuyper,' *The Banner,* 56 (17 February 1921), pp.100-101.
>The editor's review of an article and a book that extol Kuyper's contributions.

Begbie, Jeremy. *Voicing Creation's Praise: Towards a Theology of the Arts.* Edinburgh: T. & T. Clark, 1991.
>The chapter 'Kuyper and Bavinck: Art, Beauty and the Sovereignty of God' is a helpful analysis of the subject.

Benda, Harry J. 'Christiaan Snouck Hurgronje and the Foundations of Dutch Islamic Policy in Indonesia,' *Journal of Modern History,* XXX (1958), pp.338-47.
>A useful examination of the leading Dutch Islamicist and his influence on colonial policy.

Berkhof, Hendrikus. *Christian Faith: An Introduction to the Study of the Faith,* revised edition, trans. Sierd Woudstra. Grand Rapids: William B. Eerdmans Publishing Co., 1986 (1979).
>A liberal theologian shows respect for Kuyper, especially his book about the Holy Spirit and his works on common grace.

Two Hundred Years of Theology: Report of a Personal Journey, trans. John Vriend. Grand Rapids: William B. Eerdmans Publishing Co., 1989.
>Contains a helpful chapter about the development of liberal and modernist theology in the Netherlands; makes only passing mention of orthodox scholars.

Berkhof, Louis. *The Church and Social Problems.* Grand Rapids: Eerdmans-Sevensma Co., 1913.
>A lecture to a Calvin College and Seminary gathering; affirms the church's social responsibility as adjunct to her evangelistic role; emphasizes principles but not specific programmes; unclear about socialism.

'Dr. Kuyper and the Revival of Calvinistic Doctrine,' *The Calvin Forum,* 3 (1937-38).
>An appreciative, critical tribute to Kuyper's role in the resurgence of Reformed theology.

Berkouwer, G. C. *General Revelation.* Grand Rapids: William B. Eerdmans Publishing Co., 1955.
>Explains Kuyper's advocacy of the study of comparative religion; clarifies his conception of natural theology.

A Half-Century of Theology, trans. & ed. Lewis B. Smedes. Grand Rapids: William
B. Eerdmans Publishing Co., 1977.
This work relates Kuyper to his contemporaries and to his descendants and
critics in theology.

Man: The Image of God. Grand Rapids: William B. Eerdmans Publishing Co., 1962.
A Reformed analysis of anthropology with many critiques of various scholars; useful coverage of Kuyper on the subject of common grace.

The Sacraments, trans. Hugo Bekker. Grand Rapids: William B. Eerdmans Publishing Co., 1969.
Rejects Kuyper's concept of presumed regeneration as the basis for infant
baptism.

Bernbaum, John A., ed. *Economic Justice and the State: A Debate Between Ronald H.
Nash and Eric H. Beversluis.* Grand Rapids: Baker Book House, 1986.
An argument over means to help the poor and needy, whether by market
forces and charity or by state intervention; Nash's superior logic and writing
ability make a convincing case for the market.

Blok, Petrus Johannes. *History of the People of the Netherlands*, V, 5. New York: G. P.
Putnam's Sons, 1912.
A substantial survey, but one that slights Kuyper and the contributions of the
Anti-Revolutionary Party; undocumented.

Bloomberg, Charles. *Christian-Nationalism and the Rise of the Afrikaner Broederbond,
1918-48,* ed. Saul Dubow. Bloomington, IN: Indiana University Press, 1989.
An attempt by a liberal Jewish author from South Africa to expose the
Broederbond. Cites Kuyper's concept of spheres as the theological basis for apartheid, although the author admits that Afrikaners may have misapplied Kuyper's
ideas to some extent. Bloomberg did not have a clear understanding of Kuyper
and opposed his vision for Christian society.

Boer, Jan Harm. *Missionary Messengers of Liberation in a Colonial Context.* Amsterdam: Rodopi Publishers, 1979.
A missionary to Nigeria cites Kuyper as an advocate of colonial trusteeship
who favoured enlightened policy towards the Indies.

Bolt, John. *Christian and Reformed Today.* Jordan Station, Ontario: Paideia Press, 1984.
An exposition of the Reformed world-view which cites Kuyper's contributions
in common grace, the antithesis and education. Clear, insightful essays.

'Kuyper and Herman Bavinck,' *The Kuyper Newsletter,* 2 (Winter 1981-2), pp.1-2.
An interesting account of Kuyper's impatience with the peace-loving Bavinck
in the latter's attitude towards doctrinal liberals.

Boogman, J. C. 'J. Thorbecke, Challenge and Response,' in *Acta Historiae Neerlandicae:
Studies on the History of the Netherlands,* VII, ed. B. H. Sicher van Bath. The
Hague: Martinus Nijhoff, 1974.
Places Thorbecke in the context of German idealism-romanticism and shows
how his political philosophy developed under that influence.

'Thorbecke, a Liberal Statesman,' in *Acta Historiae Neerlandicae: Studies on the History of the Netherlands,* VII, ed. B. H. Slicher van Bath. The Hague: Martinus Nijhoff, 1974, pp.122-5.
   A brief biographical introduction with reference to Thorbecke's political philosophy.

Bornewasser, J. A. 'Thorbecke and the Churches,' in *Acta Historiae Neerlandicae: Studies on the History of the Netherlands,* VII, ed. B. H. Slicher van Bath. The Hague: Martinus Nijhoff, 1974, pp.146-69.
   One of the few studies of this subject in English; portrays Thorbecke as a liberal idealist with inconsistent policies towards churches, a person who despised intolerance based on firm religious beliefs.

Bosch, David J. 'Afrikaner Civil Religion and the Current South African Crisis,' *Princeton Seminary Bulletin,* 7 (1986), pp.1-14.
   A south African theologian contends that Reformed evangelicalism, Neo-Calvinism and romantic nationalism combined have produced the Afrikaner attitude towards blacks; he holds that Afrikaners have distorted Kuyper's teachings as they have adapted them to the South African situation.

'The Roots and Fruits of Afrikaner Civil Religion,' in *New Faces of Africa,* eds. J. W. Hofmeyer & W. S. Vorster. Pretoria, South Africa: University of South Africa, 1984, pp.14-35.
   The author rejects the Calvinist paradigm interpretation of Afrikaner history, but shows how Afrikaner leaders have misapplied Kuyper's Neo-Calvinism in the service of nationalism.

Bouma, Clarence. 'Abraham Kuyper: Kingdom Warrior and Kingdom Builder,' *The Banner,* 72 (1937), pp.1013-14.
   Extols Kuyper for his ecclesiastical leadership and for founding the Free University.

'The Centenary of Abraham Kuyper's Birth,' *The Calvin Forum,* 3 (1937), p.51.
   Tributes to Kuyper as a model defender of the faith.

Bouma, Clarence *et al. God-Centered Living or Calvinism in Action.* Grand Rapids: Baker Book House, 1951.
   An important collection of essays by Kuyperian scholars who apply his teachings to education, economics, politics, business, etc.

Bouma, Hendrik. *Secession,* Doleantie, *and Union* 1834-1892, trans. Theodore Plantinga, with appendices by Peter Y. De Jong. Neerlandia, Alberta: Inheritance Publications, 1995.
   A partisan but thorough study of Reformed efforts to preserve orthodoxy in the face of modernism; valuable comparisons of the *Afscheiding* and the *Doleantie* leading to the formation of the *Gereformeerde Kerken;* duly critical of some of Kuyper's beliefs. Appendices are especially useful.

Bousquet, G. H. *A French View of the Netherlands Indies,* trans. P. E. Lilienthal. London: Oxford University Press, 1940.

A somewhat impressionistic comparison of French, British and Dutch colo-nial policies, together with an admiring but critical appraisal of Dutch rule in the East Indies. Most of the book deals with the post-World War I period, but there is some historical information about the development of Dutch policy. Nothing specific about Kuyper.

Bratt, James D. 'Abraham Kuyper, American History, and the Tensions of Neo-Calvin-ism,' in *Sharing the Reformed Tradition*, eds. George Harinck & Hans Krabbendam. Amsterdam: VU Uitgeverij, 1995, pp.97-114.

'Abraham Kuyper, J. Gresham Machen, and the Dynamics of Reformed Anti-Mod-ernism', *Journal of Presbyterian History,* 74 (1997), pp.247-58.
An insightful comparison and contrast of Kuyper and Machen.

'Abraham Kuyper's Public Career,' *Reformed Journal,* 37 (1987), pp.9-12.
A rather critical article that compares Kuyper to Jerry Falwell and Martin Luther King, Jr.

Dutch Calvinism in Modern America. Grand Rapids: William B. Eerdmans Publish-ing Co., 1984.
An important survey of the European background to Dutch settlement in America precedes the major part of the book; contains numerous references to Kuyper and his supporters.

'The Dutch Schools,' in *Reformed Theology in America,* ed. David F. Wells. Grand Rapids: William B. Eerdmans Publishing Co., 1985.
An interesting account of Kuyper's influence among Dutch Americans and the disputes that arose as they sought to apply his ideas of antithesis and com-mon grace.

'In the Shadow of Mt. Kuyper: A Survey of the Field,' *Calvin Theological Journal,* 31 (1996), pp.51-66.
An analysis of five recent studies of Kuyper, two of them unpublished disser-tations; filled with keen insights.

'Raging Tumults, the Private Life of Abraham Kuyper,' *Reformed Journal,* 37 (1987), pp.9-13.
A rather critical analysis that emphasizes his mental and nervous disorders and cites character flaws.

Brinks, Herb, 'Kuyper in Michigan, 1898,' *The Kuyper Newsletter,* 2 (1981-2), pp.2-3.
Relates that Kuyper spoke to large crowds in Michigan, Iowa, Illinois and Ohio before going to Princeton to deliver the Stone Lectures.

Bristley, Eric D. 'From Probability to Certainty: The Witness of the Holy Spirit and the Defense of the Bible in Presbyterian and Reformed Apologetics, 1870-1920.' Th.M. thesis, Westminster Theological Seminary, 1989.
Contains important analyses and critiques of Warfield, Kuyper and Bavinck when compared with Calvin; defends presuppositionalism; convincing argument.

British and Foreign State Papers, 1901-1902, XCV, ed. Richard Brant & Willoughby Maycock. London: His Majesty's Stationery Office, 1902.
> This contains the diplomatic correspondence between the Dutch and British governments pertaining to Kuyper's efforts to mediate an end to the Anglo-Boer War.

Brunt, L. 'The "Kleine Luyden" as a Disturbing Factor in the Emancipation of the Orthodox Calvinists *(Gereformeerden)* in the Netherlands,' *Sociologia Neerlandica,* VIII (1972), pp.89-102.
> A sociological study that questions the view that Kuyper's followers were mostly poor, unlearned people; portrays him as a populist politician.

Bulhof, Ilse N. 'The Netherlands,' in *The Comparative Reception of Darwinism,* ed. Thomas F. Glick. Austin, TX: University of Texas Press, 1972, pp.269-306.
> Cites Kuyper's opposition to evolution as dogma and shows how receptivity to Darwinism among the liberals prepared the way for socialism.

Burggraaff, Winfred. 'The Revival of Evangelical Theology in the Netherlands,' *The Evangelical Student,* 4 (1930), pp.6-17.
> Contains a survey of Dutch theology in the nineteenth century with due recognition of Kuyper's contributions to orthodoxy.

Cairns, John. 'The Present Struggles in the National Church of Holland,' *The Presbyterian Review,* 9 (1887), pp.87-108.
> A Scottish Presbyterian's sympathetic analysis of the secession of 1886; decidedly pro-Kuyper.

Conradie, A. L. *The Neo-Calvinistic concept of Philosophy.* Natal, South Africa: The University Press, 1960. Cites Kuyper as founder of genuine Calvinistic philosophy and presents an exposition of his Stone Lectures.

Daalder, Hans, 'The Netherlands: Opposition in a Segmented Society,' in *Political Oppostions in Western Democracies,* ed. Robert A. Dahl. New Haven, CT: Yale University Press, 1966, pp.188-247.
> An important analysis of Dutch parties since 1814; explains pluralism in terms of causative factors. Helpful information about the Anti-Revolutionary Party.

'Parties and Politics in the Netherlands,' *Political Studies,* 3 (1955), pp.1-16.
> A helpful explanation of how parties function and how religious groups have formed them; some information about the Anti-Revolutionary Party and the Christian Historical Union.

Davies, Alan. *Infected Christianity: A Study of Modern Racism.* Montreal: McGill-Queen's University Press, 1988.
> The chapter entitled 'The Afrikaner Christ' says that Kuyper's Neo-Calvinism, with its spheres of authority, encouraged racial separation, even though Kuyper was not a racist.

Day, Clive. *The Dutch in Java,* intro. John Bastin. Kuala Lumpur: Oxford University Press, 1966 reprint of 1904 edition.

A useful account of the background against which Kuyper introduced the Ethical Policy.

De Gaay Fortman, W. F. 'Kuyper and the Social Problem,' *Perspective Newsletter,* 7 (1973), pp.12-15.
A tribute to Kuyper's concerns and his proposals to apply the faith to society.

De Graaff, Arnold. *The Educational Ministry of the Church.* Phillipsburg, NJ: Craig Press, 1968.
Pages 66-71 contain a helpful explanation of Kuyper's doctrine of the church and how he used the terms 'organism' and 'institute'.

De Gruchy, John W. 'Bonhoeffer, Calvinism, and Christian Civil Disobedience in South Africa,' *Scottish Journal of Theology,* 34 (1981), pp.245-62.
Contends that South African Calvinists have sometimes distorted Kuyper's sphere-sovereignty to support apartheid and have thereby constructed a civil religion that Kuyper would not have endorsed.

De Jong, A. C. *The Well-Meant Offer of the Gospel: The Views of H. Hoeksema and K. Schilder.* Franeker, Netherlands: T. Wever, 1954.
A careful study of Reformed scholars who rejected Kuyper's doctrine of common grace.

De Jong, James A. 'Abraham Kuyper's Edition of the *Institutes,*' *Calvin Theological Journal,* 21 (1986), pp.231-2.
Relates that Kuyper improved on an earlier Dutch version and included Beza's life of Calvin; the Battles and McNeill edition used Kuyper's work in preparing the latest English version.

'Henricus Beuker and *De Vrij Kerk* on Abraham Kuyper and the Free University,' in *Building the House: Essays on Christian Education,* eds James A. De Jong & Louis Y. Van Dyke. Sioux Center, IA: Dordt College Press, 1981, pp.27-45.
Relates support and criticism of Kuyper's project for a university free from church as well as state.

De Jong, Norman. 'Sphere-Sovereignty — Is It Politics?' *The Banner,* 109 (1974), pp.14-15.
A helpful summary of Kuyper's development as a Christian political thinker.

'Sphere Sovereignty Re-examined,' *The Outlook,* 24 (1974), pp.2-5.
This author appears to have misunderstood Kuyper's concept and therefore to have drawn false conclusions from it.

De Jong, Peter. '1886 — A Year to Remember,' *Midwestern Journal of Theology,* 2 (1986), pp.7-52.
A substantial survey of events that led to the secession of 1886 and the union of 1892.

'The Bible and Church Doctrine,' *The Outlook,* 22 (1972), pp.8-9.

Compares Kuyper and G. Vos on the relationship of Reformed dogma to authority of Scripture and holds that the former did not always establish dogma from Scripture but extolled Calvinistic 'principles' he assumed to be scriptural.

'Comments on Criticism of Kuyper,' *The Outlook,* 23 (1973), pp.10-11.
A reply to the charge that Kuyper was too much concerned with Calvinistic 'principles' and insufficiently concerned about exegesis of the Bible, the source of those principles.

'God's Book is our Light,' *The Outlook,* 23 (1973), pp.12-13.
Although the author admires Kuyper, he cautions against making Calvinistic 'principles', rather than Scripture, the priority.

'Kuyper on the American Church Scene,' *Torch and Trumpet,* 16 (1966), p.14.
Shows that Kuyper hailed the American separation of church and state but lamented the individualism that often negates the covenant community of God's people.

'Kuyper on the Social Struggle,' *The Federation Messenger,* 22 (1950-51), pp.33-4.
A tribute to Kuyper's vision for social justice as expressed in his book *Christianity and the Class Struggle.*

'Where are we Going — with the Kingdom?,' *The Outlook,* 24 (1974), pp.2-6.
A critique of those Kuyperians who have made his concept of spheres the basis for antinomian use of the Bible and rejection of its sole authority.

'Where are we Going — with Sphere Sovereignty?,' *The Outlook,* 24 (1974), pp.18-22.
Accuses Kuyper of overstating the authority of independent spheres and shows how recent Kuyperians have misapplied the concept to justify unscriptural ideas and action.

De Jong, Peter Y. & Nelson D. Kloosterman, eds. *The Reformation of 1834: Essays in Commemoration of the Act of Secession and Return.* Orange City, IA: Pluim Publishing, Inc., 1984.
Chiefly an assessment of *Afscheiding* influence in USA, but helpful for European background as well.

De Jongste, H. & J. M. Van Krimpen. *The Bible and the Life of the Christian,* 5th ed. Nutley, NJ: Presbyterian & Reformed Publishing Co., 1978.
An application of Kuyper's principles to many spheres of authority and responsibility.

De Kat Angelino, A. D. A. *Colonial Policy,* 2 vols, trans. G. J. Reiner. Chicago: University of Chicago Press, 1931, pp. 530, 674.
A thorough topical analysis of theory and practice in the East Indies; the author died before reaching Kuyper's administration.

De Klerck, E. S. *History of the Netherlands East Indies,* 2 vols. Rotterdam: W. L. & J. Brusse, 1938.

Writes in an awkward style about Dutch history and policy in East Indies; much helpful information, but little about Kuyper.

De Klerk, Peter, comp. & ed. *A Bibliography of the Writings of the Professors of Calvin Theological Seminary.* Grand Rapids: Calvin Theological Seminary, 1980.
Useful for locating Dutch and English articles about Kuyper.

De Klerk, Willem. *The Puritans in Africa: a Story of Afrikanerdom.* London: Rex Collings, 1975.
Contends that the Boers drew upon the doctrine of sphere authority to justify apartheid; cites Kuyper and Dooyeweerd as providing a basis for Afrikaner claims.

De Koster, Lester Ronald. 'Sphere-Sovereignty: Ideology: Neither Biblical nor Reformed,' *The Banner,* 109 (1974), pp.4-5.
A categorical rejection of cosmonomic ideology, with the claim that its exponents have twisted Kuyper's concept of sphere-authority.

De Savornin Lohman, Witsius H. 'Dr. Abraham Kuyper,' *The Presbyterian and Reformed Review,* IX (1898), pp.561-609.
Mainly a summary of Kuyper's views about church and state, with specific reference to his concept of reformation and just procedures in government, colonies, suffrage, etc.; an important work by a contemporary observer who refrained from judgements about Kuyper's proposals.

De Vries, Simon John. *Bible and Theology in the Netherlands: Dutch Old Testament Criticism under Modernist and Conservative Auspices.* Wageningen, Netherlands: H. Veenman & N. V. Zonen, 1968.
A survey of Higher Criticism that extols the work of Kuenen and other modernists, but holds that mediating theologians saved Christianity from secularists and from anti-progressive orthodox Calvinists. Readable and interesting but decidedly biased against orthodoxy.

Deenick, J. W. 'Christocracy in Kuyper and Schilder,' *The Reformed Theological Review,* 43 (1984), pp.42-50.
Helpful background about Kuyper and a comparison between him and Schilder, who denied common grace.

Dengerink, J. D. 'The State and Christian Education in the Netherlands,' *International Reformed Bulletin,* 13 (1963), pp.11-15.
An explanation of the Dutch schools, public and private, that credits Kuyper with aiding the cause of Christian education with public funding.

Dennison, William D. 'Dutch Neo-Calvinism and the Roots for Transformation: An Introductory Essay,' *Journal of the Evangelical Theological Society,* 42 (1999), pp.271-91.
A critical study of Neo-Calvinists since Kuyper who have taken his views to ends he might not have approved.

'Domela Nieuwenhuis, a Great Dutch Socialist,' *American Monthly Illustrated Review of Reviews,* XXIX (1904), pp.746-7.

A liberal American journal extols a radical Lutheran pastor who defected from Christ to become an advocate of social revolution.

'Dr. Kuyper,' *The Presbyterian,* LXVIII (1898), p.7.
Hails Kuyper as a Christian theologian and statesman and celebrates his visit to Princeton in 1898.

'Dr. Kuyper,' *The Princeton Press* (1 October 1898).
A notice of the forthcoming Stone Lectures with a commendation of Kuyper as a worthy recipient of an honorary degree from Princeton University.

Dooyeweerd, Herman. *A New Critique of Theoretical Thought,* 4 vols, trans. David H. Freeman and William S. Young. Nutley, NJ: Presbyterian and Reformed Publishing Co., 1969.
Contains some helpful clarifications and applications of Kuyper's teachings.

Roots of Western culture, trans. John Kraay, eds. Mark Vander Vennen & Bernard Zylstra. Toronto: Wedge Publishing Foundation, 1979.
An heir to Kuyper's legacy has analysed conditions in post-World War II Europe, especially in the Netherlands. Difficult reading.

Douma, J. *Infant Baptism and Conversion.* Winnipeg, Manitoba: Premier Publishing, 1979.
Contains a pertinent critique of Kuyper's view of presumed regeneration; a reply to David Kingdon and Reformed Baptists.

Du Toit, André. 'No Chosen People: The Myth of the Calvinist Origins of Afrikaner-Nationalism and Racial Ideology,' *American Historical Review,* 88 (1983), pp.920-52.
Shows clearly that David Livingstone initiated the popularity of the Calvinist paradigm of Afrikaner nationalism without adequate evidence; numerous scholars have assumed the validity of that thesis without testing it and have thereby perpetuated the myth.

Durand, Jaap. 'Afrikaner Piety and Dissent,' in *Resistance and Hope: South African Essays in Honour of Beyers Naude,* ed. Charles Villa-Vicencio and John W. De Gruchy. Grand Rapids: William B. Eerdmans Publishing Co., 1985, pp.39-51, 200.
A critique of Kuyperian theologians who justified apartheid; the author laments that Barth's theology has not made greater gains to offer an alternative to Neo-Calvinism.

'Church and State in South Africa: Karl Barth vs. Abraham Kuyper,' in *On Reading Karl Barth in South Africa,* ed. Charles Villa-Vicencio. Grand Rapids: William B. Eerdmans Publishing Co., 1988, pp.121-37, 169-70.
A decidedly pro-Barth analysis, one that credits him with advocating a prophetic role for the church, while holding that Kuyper's concept of common grace denied the church that role.

Ericson, Edward E. 'Abraham Kuyper: Cultural Critic,' *Calvin Theological Journal*, 22 (1987), pp.21-7.
Shows clearly that Kuyper rejected romanticism, as well as rationalism, in favour of a biblical world-view; portrays his opposition to the influence of the French Revolution.

Ericson, Edward E., Jr. 'Remembering the Antithesis,' *Perspectives*, 8 (1993), pp.3-5.
A contemporary academician's warning to apply the antithesis and not to allow belief in common grace to justify approval of evil.

Edmundson, George. 'Holland,' in *Cambridge Modern History*, XII, ed. A. W. Ward *et al.* Cambridge: The University Press, 1910, reprinted 1969, pp.243-50.
Some insights into the period of Kuyper's greatest influence; hails him as a democratic Calvinist.

Faber, J. *Essays in Reformed Doctrine*. Neerlandia, Alberta: Inheritance Publications, 1990.
Contains an essay about Kuyper's understanding of the incarnation and contends that he expressed his view improperly and thereby failed to do justice to Jesus' humiliation.

'The Fall of the Kuyper Ministry in Holland,' *American Monthly Illustrated Review of Reviews*, XXXII (1905), pp.356-7.
A liberal American journal applauds the defeat of the Anti-Revolutionary Party in 1905 as a triumph over 'clerical' government.

Fernhout, Harry. 'Man, Faith, and Religion in Bavinck, Kuyper, and Dooyeweerd,' unpublished M. Phil. thesis at the Institute for Christian Studies, 1975.
A highly technical and awkwardly written comparison of three great Reformed thinkers; sheds some light on Kuyper's understanding of faith in its relation to all knowledge and learning.

Frame, John M. *Cornelius Van Til: An Analysis of his Thought*. Phillipsburg, NJ: Presbyterian and Reformed Publishing Co., 1995.
A careful, thorough study by a grateful but duly critical disciple who finds Van Til's lack of communication skills a major cause of confusion about his ideas.

Friedman, David. 'Philosophy and Religious Trends,' in *The Netherlands*, ed. Bartholomew Landheer. Berkeley, CA: University of California Press, 1944, pp.205-25.
A concise survey of philosophical currents from the fifteenth to the twentieth century, with remarks about their effects upon religion. Kuyper receives only a passing mention.

'Political Parties,' in *The Netherlands*, ed. Bartholomew Landheer. Berkeley, CA: University of California Press, 1944, pp.107-31.
Although Friedman credits Kuyper and Anti-Revolutionaries with progressive policies, he refers to them and their allies as 'right wing'.

Fuhrmann, Paul T. *God-Centered Religion — Essays Inspired by Some French and Swiss Protestant Writers.* Grand Rapids: Zondervan Publishing House, 1942.
    Although chiefly an exposition of historic Calvinism, this work hails Kuyper as one of its greatest exponents; the author was confused about Barthian theology, which he regarded as a valid expression of Reformed faith.

Furnivall, J. S. *Netherlands India, A Study of Plural Economy,* intro. Jonkheer MR. A. C. D. De Graeff. Cambridge: The University Press, 1967 reprint of 1939 edition.
    A thorough study of Dutch policy in the East Indies up to 1929; incorrectly refers to the Anti-Revolutionary Party as a 'clerical' party.

Gaffin, Richard B., Jr. 'Geerhardus Vos and the Interpretation of Paul,' in *Jerusalem and Athens,* ed. E. R. Geehan. Nutley, NJ: Presbyterian & Reformed Publishing Co., 1971, pp.228-43.
    Sheds light upon Kuyper's reluctance to acknowledge the discipline of biblical theology.

    'Old Amsterdam and Inerrancy,' *Westminster Theological Journal,* 44 (1982), pp.250-89.
    A thorough and convincing reply to Rogers and McKim, who attempted to portray Kuyper as believing that the Bible is not inerrant in form as well as in saving content.

    'Old Amsterdam and Inerrancy,' *Westminster Theological Journal,* 45 (1983), pp.219-72.
    A defence of Herman Bavinck against misuse of his writings by Rogers and McKim.

Geehan, E. R. ed. *Jerusalem and Athens: Critical Discussions on the Philosophy and Apologetics of Cornelius Van Til.* Nutley, NJ: Presbyterian and Reformed Publishing Co., 1977.
    Several contributors relate Van Til's debt to Kuyper and show how he amplified Kuyper's position.

Gerstner, John H. 'Warfield's Case for Biblical Inerrancy,' in *God's Inerrant Word,* ed. John Warwick Montgomery. Minneapolis: Bethany Fellowship, Inc., 1974, pp.115-42.
    Shows that the disagreement between Warfield and Kuyper about apologetics was friendly.

Geyl, Pieter. *The Netherlands in the Seventeenth Century,* V. 1. London: Ernest Benn Limited, 1961 (1936).
    Contains helpful coverage of the Dutch Reformed Church in its formative period; an especially useful account of the Calvinist-Remonstrant issue.

Glenn, Charles Leslie, Jr. *The Myth of the Common School.* Amherst, MA: University of Massachusetts Press, 1988.
    Contains a valuable description of education in the Netherlands; extensive bibliography.

Godfrey, W. Robert. 'Calvin and Calvinism in the Netherlands,' in *John Calvin: His Influence in the Western World,* ed. W. Stanford Reid. Grand Rapids: Zondervan Publishing House, 1982, pp.93-120.
    A reliable survey of the subject with a little about Kuyper.

'Kuyper and Materialism,' *The Outlook,* 41 (1991), pp.17-28.
    A concise summary of Kuyper's arguments against capitalism and socialism and his call for Christian social action.

Goudzwaard, Bob. 'Christian Higher Education in the Netherlands,' *Reformed Ecumenical Synod Theological Forum,* XX (1992), pp.5-9.
    A rather vague analysis of Kuyper's legacy and the demise, or at least modification, of his projects, especially in university education.

A Christian Political Option, trans. Herman Praamsma. Toronto: Wedge Publishing Foundation, 1972.
    A contemporary Kuyperian's argument for state intervention to assure social justice in domestic economy and world affairs. Unclear in places; the author fails to distinguish adequately between law and gospel.

'Christian Social Thought in the Dutch Neo-Calvinist Tradition,' in *Religion, Economics, and Social Thought,* eds. Walter Block & Irving Hexham. Vancouver, BC: The Fraser Institute, 1986, pp.251-79.
    An explanation of sphere authority and the antithesis by a contemporary disciple of Abraham Kuyper.

Groen van Prinsterer, Guillaume. *The Anti-Revolutionary Principle,* trans. J. Faber. Amsterdam: The Groen van Prinsterer Fund, 1956.
    A succinct statement of the gospel and the Anti-Revolutionary principle; rejects uncritical conservatism as well as liberalism, Roman Catholicism and socialism; shows appreciation for Burke, de Maistre, Guizot, *et al.*

The History of the Revolution in its First Phase, trans. Harry Van Dyke & Donald Morton. Amsterdam: The Groen Van Prinsterer Fund, 1973.

Unbelief and Revolution, Lectures VIII & IX, trans. Harry Van Dyke with Donald Morton. Amsterdam: The Groen Van Prinsterer Fund, 1974.
    Kuyper's mentor contended that revelation and divine sovereignty opposed human reason and autonomy, and the French Revolution was the collision between them.

Unbelief and Revolution, Lecture XI, ed. & trans. Harry van Dyke with Donald Morton. Amsterdam: The Groen van Prinsterer Fund, 1973.
    An overtly interpretive argument that the doctrine of popular sovereignty caused the French Revolution and infected most European nations and governments long before 1789.

Haas, Guenther. 'Kuyper's Legacy for Christian Ethics,' *Calvin Theological Journal,* 33 (1998), pp. 320-49.

Haas contends that Neo-Calvinism has the resources to combat the relativism of post-modern philosophy, especially in ethics. Awkward writing and much jargon.

Hansen, Erik & Peter A. Prosper, Jr. 'Religion and the Development of the Dutch Trade Union Movement, 1872-1914,' *Social History,* 9 (1976), pp.357-83.
An interesting survey of how Protestant and Roman Catholic leaders led in the formation of unions related to their respective political parties, with the Anti-Revolutionary Party leading the way.

Hansen, Maurice G. *The Reformed Church in the Netherlands Traced from A.D. 1340 to A.D. 1840.* New York: Board of Publication of the German Reformed Church in America, 1884.
A readable survey of the period leading up to the Secession of 1834 and its consequences.

Harinck, George. ' " Give us an American Kuyper." Dutch Calvinist Responses to the Founding of Westminster Theological Seminary in Philadelphia,' *Calvin Theological Journal,* 33 (1998), pp. 299-319.
An interesting account of Dutch perceptions of Machen and Presbyterian conflicts in the US; relates Machen's admiration for Kuyper.

Henderson, R. D. 'How Abraham Kuyper Became a Kuyperian,' *Christian Scholar's Review,* XXII (1992), pp.22-35.
An excellent biographical sketch documented from primary sources; especially helpful in relating Kuyper's conversion from modernism to orthodoxy.

Heslam, Peter Somers. *Creating a Christian Worldview.* Grand Rapids: William B. Eerdmans Publishing Co., 1998.
An appreciative but critical analysis of Kuyper as an exponent of common grace, the antithesis, etc., and as a critic of art and science. Readable despite some awkward passages; helpful interpretations of why Kuyper argued as he did.

'The Christianization of the East Indies: The Ideas of Abraham Kuyper on Dutch Colonial Policy,' *Reflection: An International Reformed Review of Missiology,* 2 (1989), pp.15-17.
An undocumented summary of the Anti-Revolutionary Party and the Ethical Policy from Kuyper's perspective; a superficial treatment.

Hesselink, I. John. *On Being Reformed.* Ann Arbor, MI: Servant Books, 1983.
This collection of essays to rebut misunderstandings of the Reformed faith pays tribute to Kuyper's contributions but criticizes his concept of sphere authority.

Hexham, Irving. 'Christian Politics According to Abraham Kuyper,' *Crux,* 19 (1983), pp.2-7.
A helpful analysis based upon Kuyper's *Lectures on Calvinism;* finds inconsistencies and lack of coherence at some points in Kuyper's presentation but extols his political philosophy as a Christian alternative to capitalism and socialism.

'Christianity and Apartheid: An Introductory Bibliography,' *Reformed Journal*, 30 (1980), S-2-2-11.
> A very useful annotated bibliography for the study of South African Calvinism and Kuyper's influence upon it.

'Dutch Calvinism and the Development of Afrikaner Nationalism,' *African Affairs*, 79 (1980), pp.195-208.
> Contends that S. J. Du Toit and the Reformed Church are the sources of Afrikaner nationalism, i.e., from about 1902 onwards the Doppers' view encouraged nationalism as an outgrowth of a Calvinist world-view.

The Irony of Apartheid: The Struggle for National Independence of Afrikaner Calvinism against British Imperialism. Lewiston, NY: Edwin Mellen Press, 1981.
> Contains a useful summary of Kuyper's belief and argues that Afrikaners misapplied his concept of sphere authority to justify apartheid.

Heyns, W. *Manual of Reformed Doctrine.* Grand Rapids: William B. Eerdmans Publishing Co., 1926.
> Contains a clear treatment of traditional Reformed belief about the covenant of grace and infant baptism from which Kuyper deviated.

Hoekema, Anthony A. 'Kuyper, Bavinck, and Infallibility,' *Reformed Journal*, 11 (1961), pp.18-22.
> Speaks to a controversy in the Christian Reformed Church to show that infallibility, biblically stated, is not the same as precision of expression; invokes Kuyper and Bavinck in support of this contention.

Hoeksema, Herman. *Reformed Dogmatics.* Grand Rapids: Reformed Free Publishing Association, 1966.
> Expresses many criticisms of Kuyper on a variety of subjects; by an author who denied common grace.

Hoeksema, Homer C. 'Kuyper's Prayer for the "Free",' *The Standard Bearer*, 57 (1980), pp.126-7.
> A lament about defection from Kuyper's legacy at the Free University of Amsterdam.

Hospers, Gerrit Hendrik. *Apologetics: A Study and a Critique.* Ontario, NY: published by the author, 1924.
> A ringing affirmation of Kuyper's position which includes at the end a brief essay by Kuyper.

'Groen Van Prinsterer and his Book,' *Evangelical Quarterly*, 7 (1935), pp.267-86.
> A laudatory introduction to Groen's life with translations of excerpts from *Unbelief and Revolution;* uncritical appraisal of Groen as a historian.

The Reformed Principle of Authority. Grand Rapids: The Reformed Press, 1924.
> A vigorous defence of the inspiration and authority of the Bible against the modernism of the 1920s. Many references to Abraham Kuyper and numerous excerpts from his writings; chapter 2 is Kuyper's 'Modernism, a Fata Morgana in the Christian World'.

House, H. Wayne and Thomas Ice. *Dominion Theology: Blessing or Curse?* Portland, OR: Multnomah Press, 1988.
    Chapter 15, 'Dangers of Christian Reconstructionism,' shows that Kuyper's amillennialism and pluralistic political and social philosophy negate the claim that he was a forerunner of theonomists.

'How Dr. Abraham Kuyper has Influenced our Churches in America,' *The Banner,* 72 (1937), 1060.
    An unsigned editorial extolling Kuyper on the centennial of his birth; calls for maintaining his legacy through attendance at the Free University and translations of his works.

Idenburg, Philip J. 'Church and State in the Netherlands,' in *The World Year Book of Education,* 1966, ed. George Z. F. Bereday and Joseph A. Lauwerys. New York: Harcourt, Brace, and World, Inc., 1966, pp.78-91.
    A helpful explanation of pluralism in education as the outgrowth of Kuyper's accomplishments.

Jellema, Dirk. 'Abraham Kuyper: Forgotten Radical?' *Calvin Forum,* 15 (1950), pp.211-13.
    Portrays Kuyper as an opponent of liberalism and socialism and an exponent of Calvinist corporatism; the following article explains his proposed solution to the class struggle.

'Abraham Kuyper: Forgotten Radical?' *The Calvin Forum,* 15 (1950), pp.241-2.
    Part II of a study that portrays Kuyper as an opponent of both capitalism and socialism and an advocate of Calvinistic corporatism based on spheres over which the state should not have control.

'Abraham Kuyper's Answer to "Liberalism",' *Reformed Journal,* 15 (1965), pp.10-14.
    The author contends that Kuyper's concept of sphere authority militates against the individualism of capitalism and requires state intervention to assure justice.

'Abraham Kuyper's Attack on Liberalism,' *The Review of Politics,* 19 (1957), pp.472-85.
    A summary of Kuyper's political philosophy of Christian Socialism and examples of how he implemented it. The notes are rich in suggestions for additional reading.

'Groen van Prinsterer,' *Calvin Forum,* 19 (1954), pp.114-16.
    A concise introduction to Groen's critique of revolution, socialism and capitalism, and his appeal for Christian democracy; a readable place to begin a study of Groen.

'Kuyper and the Crisis of the West,' *The Banner,* 85 (1950), pp.156-7.
    Cites Kuyper's diagnosis of moral, social and political conditions at the turn of the century and relates them to the worsening situation in mid-century.

'Kuyper's Visit to America in 1898,' *Michigan History,* 42 (1958), pp.227-36.
    A summary of life in America and reservations about some political developments.

Kalsbeek, L. *Contours of a Christian Philosophy,* eds. Bernard and Josina Zylstra. Toronto: Wedge Publishing Foundation, 1975.
Contains some insightful references to Kuyper as the progenitor on whose
work Dooyeweerd and others have built.

Keizer, P. K. *Church History,* trans. M. P. Vander Ven. Neerlandia, Alberta: Inheritance
Publications, 1990.
This superficial survey from a highly partisan, Reformed perspective con-
tains a critical analysis of Kuyper; many errors of fact and dubious interpretation.

Kennedy, Jon R. *The Reformation of Journalism.* Nutley, NJ: The Craig Press, 1972.
Pays tribute to Kuyper for his leadership of the Christian political movement
and cites him as a model of biblically sound journalism.

Kijphart, Arend. *The Politics of Accommodation, Pluralism and Democracy in the Netherlands.* Berkeley, CA: University of California Press, 1968.
Although this work slights Kuyper, it covers the development of his political
idea for pluralistic democratic arrangements.

Kistemaker, Simon. *Calvinism: History — Principles — Perspectives.* Grand Rapids: Baker
Book House, 1966.
A modern Kuyperian survey with proposals for applications of sphere
authority.

Klapwijk, Jacob. 'Antithesis and Common Grace,' in *Bringing into Captivity Every Thought,*
ed. Jacob Klapwijk, Sander Griffoen, & Gerben Groenewoud. Lanham, MD:
University Press of America, 1991, pp.169-90.
The author criticizes Kuyper's concept of common grace and finds scholastic precedents and shared attributes for it.

'Dooyeweerd's Christian Philosophy: Antithesis and Critique,' *Reformed Journal,*
30 (1980), pp.20-24.
An appreciative and critical analysis of Kuyper and Dooyeweerd with regard to the antithesis between Christian and non-Christian world-views as they
affect scholarship.

'Rationality in the Neo-Calvinian Tradition,' in *Rationality in the Calvinian Tradition,*
ed. H. Hart, *et al.* Lanham, MD: University Press of America, 1983, pp.93-111.
An important critique of Kuyper which finds tension between his view of
common grace and the antithesis between regenerate and unregenerate
scholarship.

'The Struggle for a Christian Philosophy: Another Look at Dooyeweerd,' *Reformed
Journal,* 30 (1980), pp.12-15.
A useful analysis and critique of Kuyper's concept of sphere authority and
Dooyeweerd's development and application of it.

Klooster, Fred H. 'The Kingdom of God in the History of the Christian Reformed Church,'
in *Perspectives on the Christian Reformed Church: Studies in its History, Theology, and Ecumenicity,* eds. Peter De Klerk & Richard R. De Ridder. Grand Rapids: Baker Book House, 1983, pp.203-23.

An interesting study of social responsibility as reflected in the work of Kuyper, G. Vos, L. Berkhof and Samuel Volbeda.

Kobes, Wayne A. 'Sphere Sovereignty and the University: Theological Foundations of Abraham Kuyper's View of the University and its Role in Society,' Ph.D. dissertation at Florida State University, 1993.
A thorough study of the subject, rich with biographical information; the appendix includes a translation of Kuyper's speech at the opening of the Free University in 1880; helpful bibliography.

Kolfhaus, Wilhelm. 'The Significance of Abraham Kuyper for Reformed Theology,' *Evangelical Quarterly,* 2 (1930), pp.302-12.
A succinct, readable introduction to Kuyper as a theologian.

Kossmann, E. H. *The Low Countries 1780-1940.* Oxford: Clarendon Press, 1978.
A critical but appreciative study of Kuyper's efforts; puts the work of Groen and Kuyper in context and compares Dutch and Belgian developments.

Kromminga, D. H. *The Christian Reformed Tradition.* Grand Rapids: William B. Eerdmans Publishing Co., 1943.
A useful survey which includes much material about the religious history of the Netherlands from the Reformation to the late nineteenth century.

'Dr. Abraham Kuyper, Sr.,' *The Banner,* 72 (1937), pp.1012-13. A laudatory biographical sketch.

Kromminga, John. 'Abraham Kuyper (1837-1920),' in *A History of Religious Educators,* ed. Elmer L. Towns. Grand Rapids: Baker Book House, 1975, pp.288-96.
A brief introduction to Kuyper's philosophy of education.

'*De Afscheiding*— Review and Evaluation,' *Calvin Theological Journal,* 20 (1985), pp.43-57.
A critical but appreciative appraisal of the 1834 Seceders from the *Hervormde Kerk.* Readable and interesting.

The Christian Reformed Church: A Study in Orthodoxy. Grand Rapids: Baker Book House, 1949.
Contains some interesting reports of Kuyper's influence on Reformed thinking and actions in America.

Kruger, Paul. *The Memoirs of Paul Kruger,* trans. A. Teixeira. London: T. Fisher Unwin, 1902.
Shows diversity among the Reformed churches in South Africa and Kruger's deep Calvinistic faith.

Kruijt, J. P. 'The Influence of Denominationalism on Social Life and Organizational Patterns,' *Archives de Sociologie des Religions,* 4 (1959), pp.105-11.
An interesting account of how Dutch political parties accommodate one another in crucial questions so as to avoid confrontation; shows how Kuyper and the Anti-Revolutionary Party laid the basis for this practice.

Kuenen, Abraham. *The Prophets and Prophecy in Israel,* trans. Adam Milroy. London: Longmans, Green, & Co., 1877.
> A fine example of Dutch modernist theology.

The Religion of Israel to the Fall of the Jewish State, trans. Alfred Heath May. London: Williams & Norgate, 1874-5.
> This use of German Higher Criticism of the Old Testament shows how it influenced theological studies in the Netherlands.

Kuiper, B. K. *The Church in History.* Grand Rapids: Eerdmans Publishing Co., 1951.
> A little biographical information of use.

Kuiper, D. Th. 'Historical and Sociological Development of ARP and CDA,' in *Christian Political Options*, ed. C. den Hollander, *et al.,* trans. A. J. van Dijk and G. Groenewoud. The Hague, Netherlands: AR-Partijstichting, 1980, pp.10-33.
> Awkward translation makes this analysis of developments in the Anti-Revolutionary Party difficult reading. The author shows the course of Anti-Revolutionary politics since the death of Kuyper and accommodations that have led to the formation of the Christian Democratic Appeal.

'Theory and Practice in Dutch Calvinism on the Racial Issue in the Nineteenth Century,' *Calvin Theological Journal*, 21 (1986), pp.51-78.
> A critique of Groen and Kuyper for their views about race; shows that South African Calvinists altered Kuyper's position illegitimately so as to make it seem to support apartheid.

Kuiper, Herman. *Calvin on Common Grace.* Grand Rapids: Smitter Book Co., 1928.
> An appendix pays tribute to Kuyper for developing the doctrine of common grace with application to modern times.

Kuiper, R. *Zelfbeeld en Wereldbeeld: Antirevolutionairen en Het Buitenland.* Kampen, Netherlands: J. H. Kok, 1992.
> Contains, at the end of the book, a brief summary in English of the Anti-Revolutionary world-view.

Kuiper, R. B. *To Be or Not to Be Reformed.* Grand Rapids: Zondervan Publishing House, 1959.
> Contains a helpful application of common grace and the antithesis to the Christian Reformed Church in the twentieth century.

Kuitenbrouwer, Maarten. *The Netherlands and the Rise of Modern Imperialism: Colonies and Foreign Policy, 1870-1902,* trans. Hugh Beyer. New York: Berg Publishers, 1991 (1985).
> An important examination of colonial and international affairs with reference to the East Indies and South Africa; many references to Kuyper. A balanced and fair treatment; extensive bibliography.

Kuyper, Catherine M. E. 'Abraham Kuyper: His Early Life and Conversion,' *International Reformed Bulletin,* 5 (1960), pp.19-25.

Kuyvenhoven, Andrew. 'An Old Sermon on a Timely Topic.' *The Banner,* 121 (1986), p.4.
    A reminder that Kuyper did not equate conservatism with orthodoxy.

Lagerwey, Walter. 'The History of Calvinism in the Netherlands,' in *The Rise and Development of Calvinism,* ed. John H. Bratt. Grand Rapids: William B. Eerdmans Publishing Co., 1959, pp. 63-102.
    An excellent survey which explains the roots of Kuyper's heritage and shows how and why Calvinists have organized their efforts.

Landheer, Bartholomew. 'Modern Development,' in *The Netherlands,* ed. Bartholomew Landheer. Berkeley, CA: University of California Press, 1944, pp.71-87.
    A rather harsh treatment of Kuyper as a religious and political leader.

Langley, McKendree R. 'Abraham Kuyper: A Christian Worldview,' *New Horizons,* 20 (January 1999), pp. 20-21.
    A concise introduction to Kuyper's thinking.

'Creation and Sphere Sovereignty in Historical Perspective,' *Pro Rege,* IX (1981), pp.12-22.
    Traces the development of Kuyper's concept into the twentieth century through Dooyeweerd and Goudzwaard.

'Emancipation and Apologetics: The Formation of Abraham Kuyper's Anti-Revolutionary Party in the Netherlands,' Ph.D. dissertation at Westminster Theological Seminary, 1995.
    A thorough analysis of Kuyper's political philosophy and his efforts to implement it in the Netherlands; duly critical but very supportive.

'Groen van Prinsterer: What Does it Mean to be a Christian in the World?' *The Presbyterian Guardian,* 46 (1976), pp.8-9, 12-13.
    A clear and insightful introduction to Groen as father of the Anti-Revolutionary philosophy.

'The Kuyper Memorial: An Evangelical Birthday,' *Eternity,* 39 (1988), p.16.
    A report of the celebration of the 150th anniversary of Kuyper's birth; Prime Minister Ruud Lubbers and others pay tribute to his influence in national life.

'The Legacy of Groen van Prinsterer,' *Reformed Perspective,* 4 (1985) pp.25-8.
    A helpful account of Groen's political philosophy and proposals to reform society along biblical lines.

'Pioneers of Christian Politics,' I, *The Vanguard,* 2 (1971), pp.7-9,22.
    A clear introduction to Groen van Prinsterer and his foundational contribution to the formation of a biblical philosophy of politics.

'Pioneers of Christian Politics,' II, *The Vanguard,* 2 (1971), pp.7-10, 22. A helpful summary of Kuyper's political philosophy and leadership of the Anti-Revolutionary Party.

'The Political Spirituality of Abraham Kuyper,' *International Reformed Bulletin*, 76 (1979), pp.4-9.
> Insightful analysis of Kuyper's socio-economic views as outgrowths of his biblical faith.

The Practice of Political Spirituality. Jordan Station, Ontario: Paideia Press, 1984.
> An excellent analysis of Kuyper's political philosophy as a consequence of his Reformed faith; traces his career in politics from 1879-1918; readable; not documented; useful bibliography.

'A Sketch of Abraham Kuyper's Life,' *Reformed Ecumenical Synod Theological Forum*, XVI (1988), pp.4-8.
> An appreciative but duly critical essay that emphasizes Kuyper's journalism; cites personality faults that impaired his ability to work with others.

'The Unknown Kuyper,' *New Reformation*, 4 (1973), pp.7-9.
> A friendly critic's appraisal of Kuyper's contributions and faults.

'The Witness of a World View,' *Pro Rege*, VIII (1979, pp.2-11.
> A highly insightful analysis of Groen van Prinsterer's importance for the revival of Reformed influence in the Netherlands. Readable and documented.

Latourette, Kenneth Scott. *Christianity in a Revolutionary Age*, II & III. Grand Rapids: Zondervan Publishing House, 1969 (1959).
> Useful information about missionary work by the Dutch in the nineteenth century as it reflected conditions in the churches of Kuyper's homeland. Helpful information about the *réveil* and the condition in the *Hervormde Kerk*.

A History of the Expansion of Christianity, V. New York: Harper & Brothers Publishers, 1943.
> Valuable for a view of Dutch colonial policies as they affected missions in the East Indies.

Lee, Francis Nigel. *A Christian Introduction to the History of Philosophy*. Nutley, NJ: Craig Press, 1969.
> The author cites Kuyper as the greatest influence in Christian philosophy in his day.

'The Legacy of Vision: The *Doleantie* and the Christian Reformed Church,' *The Banner*, 121 (1986), pp.12-14.
> A chapter taken from a forthcoming history of the Christian Reformed Church; a helpful review of the Dutch roots of the church through the *Afscheiding* and the *Doleantie*.

Leo XIII, Pope. 'The Condition of Labour,' in *Five Great Encyclicals*, ed. Gerald C. Treacy, S. J. New York: The Paulist Press, 1939, pp.1-30.

Lloyd-Jones. D. Martyn. 'The French Revolution and After,' in *The Christian and the State in Revolutionary Times*. Huntingdon, England: The Westminster Conference, 1975, pp.94-110.

The author holds that man now worships himself and the end times are probably near; he extols Kuyper's approach to socio-economic problems as the best means to retard evil and to promote good as believers await the return of Christ.

Lourens, Marunus Michiel. 'Labor,' in *The Netherlands,* ed. Bartholomew Landheer. Berkeley, CA: University of California Press, 1944, pp.189-202.
Brief coverage of Kuyper's role in suppressing the railway strike of 1903; generally fair.

Lovelace, Richard F. *Dynamics of Spiritual Life.* Downers Grove, IL: Inter-Varsity Press, 1979.
Cites Kuyper for his experimental Calvinism, as expressed in his endeavours to achieve social and ecclesiastical reform.

Lucas, Henry. *Netherlanders in America.* Grand Rapids: William B. Eerdmans Publishing Co., 1955, revised 1989.
This contains a useful account of the European background and Dutch immigrations into United States; it identifies Kuyper's influence upon Reformed Christians there.

McCarthy, Rockne, *et al. Society, State & Schools: A Case for Structural and Confessional Pluralism.* Grand Rapids: William B. Eerdmans Publishing Co., 1981.
Contemporary Kuyperians call for reforms in funding and organization of schools in accord with sphere authority.

McGoldrick, James Edward. 'Edmund Burke: Christian Activist,' *Modern Age,* 17 (1973), pp.275-86.
Kuyper's debt to Burke will become evident as one considers their mutual opposition to the French Revolution.

'Every Inch for Christ: Abraham Kuyper on the Reform of the Church,' *Reformation and Revival,* 3 (1994), pp.91-100.

'1776: A Christian Loyalist View,' *Fides et Historia,* XI (1977), pp.26-40.

McKim, Donald K.. 'Reformed Perspective on the Mission of the Church in Society,' *The Reformed World,* 38 (1985), pp.405-21.
A few references to Kuyper but most attention is given to Calvin and modern 'Reformed' theologians such as Barth.

McNeill, John T. *The History and Character of Calvinism.* New York: Oxford University Press, 1967 (1954).
Contains only a few scattered references to Kuyper; portrays him as hyper-Calvinist supralapsarian.

Machen, J. Gresham. 'History and Faith,' *Princeton Theological Review,* 13 (1915), pp.337-51.
A clear affirmation of Christianity's historic validity and a clear delineation between it and modernism.

Mackay, James Hutton. *Religious Thought in Holland During the Nineteenth Century.* London: Hodder and Stoughton, 1911.

    Although this work mentions Kuyper and expresses some admiration for him, it contains little about his work; useful for its coverage of rationalism, the Gronigen and Ethical schools of thoughts and modernism, all of which Kuyper opposed.

Maffet, Gregory John. 'The Educational Thought of Cornelius Van Til: An Analysis of the Ideological foundations of his Christian Philosophy of Education,' Ed.D. dissertation at the University of Akron, 1984.

Mason, Caroline Atwater. 'The New Premier of Holland,' *The Outlook,* 70 (1902), pp.333-7.

    An American journalist's account of her visit to the Kuyper home and her impression of the man and his abilities.

Masselink, William. *General Revelation and Common Grace.* Grand Rapids: William B. Eerdmans Publishing Co., 1953.

    Portrays Van Til as contradicting Kuyper. Difficult reading; unconvincing argument.

    'New Views of Common Grace in the Light of Historic Reformed Theology,' *The Calvin Forum,* 19 (1954), pp.194-204.

    A critique of Van Til and a defence of Kuyper on particular points of general revelation, common grace and apologetics; approves of the Princeton approach to apologetics.

Mayers, Ronald B. *Both/And: A Balanced Apologetic.* Chicago: Moody Press, 1984.

    Depicts Kuyper as a fideist for whom apologetics had little value because sinners have no capacity for belief apart from preceding regeneration.

Meeter, H. Henry. *The Basic Ideas of Calvinism,* 5th edition, revised. Grand Rapids: Baker Book House, 1956, reprinted 1975.

    Pays tribute to Kuyper as a pioneer exponent of common grace and sphere authority; Meeter's exposition and applications of these concepts are very helpful.

Mennega, Aaldert. 'Science, Evolution, and Abraham Kuyper,' *The Outlook,* 21 (1971), pp.23-4.

    A ringing affirmation of Kuyper's stand against evolution by a biologist at Dordt College; clarifies Kuyper's opposition to theistic as well as Darwinian evolutionism.

Menninga, Clarence. 'Critical Reflections on Abraham Kuyper's *Evolutie* Address,' *Calvin Theological Journal,* 33 (1998), pp. 435-53.

    An attempt to make Kuyper support some degree of evolution, while admitting that he opposed theistic evolution and Darwinism as a world-view. Unclear and apparently incoherent argument.

Meyer, Steven E. 'Calvinism and the Rise of the Protestant Political Movement in the Netherlands,' Ph.D. dissertation at Georgetown University, 1976.

A useful analysis of the Anti-Revolutionary philosophy and Kuyper's contribution to the political life of his homeland.

Monsma, Timothy. 'Kuyper and Orange City,' *The Banner,* 117 (1982), pp.2,4.
A supporter of Mid-America Reformed Seminary cites Kuyper to justify dissidence from the Christian Reformed Church in America on the matter of theological education.

Moodie, T. Dunbar. *The Rise of Afrikanerdom.* Berkeley, CA: University of California Press, 1975.
Argues that Afrikaner civil religion created the justification for apartheid and blames Kuyper's concept of sphere authority to some extent; André Du Toit, 'No Chosen People,' offers a rebuttal.

Mouw, Richard J. 'Abraham Kuyper: a Man for this Season,' *Christianity Today,* 42 (October 1998), pp. 86-7.
A helpful introduction to Kuyper's career, but the author wrongly attributes racist ideas to Kuyper.

'Dutch-Calvinist Philosophical Influences in North America,' *Calvin Theological Journal,* 24 (1989), pp.93-120.
An insightful analysis of philosophical currents which include the effect of Kuyper's endeavours based on common grace and the antithesis.

Uncommon Decency: Christian Civility in an Uncivil World. Downers Grove, IL: InterVarsity Press, 1992.
The chapter 'Abraham Kuyper Meet Mother Teresa' is a call for a combination of Kuyper's theology of Christ's kingship and Mother Teresa's compassion; the author implies that Kuyper was not deeply concerned with social needs.

Multati (Eduard Douwes Dekker). *Max Havelaar,* trans. Roy Edwards. Amherst, MA: University of Massachusetts Press, 1982.
A partly autobiographical, satirical attack upon abuses in Dutch colonialism by one who served the administration in the East Indies.

Murray, John. 'Common Grace,' in *Collected Writings of John Murray,* ed. Iain Murray. Edinburgh: Banner of Truth Trust, 1977.
Clear explanation but no explicit references to Kuyper.

Nicole, Roger. 'Theology,' in *Contemporary Evangelical Thought,* ed. Carl F. H. Henry. Great Neck, NY: Channel Press, 1957, pp. 67-106.
Contains an important survey of Dutch dogmaticians, including Kuyper.

Nichols, Anthony H. 'Abraham Kuyper — A Summons to Vision in Christian Education,' *Journal of Christian Education,* 16 (1973), pp.78-94.
A valuable summary of Kuyper's accomplishments in education; sparsely documented.

'The Educational Doctrines of Abraham Kuyper: An Evaluation,' *Journal of Christian Education,* Papers, 52 (1975), pp.26-38.
A few insightful glimpses into Kuyper's thinking and influence.

Nichols, James Hastings. *History of Christianity 1650-1950.* New York: Ronald Press, 1956.
> Contains some observations about the Dutch ecclesiastical situation in Kuyper's day and his leadership of the Reformed party and the Anti-Revolutionaries; some useful information about the East Indies.

Nieuwenhys, Rob. *Mirror of the Indies: A History of Dutch Colonial Literature,* trans. Frans van Rosevelt, ed. E. M. Beekman. Amherst, MA: University of Massachusetts Press, 1982.
> Some helpful information about Edouard Douwes Dekker, author of *Max Havelaar.*

Notaro, Thom. *Van Til and the Use of Evidence.* Phillipsburg, NJ: Presbyterian & Reformed Publishing Co., 1980. Explains Van Til's debt to Kuyper and shows how the former developed the apologetic of the latter.

Notenboom, J. W. 'Kuyper's significance for Christian Politics,' *Calvin Forum,* 2 (1937), pp.88-90.
> Hails Kuyper as a champion of limited government, freedom of religion and social justice apart from socialism.

Nymeyer, Frederick. 'The Anti-Revolutionary Party; the Founder was Confusilated from the Beginning and now they seem to have Made a *Volte Face,*' *Progressive Calvinism,* I (1955), pp.195-200.
> A critique of Kuyper's subscription to state interventions to assure social and economic benefits; contends that the Free University of Amsterdam has become socialistic due to Kuyper's influence.

'The Origin of *Trouw,* the Successor to *De Standaard,*' *Progressive Calvinism,* I (1955), pp.326-8.
> Laments the fact that unbiblical reverence for the post-war socialist government has led this newspaper to follow its predecessor's mistakes.

'What Happened to the Daily Newspaper Abraham Kuyper Founded?' *Progressive Calvinism,* I (1955), pp.324-8.
> Relates that *De Standaard* is defunct because it failed to resist the Nazi occupation, which it saw as a government ordained by God.

Oppewal, Donald. *The Roots of the Calvinistic Day School Movement.* Grand Rapids: Calvin College Monograph Series, 1963.
> A historical and theoretical analysis of Reformed Christian education that pays appropriate tribute to Kuyper's influence.

Osterhaven, M. Eugene. 'The Calvinistic Attitude Towards the World,' *Reformed Review,* 18 (1965), pp.30-36.
> A vigorous call for Calvinistic social responsibility with an implied criticism of Kuyper's doctrine of the antithesis.

Plantinga, Cornelius, Jr. *A Place to Stand: A Reformed Study of Creeds and Confessions.* Grand Rapids: Board of Publications of the Christian Reformed Church, 1979.

A valuable study of the historic creeds and doctrinal standards for which Kuyper contended vigorously.

Platt, Frederic. 'The Renaissance of Calvinism,' *London Quarterly and Holborn Review,* 96 (1901), pp.219-42.
    Written soon after Kuyper's Stone Lectures, this article predicted a resurgence of Calvinism as the basis for a Christian world-view and cited Kuyper's work as evidence of such a revival.

Praamsma, Louis. *The Church in the Twentieth Century,* v. VII of *Elect From Every Nation.* St. Catherines, Ontario: Paideia Press, 1981.
    Contains some references to Kuyper and defends him against critics of common grace.

'A Great Enterprise,' *Christian Renewal,* 5 (1986), pp.10-11.
    A summary of Kuyper's reasons for founding the Free University of Amsterdam and his objections to the Higher Criticism of the Bible.

Let Christ be King: Reflections on the Life and Times of Abraham Kuyper. Jordan Station, Ontario: Paideia Press, 1985.
    A somewhat vaguely written examination of Kuyper's life and thought; unclear about his specific political philosophy and social programmes.

'Let Christ be King,' *Christian Renewal,* 3 (1985), pp.1-2, 13.
    A brief excerpt from a book by the same title; a helpful introduction to Kuyper's *Pro Rege.*

'The Reformed First Principles,' *Christian Renewal,* 5 (1986), pp.1-11.
    An incisive and duly critical appraisal of Kuyper's flirtations with Methodism and his work as a historian and social critic.

Pronk, Cornelis. 'Neo-Calvinism', *Reformed Theological Journal,* 11 (1995), pp.42-56.
    A highly critical analysis of common grace which contends that Kuyper's concept led to a decline in evangelistic fervour and unwarranted attention to cultural-social matters.

'This Dutch Puritan,' *Banner of Truth,* 154-155 (1976), pp.1-10.
    An appreciative but critical appraisal of Kuyper and the Neo-Calvinists; contends that his emphasis on the cultural mandate and common grace led to a decline of vital, experiential religion.

'F. M. Ten Hoor: Defender of Secessionist Principles against Abraham Kuyper's *Doleantie* Views,' Th.M. Thesis at Calvin Theological Seminary, 1987.
    A penetrating study of objections to Kuyper's ecclesiology and its implications for regeneration, baptism, the covenant, etc.

Ramm, Bernard L. *The Christian College in the Twentieth Century.* Grand Rapids: William B. Eerdmans Publishing Co., 1963.
    Contains important coverage of Kuyper as educator and the development of the Free University of Amsterdam.

The Evangelical Heritage. Waco, TX: Word Books, 1973.
Contains several tributes to Kuyper and hails him as the greatest Calvinist since Calvin.

Special Revelation and the Word of God Grand Rapids: William B. Eerdmans Publishing Co., 1961.
Ramm hails Kuyper's view of Scripture as the proper alternative to bibliolatry and to the neo-orthodox depreciation of revelation as knowledge.

Varieties of Christian Apologetics. Grand Rapids: Baker Book House, 1961.
Contains a lucid chapter about Kuyper's conception and method of apologetics.

The Witness of the Spirit. Grand Rapids: William B. Eerdmans Publishing Co., 1959.
The author hails Kuyper as one of the most profound writers about the Holy Spirit.

Ratzsch, Del. 'Abraham Kuyper's Philosophy of Science,' *Calvin Theological Journal,* 27 (1922), pp.277-303.
A succinct summary and analysis of Kuyper's understanding about what believing and unbelieving scientists can have in common and what must inevitably separate them.

Reid, Anthony. *The Contest for North Sumatra.* Kuala Lumpur, Singapore: University of Mayla Press, 1969.
A scholarly account of Dutch policy up to 1898, with emphasis upon the war against Acheh; makes only passing reference to Kuyper's government, but important for understanding historic developments in the Indies.

Remelt, Glenn A., 'The Christian Reformed Church and Science, 1900-1930,' *Fides et Historia,* 21 (1989), pp.70-80.
A little background information about Kuyper.

Reville, Jean. *Liberal Christianity: Its Origin, Nature and Mission,* trans. & ed. Victor Leuliette. New York: G. P. Putnam's Sons, 1903.
An eloquent, impassioned description of religious rationalism as an alternative to orthodoxy; dismisses the miraculous nature of the Bible and calls for adoption of Christ's ethical teachings; assumes that modern science has made belief in supernatural revelation untenable.

Rewerts, Ronald M. 'The Significance of Abraham Kuyper for Reformed Theology,' *Trinity Journal,* 7 (1977), pp.149-71.
A survey and critique of Kuyper's major beliefs; helpful in appraising his influence.

Rian, Edwin H. *The Presbyterian Conflict.* Grand Rapids: William B. Eerdmans Publishing Co., 1940.
Provides the context for Kuyper's opposition to revision of the Westminster Standards of the Presbyterian Church in the USA.

Rodgers, R. E. L. *The Incarnation of the Antithesis: An Introduction to the Educational Thought and Practice of Abraham Kuyper.* Durham, England: The Pentland Press, 1992.

    An enthusiastic analysis of Kuyper's ideas; based mostly on secondary sources; suitable for beginners; readable; incomplete bibliographic data make verification difficult.

Rogers, Jack B. & Donald K. McKim. *The Authority and Interpretation of the Bible.* New York: Harper & Row Publishers, 1979.

    An effort by followers of Barth to affirm that the sixteenth-century Reformers did not hold to inerrancy; pages 388-93 deal with Kuyper and Bavinck, where the authors try to depict them as rejecting the inerrancy of Scripture.

Rookmaker, H. R. *Gaugin and 19th Century Art Theory.* Amsterdam: Swets & Zeitlinger, 1972.

    Contains a brief analysis of Kuyper's view of art, symbolism and revelation.

Rooy, Sidney H. 'Kuyper vs. Warfield: An Historical Approach to the Nature of Apologetics,' S.T.M. thesis, Union Theological Seminary, 1956.

    An interesting comparison which stresses the role of reason in authenticating the authority of Scripture. Readable.

Rullmann, J. C., ed. with introduction by H. Colijn. *Kuyper-Bibliographie*, 3 vols. TE's-Gravenhage Bij Js. Bootsma and Kampen: N. V. Uitgevers Mij J. H. Kok, pp.1923-40.

    A chronological listing of Kuyper's works with extensive editorial commentary; thorough index.

'Past and Present of the Reformed Churches in Holland,' *Evangelical quarterly*, 2 (1930), pp.162-78.

    A succinct survey of church history from 1816 to 1930 which applauds the *Aufscheiding* and the *Doleantie*; calls for vigilance to guard orthodoxy.

Runner, H. Evan. 'Abraham Kuyper's Influence on Dr. Vollenhoven,' *Perspective Newsletter*, 6 (1972), pp.7-10.

    An impressionistic account of a meeting with Vollenhoven.

'The Christian and the World, *Torch and Trumpet*, 5 (1955).

    A series of five articles in April, May, July, September and October. This provides an excellent survey and analysis of Christian attitudes towards culture from ancient times through Kuyper's construction of the antithesis and common grace.

'The Christian and the World,' part I, *Torch and Trumpet*, 5 (1955), pp.9-11, 15; part II, pp.17-20.

    Although these articles do not deal with Kuyper specifically, they offer an excellent summary of Christian thinking about the antithesis and common grace in the ancient and medieval periods.

The Relation of the Bible to Learning. Toronto: Wedge Publishing Foundation, 1970.

The final chapter contains a lecture entitled 'Sphere-sovereignty,' and it offers helpful insights into Kuyper's contributions to the development of that view.

Scriptural Religion and Political Task. Toronto: Wedge Publishing Foundation, 1974.
A contemporary Kuyperian appeal for principled political organization and action.

'Sphere-Sovereignty,' in *Christian Perspectives 1961,* ed. François Kouwenhoven. Hamilton, Ontario: Guardian Publishing Company for the Association for Reformed Scientific Studies, 1961.
An amplification and application of Kuyper's contention that all of life is religion.

Rüter, J. C. *Spoorwegstrakingen Van 1903: Een spiegel der Arbeidersbweging in Nederland.* Leiden: E. J. Brill, 1935.
An English summary by M. R. Langley gives an outline of events connected with the major strike of 1903.

Saayman, Willem. 'Rebels and Prophets: Afrikaners against the System,' in *Resistance and Hope: South African Essays in Honour of Beyers Naude,'* ed. Charles Villa-Vicencio & John W. De Gruchy. Grand Rapids: William B. Eerdmans Publishing Co., 1985. pp.52-60, 200-201.
The author contends that Afrikaners made Neo-Calvinism their civil religion but distorted the teachings of both Calvin and Kuyper in doing so.

Schama, Simon. *Patriots and Liberators: Revolution in the Netherlands,* 1789-1813. London: Collins, 1977.
Thorough coverage of the effects of the French Revolution and Napoleonic rule.

Schilder, Klass. *Christ and Culture,* trans. G. van Ronger & W. Helder. Winnipeg, Ontario: Premier Printing, Ltd, 1977.
The author denies Kuyper's concept of common grace; shows how depravity produces disunity among men and fragments culture; calls Christians to deliberate efforts to compose cultural endeavours. Clumsy translation makes for difficult reading.

Schlossberg, Herbert. *Idols for Destruction: Christian Faith and its Confrontation with American Society.* Nashville: Thomas Nelson Publishers, 1983.
A penetrating analysis and powerful critique of secular humanism as a worldview and religious system which sponsors civil religion; although the author does not mention Kuyper, he seems to subscribe to sphere authority as a defence against tyranny.

Schouls, Carl. 'The Development of the Dutch Calvinistic Churches,' *Banner of Truth,* 359-60 (1993), pp.46-52.
A concise survey of Reformed history in the Netherlands that relates Kuyper's role appreciatively but critically.

Schrotenboer, Paul G. 'Abraham Kuyper: His International Influence,' *Reformed Ecumenical Synod Theological Forum,* SVI (1988), pp.1-2.

A laudatory introduction to a series of articles issued upon the 150th anniversary of Kuyper's birth.

Seel, David John, Jr. 'A Critical Comparison of Abraham Kuyper's and Klaas Schilder's Views of the Basis of Christian Cultural Responsibility,' *Salt*, 9 (1981), pp.20-29. An awkwardly written analysis of the significance of common grace.

Seerveld, Calvin. *A Christian Critique of Art and Literature.* Toronto: Association for the Advancement of Christian Scholarship, 1968. This obscurely written work contains some unclear criticisms of Kuyper's understanding of common grace.

Shetter, William Z. *The Pillars of Society: Six Centuries of Civilization in the Netherlands.* The Hague: Martinus Nijhoff, 1971. A helpful survey that relates the development of the pluralism that Kuyper advocated for Dutch society.

Skillen, James W. 'The Development of Calvinistic Political Theory in the Netherlands with Special Reference to the Thought of Herman Dooyeweerd,' Ph.D. dissertation at Duke University, 1973. A valuable analysis of the Anti-Revolutionary philosophy in general with much material about Kuyper.

'From Covenant of Grace to Equitable Public Pluralism: The Dutch Calvinist Contribution,' *Calvin Theological Journal,* 31 (1996), pp.67-96. An analysis of sphere authority and pluralism in religion from Althusius to Dooyeweerd, with due credit to Kuyper.

'God's Ordinances: Calvinism in Revival,' *Pro Rege,* VIII (1980), pp.24-33. An exposition of sphere sovereignty as espoused by Kuyper and interpreted by Dooyeweerd, Goudzwaard, *et al.*; calls for Christians to accept their obligation to implement God's ordinances for all creation.

'Kuyper Was on Time and ahead of his Time,' *Reformed Ecumenical synod Theological Forum*, XVI (1988), pp.15-19. An enthusiast's thesis that Kuyper's contention that all of life is religion is the only basis for truly Christian social actions.

'Politics, Pluralism, and the Ordinances of God,' in *Life is Religion: Essays in Honor of H. Evan Runner*, ed. Henry Vander Groot. St Catherines, Ontario: Paideia Press, 1981, pp.195-206. Shows that sphere authority affirms the sovereignty of God and thereby retards totalitarianism; calls for Christians to implement this principle throughout society.

'Societal Pluralism: Blessing or Curse for the Public Good?' in *The Ethical Dimension of Political Life*, ed. Francis Canavan. Durham, NC: Duke University Press, 1983, pp.166-72. A contemporary application of Kuyperian sphere authority.

'Sphere Sovereignty, Creation Order, and Public Justice: An Evaluation,' in *Political Order and the Plural Structure of Society,* eds. James W. Skillen & Rockne McCarthy, Atlanta: Scholars Press, for Emory University, 1991, pp.397-417.
    Brief introductions to Kuyper and his heirs Dooyeweerd, Runner, Zylstra and Goudzwaard.

Skillen, James W. & Stanley W. Carlson-Thies, 'Religion and Political Development in Nineteenth-Century Holland,' *Publius* (1982), pp.43-64.
    Contends that the Dutch experience of pluralism and confessional political parties contradicts the theory that modernization requires secularization; some helpful bibliography.

Smit, Kobus, 'Kuyper and Afrikaner Theology,' *Reformed Ecumenical Synod Theological Forum,* XVI (1988), pp.20-28.
    A South African scholar shows clearly that advocates of apartheid misused Kuyper, but his own lack of precision in expressing the concept of spheres allowed them to do so.

Smith, Gary Scott. *The Seeds of Secularization: Calvinism, Culture, and Pluralism in America,* 1870-1915. Grand Rapids: Christian University Press, 1985.
    Some valuable insights about Kuyper and many bibliographic items in notes.

Snouck Hurgronje, C. *The Achehnese*, 2 vols, trans. A. W. S. O'Sullivan. Leiden, the Netherlands: E. J. Brill, 1906, pp.439-84.
    A thorough study of Islam in the Dutch East Indies by a colonial official and leading scholar of the Muslim religion.

Selected Works of C. Snouck Hurgronje, eds G. H. Bousquet and J. Schacht. Leiden, Netherlands: E. J. Brill, 1957.
    Essays in French and English that illustrate the author's expertise about Islam in general and the East Indies in particular.

Spencer, Stephen R. 'A Comparison of the Old Princeton and Amsterdam Apologetic.' Th.M. thesis, Grand Rapids Baptist Seminary, 1980.
    An insightful analysis from a Van Tilian perspective; shows the incompleteness of Kuyper's view.

Spier, J. M. *An Introduction to Christian Philosophy,* trans. David Hugh Freeman. Philadelphia; Presbyterian & Reformed Publishing Co., 1954.
    This author builds on the foundation Kuyper laid for the formulation and explication of a Christian world-view.

Spykman, Gordon J. 'Pluralism: Our Last Best Hope,' *Christian School Review,* 10 (1981), pp.99-115.
    A helpful examination of Calvin and Kuyper on sphere authority and the maintenance of a Christian position in pluralistic society.

Reformational Theology: A New Paradigm for Doing Dogmatics. Grand Rapids: William B. Eerdmans Publishing Co., 1992.
    In this alternative to the 'scholastic' method of Berkhof, the author draws on Kuyper appreciatively but critically; marred by obscure academic jargon.

'Sphere-Sovereignty in Calvin and the Calvinist Tradition,' in *Exploring the Heritage of John Calvin,* ed. David E. Howerda. Grand Rapids: Baker Book House, 1976. pp.163-208.
> A thorough analysis of developments from Calvin's premises into the Dutch Reformed works of Kuyper and Bavinck; the emphasis is upon Calvin's foundation.

Star, Ring. 'Appeals to Kuyper for a Literal Genesis,' *The Banner,* 107 (1972), p.20.
> A brief reminder that Kuyper took the Genesis account of creation literally in opposition to theistic evolution.

Steffens, Nicholas M. 'Calvinism and the Theological Crisis,' *Presbyterian and Reformed Review,* 11 (1901), pp.211-25.
> An American Presbyterian's analysis and critique of the threat from modernism and secular humanism. A few references to the Dutch situation; the author expresses the same concerns as those of Kuyper.

Stob, Henry. 'Observations on the Concept of the Antithesis,' in *Perspectives on the Christian Reformed Church: Studies in its History, Theology, and Ecumenicity,* eds. Peter DeKlerk & Richard R. De Ridder. Grand Rapids: Baker Book House, 1983, pp.241-58.

Stoeffler, F. Ernest. *The Rise of Evangelical Pietism.* Leiden, Netherlands: E. J. Brill, 1965.
> Valuable coverage and analysis of Protestant developments in the seventeenth century; helps to clarify the particular character of the Dutch Reformation and its effects.

Strauss, D. F. M. 'An Analysis of S. A. Calvinist Theology,' *Journal of Theology for Southern Africa,* 19 (1977), pp.29-34.
> An argument that Kuyper's concept of created spheres has served Afrikaner nationalists who have emphasized the separate development of peoples as God's will.

Strauss, P. J. 'Abraham Kuyper, Apartheid and the Reformed Churches in South Africa in their Support of Apartheid,' *Reformed Ecumenical Synod Theological Forum,* XXIII (1995), pp.4-27.
> A helpful analysis which contends that Kuyper was not a racist and would not have favoured permanent separation of races in South Africa.

'The Struggle for Christian Politics in Holland,' *Current Literature,* 40 (1906), pp.292-3.
> An unsigned tribute to Kuyper and the Anti-Revolutionary Party soon after their defeat in the election of 1905; predicted that the party would return to govern the Netherlands.

Tangelder, Johan D. 'Abraham Kuyper (1837-1920), the Antithesis Theologian,' *Christian Renewal,* 3 (1984), p.8.
> A succinct and readable introduction to a pivotal emphasis in Kuyper's beliefs.

Tanis, Edward J. 'Abraham Kuyper, Christian Statesman,' *Calvin Forum,* 3 (1937), pp.53-6.
> A succinct introduction to Kuyper's political philosophy and his achievements.

Calvinism and Social Problems. Grand Rapids: Zondervan Publishing House, 1934.
    A Kuyperian's appeal for government regulation of the economy to assure
    social justice; reflects depression-time thinking.

'My Acquaintance with Kuyper,' *The Banner,* 72 (1937), p.966.
    A call for the maintenance of Kuyper's teaching about the antithesis and
    common grace.

'The World Today,' *The Banner,* 72 (1937), p.1134.
    A tribute to Kuyper upon the 100th anniversary of his birth.

Taylor, E. L. Hebden. *The Christian Philosophy of Law, Politics, and the State.* Nutley,
    NJ: Craig Press, 1966.
    Taylor shows how Kuyper's world-view provided the basis for Dooyeweerd
    and others to develop his philosophy and apply it systematically.

Reformation or Revolution? Nutley, NJ: Craig Press, 1970.
    An exposition and development of sphere authority from Kuyper through
    Dooyeweerd and other recent thinkers.

Ten Zythoff, Gerrit J. *Sources of Secession: The Netherlands Hervormde Kerk on the Eve
    of the Dutch Migration to the Midwest.* Grand Rapids: William B. Eerdmans
    Publishing Co., 1987.
    A detailed, balanced account of the first third of the nineteenth century that
    conveys much information about the role of Bilderdijk, Da Costa, De Cock, etc.

Thielicke, Helmut. *Theological Ethics,* v. 2, ed., William H. Lazareth. Philadelphia: For-
    tress Press, 1969.
    An interesting interpretation which holds that Kuyper was the synthesizer of
    Calvinist and Lutheran concepts about church and state.

Van Andel, Henry J. 'The Christian and Culture,' *The Presbyterian Guardian,* 13 (1944),
    pp.17-18, 28-30. A succinct and insightful explanation of the Calvinistic-Kuyperian
    view of culture.

Van Baalen, Jan Karel. *The Heritage of the Fathers: a Commentary on the Heidelberg
    Catechism.* Grand Rapids: William B. Eerdmans Publishing Co., 1948.
    Contains numerous excerpts from Kuyper to elucidate the exposition of the
    catechism.

Van Brummelen, Harro W. *Telling the Next Generation: Educational Development in
    North American Calvinist Christian Schools.* Lanham, MD: University Press of
    America, 1986.
    Useful for assessing Kuyper's influence upon Christian education in America.

Van der Kroef, Justus M. 'Abraham Kuyper and the Rise of Neo-Calvinism in the Nether-
    lands,' *Church History,* 17 (1948), pp.316-34.
    A richly informative analysis of Kuyper's political philosophy and
    programmes.

'Calvinism as a Political Principle,' *Calvin Forum,* 15 (1949), pp.139-42.
     The author argues that the American situation makes pursuit of Kuyper's
     political methods and formation of an Anti-Revolutionary Party untenable.

'Dichotomy Revisited,' *Calvin Forum,* 15 (1949), pp.231-34.
     The author pointedly rejects Kuyper's political activism and contends that
     he violated Calvin's instructions and compromised the Reformed faith by al-
     liance with Roman Catholics; denies the possibility of 'Christian' political action
     in a secularist society.

Van Dyke, Harry. *Groen Van Prinsterer's Lectures on Unbelief and Revolution.* Jordan
     Station, Ontario: Wedge Publishing Foundation, 1989.
     This erudite introduction and translation is the definitive analysis of Groen's
     importance.

'How Abraham Kuyper became a Christian Democrat,' *Calvin Theological Journal,*
     33 (1998), pp.420-35.
     An appreciative account of the way in which Kuyper and the Anti-Revol-
     utionary Party adopted the Social Programme and sought to aid poor workers.

'Kuyper in Post-War Canada,' *Reformed Ecumenical Synod Theological Forum,* XVI
     (1988), pp.34-40.
     A survey of Kuyper's influence in Canada through Dutch immigrants who
     have formed schools, unions, newspapers, agricultural organizations, etc.

Van Essen, Jantje Lubbegiena. 'Guillaume Groen Van Prinsterer and his Conception of
     History,' trans. Herbert Donald Morton, *Westminster Theological Journal,* 44
     (1982), pp.205-49.
     An informative analytic essay about Groen as a historian; important to set
     the stage for the emergence of Kuyper.

Van Essen, Jantje Lubbegiena & Herbert Donald Morton. *Guillaume Groen Van Prinsterer:
     Selected Studies.* Jordan Station, Ontario: Wedge Publishing Foundation, 1990.
     Insightful interpretations of Groen as a historian and advocate of Christian
     schools.

Van Groningen, Gerard. 'Does the Bible Teach Sphere Sovereignty?' *The Outlook,* 23
     (1973), pp.18-19.
     A concise explanation of the concept and an affirmation of its biblical
     character.

'Does the Bible Teach Sphere Sovereignty?' (2) *The Outlook,* 24 (1974), pp.18-19.

'The Effect of the *Doleantie* on the Christian Reformed Church,' *Calvin Forum,* 19
     (1954), pp.227-32; 20 (1954), pp.33-40.
     Shows the composite nature of the American Christian Reformed Church
     due to the 1834 Secession and the 1892 *Doleantie.* An insightful treatment of
     Kuyper.

'What is our Stand on Morality these Days?' *The Outlook,* 23 (1973), pp.11-12.

A call for moral absolutes in the historic Reformed tradition; cites Kuyper's Stone Lectures and his example in support of the argument.

Van Leeuwen, Mary Stewart. 'Abraham Kuyper and the Cult of True Womanhood: An Analysis of *De Eerepositie der Vrouw*,' *Calvin Theological Journal*, 31 (1996), pp.97-124.
A Christian feminist analysis and critique of Kuyper's teachings about the proper roles for women.

Van Lonkhuyzen, Jan. 'Abraham Kuyper — Modern Calvinist,' *Princeton Theological Review*, 19 (1921), pp.131-47.
A tribute to Kuyper by a former student at the Free University.

Van Reest, Rudolf. *Schilder's Struggle for the Unity of the Church*, trans. Theodore Plantinga. Neerlandia, Alberta: Inheritance Publications, 1990.
A biographical and ecclesiastical study of one of Kuyper's admirers who criticized his doctrine of common grace. Helpful to appraise the demise of Kuyper's projects.

Van Riessen, H. *The Society of the Future*, trans. & ed. David High Freeman. Philadelphia: Presbyterian & Reformed Publishing Co., 1952.
A keen post-World War II analysis of sphere authority and the statist violations thereof; clarifies Kuyper's concept

The University and its Basis. Christian Perspectives 1963. St Catherines, Ontario: Association for Reformed Scientific Studies, 1963. A contemporary Kuyperian's effort to promote the development of a Canadian Christian university along the lines of the Free University of Amsterdam.

Van Ruler, Arnold A. *Calvinist Trinitarianism and Theocentric Politics*, trans. John Bolt. Lewistown, NY: Edwin Mellen Press, 1989.
Contains valuable information about Dutch pietism and its influence upon the *réveil* and the subsequent rise of Kuyper's Neo-Calvinism.

Van Tijn, Th. 'The Party Structure of Holland and the Outer Provinces in the Nineteenth Century,' in *Vaderlands Verleden In Veelvoud*, eds G. A. M. Beekelaar, *et. al.* The Hague: Martinus Nijhoff, 1975. pp.560-78.
A sketch of Dutch parties with some attention to the Anti-Revolutionaries.

Van Til, Cornelius. *A Christian Theory of Knowledge*. Philadelphia: Presbyterian & Reformed Publishing Co., 1969.
A penetrating explanation of differences between Kuyper and B. B. Warfield in apologetics.

Common Grace. Philadelphia: Presbyterian & Reformed Publishing Co., 1947.
A helpful exposition of the doctrine with analyses of Kuyper, Schilder, *et al.* Difficult reading due to clumsy style.

Common Grace and the Gospel. Phillipsburg, NJ: Presbyterian & Reformed Publishing Co., 1973.

Contains an analysis and expansion of Kuyper's doctrine with related essays on the subject.

The Defense of the Faith, 2nd edition, revised and abridged. Philadelphia: Presbyterian & Reformed Publishing Co., 1963.
Contains an appreciative critique of Kuyper's concept of 'formal faith' and its implications for apologetics.

The New Synthesis Theology of the Netherlands. Nutley, NJ: Presbyterian & Reformed Publishing Co., 1975.
A helpful explanation of the decline of Reformed theology in the nineteenth and twentieth centuries which assigns special significance to Berkouwer.

'Reflections on Dr. A. Kuyper, Sr.,' *The Banner,* 72 (1937), 1187.
A tribute to Kuyper as a defender of the Reformed faith and a model for his heirs in that tradition.

Van Til, Henry R. *The Calvinistic Concept of Culture.* Philadelphia: Presbyterian and Reformed Publishing Co., 1972.
Presents Kuyper as the most important influence in setting forth a Reformed view of culture; offers a helpful summary and analysis of his teaching.

Van Til, Nick, 'Calvinism and Art (1),' *Pro Rege,* 9, no. 3 (1981), pp.10-120.
Appropriate criticism of Kuyper's Stone Lecture about art; the author finds that Kuyper employed Platonic rather than biblical standards in his appraisal.

Vanden Berg, F. 'Seven Cities of Dr. Kuyper,' *Christian Home and School Magazine,* 19 (1940), pp.9-10.
Brief remarks about Kuyper's activities in the seven cities of his residence.

Abraham Kuyper. Grand Rapids: William B. Eerdmans Publishing Co., 1960.
The only conventional biography in English; undocumented and uncritical.

'Dr. Abraham Kuyper, 1837-1920,' *The Young Calvinist,* 18 (1937), pp.3-5, 11.
A tribute to Kuyper on the centennial of his birth; biographical sketch.

Vanden Berge, E., 'Dr. A. Kuyper,' *The Banner of Truth,* 33 (1898), p.60.
A tribute to Kuyper as exponent and defender of orthodoxy upon the occasion of his lectures at Princeton Theological Seminary.

Vandenbosch, Amry. *The Dutch East Indies: Its Government, Problems, and Politics.* Berkeley, CA: University of California Press, 1944.
Contains much information about Dutch colonial policy but does not give enough attention to Kuyper's role in the Ethical Policy.

'The Dutch in the Far East,' in *The Netherlands,* ed., Bartholomew Landheer. Berkeley, CA: University of California Press, 1944, pp.333-45.
A succinct survey of Dutch colonial history that puts the Ethical Policy of Kuyper in context.

'Missions on the Island of Bali,' *International Review of Missions,* 23 (1934), pp.205-14.
>Narrates the development of missions on Bali despite opposition, both native and Dutch; credits Kuyper with making government policy favourable towards missions there while implementing the 'Ethical Policy' in the East Indies.

Vander Groot, Henry. 'Creation and Differentiation', *Reformed Ecumenical Synod Theological Forum,* VII (1979), pp.1-16. A rather obscure essay that purports to expound Kuyper's doctrine of creation.

'Portraits of Kuyper,' *Christian Renewal,* 1 (1983), p.1.
>A pertinent reminder that Kuyper was not infallible and that his thinking developed throughout his life, so no one written work should be regarded as his fixed position on issues.

Vander Hart, Mark, 'Abraham Kuyper and the Theonomy Debate,' *Mid-America Journal of Theology,* 2 (1986), pp.63-77.
>An interesting contrast and comparison of Kuyper's views about pluralism and current thinking about Christian Reconstruction.

Vander Kam, Henry. 'Some Thoughts on Kuyper and Common Grace', *Mid-America Journal of Theology,* 2 (1986), pp.51-60.
>Shows how Kuyper's concept of common grace led him to deny the Roman Catholic dichotomy of nature and grace and to uphold the duties of believers in all areas of life where grace operates.

Vander Stelt, John C. 'Kuyper's Semi-Mystical Conception,' in *The Idea of a Christian Philosophy: Essays in Honour of D. H. Th. Vollenhoven,* ed. K. A. Brill, H. Hart, & J. Klapwijk. Toronto: Wedge Publishing, 1973, pp.178-90.
>A philosopher's complaints about inconsistencies in Kuyper's thought and theological positions which prevented him from developing a truly biblical world-view. Very difficult reading.

Vander Werff, P. H. 'Dr. Abraham Kuyper and Evolutionism,' *The Banner,* 114 (1979), pp.23-4.
>Shows Kuyper's militant opposition to the evolutionary world-view.

'Kuyper No Evolutionist,' *The Banner,* 113 (1978), pp.23-4.
>Corrects the misuse of one of Kuyper's statements some have construed to be open to evolution.

Vander Zee, A. 'Edmund Burke,' *Calvin Forum,* 19 (1954), pp.232-34.
>A summary and appreciation of Burke's critique of the French Revolution and its anti-Christian humanism; portrays Burke as a theistic humanist.

Vanderlaan, Eldred. *Protestant Modernism in Holland.* London: Oxford University Press, 1924.

A helpful analysis of nineteenth-century scholars who controlled the universities and led the clergy away from the Reformed faith.

Veenhof, Jan. 'A History of Theology and Spirituality in the Dutch Reformed Churches
    (Gereformeerde Kerken), 1892-1992,' *Calvin Theological Journal,* 28 (1993),
    pp.266-97.
    A survey of the decline of Reformed beliefs and convictions since Kuyper's
    time; the author applauds most of the changes.

Velema, W. H. 'Abraham Kuyper — Born 150 Years Ago: A Study in Strengths and
    Pitfalls,' *Reformed Ecumenical Synod Theological Forum,* XVI (1988), pp.9-14.
    A critical analysis which finds that Kuyper never divested himself of roman-
    ticism and idealism and that these influenced his view of presumed regeneration
    and common grace; expresses praise for Kuyper, but reserves the right to dis-
    agree with him. The author sadly relates the decline of Kuyper's projects.

Villa-Vicencio, Charles. 'South African Civil Religion: An Introduction,' *Journal of Theol-
    ogy for Southern Africa,* 19 (1977), pp.5-15.
    The author holds that Afrikaner nationalists have appropriated Kuyper's
    doctrine of spheres to support apartheid, or apartheid could be the logical out-
    come of their Kuyperian concept of created spheres.

Vogel, Leroy. 'The Political Party of Abraham Kuyper,' *Calvin Forum,* 3 (1937), pp.58-60.
    A succinct and insightful summary of Kuyper's political career and its effects
    upon Netherlands.

Volbeda, Samuel. 'Dr. Abraham Kuyper as Churchman,' *Calvin Forum,* 2 (1937), pp.85-8.
    Extols Kuyper as leader of the reformation that preserved the orthodox wit-
    ness in the form of a purified church.

    'Abraham Kuyper as a Theologian,' *The Banner,* 72 (1937), pp.1014-15. Portrays
    Kuyper as a constructive dogmatic theologian who saw clearly the philosophic
    basis of his views and their implications.

    'The Reformation of 1886,' *The Calvin Forum,* 1 (1935-36), pp.273-6. An insightful
    analysis of the schism from the Dutch Reformed Church under Kuyper's
    leadership.

Vlekke, Bernard H. M. *Evolution of the Dutch Nation.* New York: Roy Publishers, 1945.
    Contains a concise, informative description of Dutch politics and party divi-
    sions; pays tribute to Groen and Kuyper but favours the Liberal position; helpful
    on colonial policy.

Vroom, H. M. 'Scripture Read and Interpreted: The Development of the Doctrine of
    Scripture and Hermeneutics in *Gereformeerde* Theology in the Netherlands,'
    Calvin Theological Journal, 28 (1993), pp.352-71.
    A survey from Kuyper, through Bavinck, to Berkouwer holds that Kuyper's
    concept of organic inspiration provided the basis for Berkouwer and others to
    deny the inerrancy of Scripture while retaining the proper concept of Christ and
    salvation; applauds recent developments away from Reformed foundations.

Warfield, Benjamin B. *Calvin as a Theologian and Calvinism Today.* Philadelphia: Presbyterian Board of Publication, 1909.
> Three lectures that laud Calvin's influence, especially his work about the Holy Spirit; incidental tribute to Kuyper and Bavinck; undocumented.

Counterfeit Miracles. Edinburgh: Banner of Truth Trust, 1976 reprint of 1918 edition.
> Cites Kuyper in support of the traditional Reformed belief that miracles ceased with the end of special revelation in the apostolic age.

'Dr. Abraham Kuyper,' in *Selected Shorter Writings of Benjamin B. Warfield I,* ed. John Meeter. Nutley, NJ: Presbyterians & Reformed Publishing Co., 1970. A laudatory and insightful introduction to Kuyper's *Principles of Sacred Theology* in English.

'Introduction to Francis R. Beattie's *Apologetics,*' in *Selected Shorter Writings of Benjamin B. Warfield II,* ed. John Meeter. Nutley, NJ: Presbyterian and Reformed Publishing Co., 1973, pp.93-105.
> A summary of Warfield's objections to Kuyper's apologetic position.

Westra, Johan G. 'Abraham Kuyper and his Influences on Church and State,' *Reformed Review,* 38 (1985), pp.119-29.
> A highly informative narrative account of Kuyper's career; the author concludes that Kuyper sought a theocracy for Netherlands; undocumented.

'Melancholia in Politics,' *Reformed Journal,* 23 (1973), pp.5-6.
> A tribute to Kuyper's political contributions.

White, William, Jr. *Van Til, Defender of the Faith.* Nashville: Thomas Nelson Publishers, 1979.
> An uncritical, authorized biography by a zealous disciple; readable and inspiring. Contains one of Van Til's brief essays about Kuyper in the appendix.

Wiersma, Stanley M. 'Curtmantle and the Philosophy of Law,' *Reformed Journal,* 27 (1977), pp.6-10.
> An interesting suggestion that Kuyper might have been under the influence of John Henry Newman and the Oxford Movement, a matter no one has investigated carefully.

Wintle, Michael. *Pillars of Piety: Religion in the Netherlands in the Nineteenth Century.* Hull, UK: Hull University Press, 1987.
> A brief survey that regards modernism as a 'progressive' movement and denigrates, at least by implication, defenders of orthodoxy; adds little to earlier books on the same subject.

Wolters, Albert M. *Creation Regained: Biblical Basis for a Reformational Worldview.* Grand Rapids: William B. Eerdmans Publishing Co., 1985.
> A Kuyperian exposition and application of common grace, antithesis and sphere authority; readable and practical; an excellent introduction to the subject.

Wolterstorff, Nicholas. 'Liberating Scholarship,' *Reformed Journal,* 31 (1981), pp.4-5.

An interesting comparison of Marx, Freud and Kuyper on the matters which keep scholars from complete objectivity in their pursuits.

Yonge, Charlotte M. *The Heir of Redclyffe*, 2 vols. New York: Garland Publishing Co., 1975 reprint of 1853 edition.

Young, William. 'Historic Calvinism and Neo-Calvinism,' *Westminster Theological Journal,* 22 (1973), pp.48-64, 156-73.
    A critical analysis of particular relevance to Kuyper's doctrine of infant baptism and presumed regeneration.

Zorn, Raymond O. *Church and Kingdom.* Philadelphia: Presbyterian & Reformed Publishing Co., 1962.
    The author draws on Kuyper with appreciation, but expresses appropriate criticisms of some of his inconsistencies about church and state.

Zuidema, S. U. *Communication and Confrontation.* Assen Kampen, Netherlands: Royal Van Gorcum Ltd & J. H. Kok Ltd, 1972.
    The chapter 'Common Grace and Christian Action in Abraham Kuyper' is an important interpretation of *De Gemenne Gratie* and *Pro Rege* in terms of the relationship of common grace and particular grace and Christian action in society.

Zwaanstra, Henry. 'Abraham Kuyper's Conception of the Church,' *Calvin Theological Journal,* 9 (1974), pp.149-81.
    An interesting, critical analysis which shows how Kuyper was unclear in distinguishing between the visible and the invisible churches, and what the implications of this were for Dutch church life.

Reformed Thought and Experience in a New World. Kampen, the Netherlands: J. H. Kok, 1973.
    Indispensable for an assessment of Kuyper's influence upon Reformed believers in America, especially the Christian Reformed Church.

Zylstra, Bernard. 'H. Evan Runner: An Assessment of his Mission,' in *Life is Religion: Essays in Honor of H. Evan Runner,* ed. Henry Vander Groot. St Catherines, Ontario: Paideia Press, 1981, pp.1-14.
    Deals with attempts by Dutch-American disciples of Kuyper to implement his principle of sphere authority.

'Thy Word our Life,' in *Will All the King's Men,* by James H. Olthuis, *et al.* Toronto: Wedge Publishing Foundation, 1972. pp.153-218.
    A Kuyperian analysis of the church and the kingdom with a call for a return to biblical patterns of responsibility for the cultural and evangelistic mandates.

Who was Groen? Grand Rapids: The Groen Van Prinsterer Society, 1956.
    A helpful summary of Groen's career and his political philosophy.

Index